CRETE 1941
EYEWITNESSED

CRETE 1941 EYEWITNESSED

Costas N. Hadjipateras - Maria S. Fafalios
Foreword by C.M. Woodhouse

EFSTATHIADIS GROUP

BY THE SAME AUTHORS

Costas N. Hadjipateras:

CENDRES, A la Baconnière, Neuchâtel, 1944 (in French).
HÉROÏSMES ET DROITS DE LA GRÈCE, Librairie générale de droit et de jurisprudence, Paris, 1946 (in French).
LA GRÈCE ET LA MER, Aix en Provence, 1963 (in French).

Maria S. Fafalios:

FORTY OLD STORIES FROM CHIOS, Athens, 1979, 2nd edition 1985 (in Greek).
FIFTY OLD STORIES FROM CHIOS, Athens, Akritas Publications, 1989 (in English).

Joint publications:

TESTIMONIES 40-41, Athens, Kedros, 1982, Academy of Athens Award, 3rd edition 1988 (in Greek).
TESTIMONIES 40-44 * WAR-OCCUPATION, Athens, Kedros, 1988 (in Greek).

"Since wars began in the minds
of men, it is in the minds of men that
the defences of peace must be constructed."

UNESCO, 1946

EFSTATHIADIS GROUP S.A.
14, Valtetsiou Str.
106 80 Athens
Tel: (01) 5154650, 6450113
Fax: (01) 5154657
GREECE

ISBN 960 226 184 6

Printed and bound in Greece

CONTENTS

GERMAN ORDER OF BATTLE
(PLANNED AND NOT ACTUAL LANDINGS)

XI AIR CORPS	VIII AIR CORPS	AIRCRAFT GROUP
7 Air Div (Para)	430 Dive Bombers	750 JU-52 tpts
1 Asst Regt (Gliderborne)	180 Fighters	80 Gliders
5 Mtn Div (+one regt from	40 Recce etc.	
6 Mtn Div)		
One Bn tks		

GROUP WEST
Maj. Gen. Meindl
1 Assault Regt (four Bns,
less half 1 Bn) etc.

GROUP CENTRE
Lt. Gen. Süsmann
Half 1 Bn — Assault Regt
I & III Bns — 2 Para Regt
I, II & III Bns — 3 Para Regt
100 Mtn Regt etc.

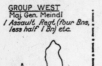

MALEME SECTOR
(2 NZ Inf Div)

5 NZ Inf Bde
21, 22, 23, 28 NZ Inf Bns.
NZ Composite Bn

10 NZ Inf Bde
20 NZ Inf Bn
NZ Composite Bn
One GREEK Bn
Arty: Ten 75mms
Six 3·7in hows
Armour: Two inf tks
Seven lt tks

4 NZ Inf Bde (Force Res)
18 NZ Inf Bn
19 NZ Inf Bn
1. WELCH

SUDA BAY SECTOR

MNBDO
1 Rangers
102 A Tk. Regt (as inf)
106 RHA (")
2/2 AUST Fd Regt (")
Two AUST Composite Bns
One GREEK Bn

_YEORYIOUPOLIS (part of
19 AUST Inf Bde)_
2/7 AUST Inf Bn
2/8 AUST Inf Bn
(Two coy str only)

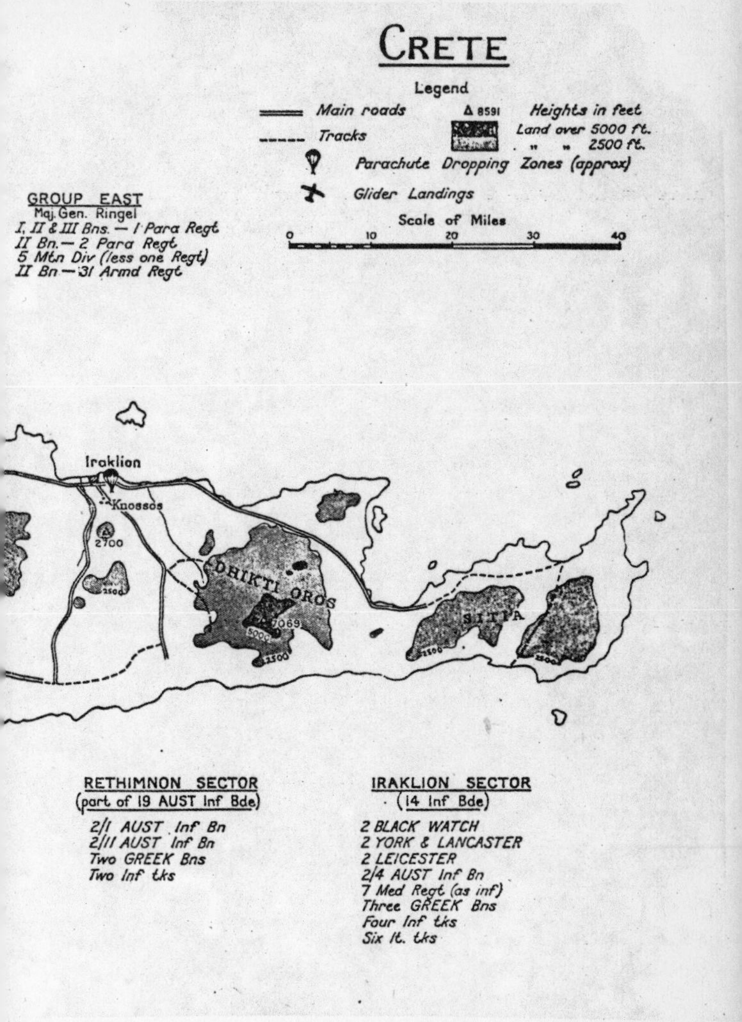
CRETE
Legend
Main roads
Tracks
Heights in feet
Land over 5000 ft.
" " 2500 ft.
Parachute Dropping Zones (approx)
Glider Landings
Scale of Miles
0 10 20 30 40
GROUP EAST
Maj. Gen. Ringel
I, II & III Bns. — I Para Regt
II Bn. — 2 Para Regt
5 Mtn Div (less one Regt)
II Bn — 31 Armd Regt
Iraklion
Knossos
2700
2500
DHIKTI OROS
7069
5000
SITIA
RETHIMNON SECTOR
(part of 19 AUST Inf Bde)
2/1 AUST Inf Bn
2/11 AUST Inf Bn
Two GREEK Bns
Two Inf tks
IRAKLION SECTOR
(14 Inf Bde)
2 BLACK WATCH
2 YORK & LANCASTER
2 LEICESTER
2/4 AUST Inf Bn
7 Med Regt (as inf)
Three GREEK Bns
Four Inf tks
Six lt. tks

"Kampf um Kreta". Der zweite Waltkrieg - Heft 29

FOREWORD

The battle of Crete in May 1941 was unique in more than one respect. It was the only major battle in the second world war which was won by airborne troops alone. Crete being an island, the German attack could obviously be reinforced only by air or by sea. An attempt was made to reinforce it by sea from mainland Greece, but the Royal Navy dispersed and destroyed the entire convoy of German ships. So the Germans were wholly dependent on the *Luftwaffe,* whether their aircraft were dropping parachutists and supplies, or towing gliders, or crashlanding themselves. It was an operation without precedent and without sequel.

The course of the battle was also very unusual, for the German attack was defeated at every point except one; but that one was crucial. It was the aerodrome at Maleme, west of Chania. Everywhere else that the Germans landed, particularly in the areas of Heraklion and Rethymno, they were soon forced to surrender. The British took many hundreds of prisoners in both areas, but they were never able to remove them from the island, since although the British controlled the sea, the Germans controlled the air. Only in the area of Maleme was the German attack successful. Its success was due partly to a failure on the part of the British commanders, but also partly to an extraordinary chance.

Here we come to another respect in which the battle of Crete was unique. It was the first operation in which the British commander on the spot had available to him a new and immensely valuable source of intelligence about the enemy. The source was known as Ultra. It was the code-name of the intelligence produced by the interception and decipherment of high-level German wireless traffic. The German telegrams were enciphered by a machine which they called Enigma; but thanks to the brilliant skill of our Polish allies, a duplicate of the Enigma machine was available to the British. It was during the Greek campaign that the products of the Ultra operation reached British commanders in the field for the first time. Among the earliest recipients, if not the very first, was General Bernard Freyberg, the New Zealand officer commanding the allied force in Crete.

Freyberg therefore had priceless intelligence on the Germans' intentions and plans. But ironically this was also his undoing. He had only taken over his command in Crete very shortly before the German attack, having previously commanded the New Zealand Division in the battle for mainland Greece. One of the first things he observed was that the aerodrome at Maleme was inadequately protected. But almost at once he was told, in great secrecy, by General Sir Archibald Wavell, the Commander-in-Chief of the Middle East, that he was about to receive the new intelligence called Ultra. Wavell also told him that the Ultra intelligence was so valuable, and the need to protect its source was so important in the long run, that once he began to receive it, he must not alter the dispositions of his troops.

One of the first things that Ultra told him, when its reports began to arrive, was that Maleme aerodrome would be the main German target in western Crete. This was indeed so logical that he would have assumed it for himself, even without the help of Ultra. If he had not received the Ultra intelligence, he would have reinforced Maleme as a simple act of military judgment. But once he had begun to receive Ultra, he felt that the strict orders which he had received from Wavell debarred him from doing so. This was the story which he told his son, now Lord Freyberg, on his deathbed.

It is at this point, by sheer chance, that I came into the story. I was in Crete, like hundreds of other junior British officers, without any organised unit, having escaped from the Greek mainland at the end of April. My billet, if one could call it that, was under an olive-tree between Chania and Maleme. Early in the morning of May 20th, I was sent to carry a message to Freyberg; why, or what about, I cannot recall. I found him in a villa on the outskirts of Chania. All was quiet at that moment, on a lovely spring morning.

After I had delivered my message to the General, he kindly invited me to stay for breakfast. It was not a luxurious meal, but it was better than I had had for some time. We sat on the small verandah of his house, just the two of us. It must have been about 7 o'clock when I happened to look up and saw the blue sky full of German aircraft and gliders. Some of the gliders were already detached and floating downwards. Hundreds of parachutes were dropping from the aircraft. The General continued quietly eating his breakfast.

What should I do? It seemed impolite, not to say insubordinate, to interrupt the General's breakfast. On the other hand, the sight was extraordinary. Eventually, very respectfully, I drew the General's attention to it. He looked up and said: "H'mph." Then he looked at his watch, and added: "They're dead on time!" He seemed mildly surprised at German punctuality. Then he went on with his breakfast.

Freyberg knew from Ultra, of course, what I did not know --- the time and the place of the German attack. He had already made his dispositions, and was not allowed to alter them. So there was nothing more for him to do until he could see how the battle developed. But the fatal weakness at Maleme, of his defensive position remained, and it had to be allowed to remain in order that the Germans should not suspect that their plan of operations had become known in advance. And so Maleme aerodrome fell into German hands.

The irony of the story is that, although the Germans knew nothing about Ultra, they did in fact suspect that their plans had become known to the British. This became clear from the German records after the war. They sensed that they were expected exactly at the time and the place where they landed. But they never suspected the real reason. They attributed the British foreknowledge to the skill of Greek agents working for the British in Athens. Nor did they ever suspect, throughout the war, that their ciphers had been broken.

This leaves my story with many unanswered and unanswerable questions. Would it still have been safe for Freyberg to alter his military dispositions, and to strengthen the defences of Maleme aerodrome, even after he began to receive the intelligence from Ultra? Would the Germans still have supposed that the source of the leakage lay in Athens, not in their ciphers? And if Freyberg had acted as he wished, and had strengthened the defences of Maleme, might the German attack on Crete have been defeated altogether? And what

13

then would have been the consequences for the rest of the war in the Mediterranean?

One can only speculate on the answers to these questions. All I know is that after finishing my breakfast with the General, I left his villa about 8 o'clock and went back to my olive-tree on the way to Maleme. Within 48 hours the battle had turned decisively against us. After that, there remained only the long march across the Levka Mountains to Chora Sphakion on the south coast. On the night of May 30th I was taken off from there by the Royal Navy. The battle of Crete was over.

But the resistance of the Greeks had already begun; for it was during the same night that two young Greeks scaled the north wall of the Acropolis to remove the Nazi flag and replace it with the Greek national flag. And for many months that followed, thousands of British, Australian and New Zealand soldiers who had escaped capture were moving freely about Crete and the mainland, protected by their Greek hosts and never betrayed.

C.M. Woodhouse

INTRODUCTION

In the early hours of Monday the 28th October 1940 Fascist Italy launched an unprovoked attack upon Greece. Expressing the will of the entire Greek nation General Ioannis Metaxas, then dictator and Prime Minister, awakened at dawn by the Italian Ambassador Emanuele Grazzi, flatly rejected the ultimatum by which Mussolini demanded the right to occupy the Greek territory.

That was one of the darkest phases of World War II. In April 1940 Hitler had unleashed his "Blitzkrieg" which in less than two months had swept out and conquered Norway, Denmark, Holland, Belgium and finally France. No country could even conceive to resist the Nazi "steamroller". England found herself isolated and fighting alone against the mightiest military force ever known, galvanized only by Churchill's exhortation for a "united strength" and braced for confronting his bleak offer of "blood, toil, tears and sweat". And when on the 15th September 1940 the heroic pilots of the RAF, by inflicting heavy losses on the German air force, prevented the Nazi invasion of the British Isles, Churchill rightly immortalised them by expressing the British nation's gratitude to "the few". Who could imagine, however, that almost a month after the RAF's Battle of Britain, the famous words of Churchill would befit another battle, the other "few", that handful of Greek soldiers who, at a time when Europe was wrapped in a shroud of despair and terror, would dare defy the mighty Axis powers by opposing Mussolini.

Despite the enormous superiority of the Italian armed forces the Greek army not only resisted fiercely the invaders of their mother-land but by a full-scale counter-attack forced the Italians to a massive retreat deep into Albania. The epic struggle of the Greek forces won the admiration of the whole world, arousing everywhere the spirit of freedom. In the words of Monty Woodhouse, who honoured us with this book's foreword, "the Greeks won the first victories of the Allies anywhere on land, ahead of the British in North Africa".

Coming reluctantly to the rescue of Mussolini's humiliated army Hitler invaded Greece on the 6th April 1941. The Greeks did not capitulate but fought, with the valuable assistance of the British and Commonwealth forces, a gallant, though hopeless battle. On the 27th April 1941, six months to the day after the beginning of the Italian invasion, Athens fell into German hands. Subsequently the Greek mainland succumbed to the Wehrmacht.

There was, however, one part of Greek soil unconquered; the island of Crete, the last stronghold of the Greek nation. The Battle for Crete, codenamed "Operation Mercury" by Hitler, which lasted from the 20th to the 31st May 1941, is the object of this book. Here, for the first time in history, an island had been captured by air-borne attack, though at very high cost. The casualties suffered by the 7th Parachute Division, the élite of the Nazi army, were heavier than the total number of Germans killed in the war to that date. Thanks to the ferocious resistance and valour of the Allied forces and of the entire Cretan population, that precious live air-borne weapon, the parachutists, had been decimated as a combat unit. For Hitler the "Pyrrhic" victory of Crete marked the end of the days of paratroops. Characterized by Winston Churchill as "a head-on collision with the very spearpoint of the German lance", the Battle for Crete was later dearly paid by the German army in the frozen mud and icy snow of Moscow and Stalingrad, due to the fateful delay of "Operation Barbarossa", that is the German invasion of Russia which was originally scheduled to be launched in spring 1941. Moreover, the costly Cretan campaign in the opinion of many historians may have prevented Hitler from invading the British Isles through air-borne troops, as advocated all along by Marshal Goering.

The aim of this book is to present the Cretan battle through the very eyes of the soldiers and civilians who lived and witnessed those historic times, that is, verbal and written testimonies of survivors, also

16

through war diaries and authentic documents mostly unpublished before, all shedding new light to that epoch-making military event. The testimonies have been given by Greeks, mainly Cretans, British, Australian and New Zealand soldiers, also by Germans who fought in Crete. This book is the result of painstaking labour and world-wide research. This is not a dry military history; it is a **living,** human, eyewitnessed history. It is the heart and spirit of people, not the guns of war. And as such, we believe, it is non-political and impartial.

The method for the presentation of our material, obviously in an edited form, is the following. Testimonies given orally are reported as "verbal testimonies". Testimonies written exclusively for the book bear simply the signature of the writer. Next to the signature of the person testifying, his or her nationality is indicated. In the case of Cretans the town or village of origin is mentioned, a detail we consider useful for the clarity of the narration. No titles of contributors are mentioned except when necessary for identification reasons. As for the names and geographic places, we left the spelling as it appears on each individual testimony. We also use the term "contributed by" for any text, material or document reported to us. Extracts of already published books refer to their author and title.

We are aware of the fact that we have omitted many persons and events either unintentionally or because of lack of space, but this does not minimise the value of their military or human contribution. The highest tribute should especially be paid to the British, Australians and New Zealanders who, though at the time exhausted and demoralised after their evacuation from mainland Greece, fought with fearless tenacity to defend the island. Cretans, and the Greek people as a whole, will never forget their lion-hearted courage and sacrifices. Many of these men have received medals which they so rightly deserve. However, for those who have not received any award for their fight in Crete one hopes that, even at this late stage, their contribution will be officially recognised.

In presenting the authentic, spontaneous and candid recollections of the survivors of this memorable battle, the book aims not only to keep alive the memory of the Battle of Crete, but also the spirit of unity and self-sacrifice of people of different nationalities united by their love for freedom and peace. War memories are now relics of the past. They have all faded away; the thunder of bombing, the crackle of machine-gunning, the shadows of death passing across the sun. Instead, today we have the splendour of the Cretan blue sky, the murmur of the waves, the clinging of wine-filled glasses between Cretans and their war-time friends and co-fighters.

But for the Cretans, friendship and hospitality are not one-sided. After almost half a century from "Operation Mercury", yesterday's enemies return regularly to the island as old comrades-in-arms. A kind of mutual respect and trust exists between the past adversaries. "I know that Cretans", writes Adolf Strauch, "are now very proud of their fight for freedom waged against us. I respect their attitude and understand the sacrifices made by them. However, as I see it, that was a senseless shedding of blood. After remembering those days I am happy that we now understand one another, that we respect each other and that we can forgive".

At the German cemetery overlooking Maleme airstrip and Chania an army of crosses strikes you with an overpowering feeling of sadness. These young parachutists, aged 19 or 20, or even younger, who were killed instantly on the 20th and 21st of May are now lying under the glorious Greek sun, united in eternity with the good earth of Crete. There are hundreds of graves and some have no names on the plaques. A Cretan is in charge of the cemetery; a custodian of these lost young men, once his enemies and now his silent everyday companions. He, too, reminds us of the futility of hatred and war.

At dusk you can often see a poignant sight; black dressed, old Cretan women lighting candles on the graves of past adversaries. When you ask them why, they reply: "They, too, have a mother, and she is far away or dead. We also lost our sons, killed or executed by the Germans. We know how a mother feels. Now, we are their mothers."

Crete is nowadays a world centre of peace. At the imposing Orthodox Academy of Crete, overlooking the blue Cretan sea, you can see the ascetic yet fiery figure of Metropolitan Eirinaios, surrounded by hundreds of people from all corners of the world. Under his inspiring leadership these devoted people meet at regular seminar sessions seeking ways and means to achieve universal peace.

During intervals, they stand on the vast terrace of the building and look far into the land. Their eyes meet a sea of olive trees, once lashed by bullets and burnt to death, but now alive and blooming again, waving in the breeze, with their sunkissed branches conveying their centuries-old message of peace.

Let the olive branch prevail over the sword and the fire. The ideal of peace must survive, durable and indestructible, as the guiding light of future generations.

Costas N. Hadjipateras   Maria S. Fafalios

Acknowledgements

We would like to thank the following institutions for granting us permission to use their archives/libraries and for enabling us to contact the Crete Veterans: Australian National Library Camberra, Benakeios Library Athens, Benaki Museum Athens, Bibliotek für Zeitgeschichte Stuttgart, British Library London, Bund Deutscher Fallschirmjäger Munich, Bundesarchiv-Militärarchiv Freiburg, Crete Veterans Association Birmingham, Crete Veterans Association Tauranga New Zealand, ELIA Archives Athens, Gennadeios Library Athens, Hellenic Philatelic Society of Great Britain Surrey, Historical Archives of Crete Chania, Imperial War Museum London, Institut für Zeitgeschichte Munich, Kameradenkreis der 5. Gebirgsdivision Koblenz, Keystone Press Agency London, Kritika Nea Newspaper Athens, Legs Eleven Minor Newsletter Maylands Australia, Mitchell Library Sydney, Museum of Contemporary History Heraclion, Museum of National Resistance Heraclion, National Archives Department of Internal Affairs Wellington, New Zealand House Library London, Penguin Books (N.Z.) Ltd., Photo Source London, Pow-Wow Magazine Christchurch New Zealand, Returned Servicemen League Campbell Australia, Alexander Turnbull Library Wellington, Verband Deutscher Soldaten Bonn, War Museum Athens, Wilson and Horton Ltd. Auckland New Zealand, among many others.

We would also like to thank all those who willingly gave us permission to use material from their private collections, or who gave us their inestimable assistance in any other way, especially: Chyssoula Bourlotou Heraclion, Kyriakos Delopoulos Athens, Effie Dolioti London, Alex Droudakis Chania, Natalia Gätlich Athens, Stavros

Georgiakakis Chania, Stergios Manouras Athens, Spyros Marnieros Athens, Leonid de Lieven London, Tassos Nollas Athens, Marcos Polioudakis Rethymnon, Jean-Louis Roba Belgium, Antonis Sanoudakis Heraclion, Mara Siambou Athens, Tom Steel Director of the film "Touch and Go" produced by Jeremy Isaacs London, Dimitrios Tsakonas Athens, and Yiannis Vassilas from Athens.

To conclude, we would like to say one more thank you: to all those who, without even knowing us sometimes, entrusted us with their memorabilia, manuscripts, sketches, photos, letters. Without them this book could not have been written.

Georgiakakis Chania, Stergios Manouras Athens, Spyros Marmieros Athens, Leonid de Lieven London, Tassos Nollas Athens, Marcos Polioudakis Rethymnon, Jean-Louis Roba Belgium, Antonis Sanoudakis Heraction, Mara Siambou Athens, Tom Steel Director of the film "Touch and Go" produced by Jeremy Isaacs London, Dimitrios Tsakonas Athens, and Yiannis Vassilas from Athens.

To conclude, we would like to say one more thank you: to all those who, without ever knowing us, sometimes, entrusted us with their memorabilia, manuscripts, sketches, photos, letters. Without them this book could not have been written.

TARGET: CRETE

Directive No 28: "Operation Mercury"

"After the occupation of the entire mainland of Greece Hitler's might turned against the last bastion of free Hellenic soil: the legendary island of King Minos, Crete, where, for eleven days, took place, in the words of Liddell Hart, "the most amazing and most daring action of the whole war". Obsessed with his plan to invade Russia the earliest possible in 1941, Hitler did not at first want to get further involved into the Greek islands, and besides he considered the conquest of Crete from the air impossible. "This affair, he said, will go wrong and will cost too many lives". But ambitious General Kurt Student, creator of the élite force of airborne troops, managed to convince him in the end. On the 25th April Hitler issued Directive no: 28 code named OPERATION MERCURY.

Crete: a jump-off base

"Operation Mercury" was conceived by Hitler in his special train on 21 April 1941 on the Semmering Pass (Austria), as a matter of fact just at the very time that the Greek divisions had laid down their arms in Larissa. The driving force at the Semmering Conference was undoubtedly General Student, that restless organizer and tactician who was called "heart of the German Parachute Arm". He had his eyes fixed on Cyprus, the Near and Middle East. The day before, he had won over to his plan Goering and Jeschonnek, Chief of the General Staff of the Air Force.

Student's plan for Crete was in the balance for about an hour when Jodl and Keitel suggested in the Fuehrer's train that it might be better to eliminate and render harmless Malta, that deadly thorn in the flesh of the German and Italian supply lines vital to the military development in North Africa. However in the end the arguments of the "jumping general" prevailed:

1. Elimination of the threat to the vital Rumanian oil wells of Ploesti by British bombers based in Crete.
2. Securing of the Eastern Mediterranean against British naval operations.
3. Threat to British bases in Egypt, particularly to the Royal Naval Base at Alexandria.
4. Creation of a German jump-off base for offensive operations against Cyprus and Palestine.

Günter Stein,
"Arms of World War II, Special Issue", Germany

"Nowadays there's nothing surprising".

The enterprise begins

One would certainly not be unfair to General Student by assuming that there was another factor weighing with him in his suggestion: He surely wanted to demonstrate what "his" paratroops were able to achieve. Thus Hitler at last gave his fiat to the assault on Crete, however not without conditions attached to it: First and foremost the enterprise would have to be begun as soon as possible and would have to be completed quickly so that the units to be committed and above all the air transport facilities could be made available readily for punctual commitment for deployment against Russia.

The final plan of attack was as follows: To capture the three airfields on the North coast Malemes, Rethymnon and Iraklion as well as Chania, the capital, together with Suda Bay, the only good port of Crete.

Der Zweite Weltkrieg, Heft 29

A curiously isolated episode

The capture of Crete in may 1941 was not part of the original German plan for the subjection of Greece. Nor did it have any direct sequel. It is a curiously isolated episode in the history of World War II but the battle had some wider consequences and is not without interest in the fuller context of the war.

German intentions were known to us in considerable detail, while vague indications of some such operation in some such area had been gleaned as far back as late March. In order to explain this awareness I need to say something about the source of our information, which was Ultra intelligence. I was not a cryptographer myself but an intelligence officer, which means that I was interpreting the already deciphered texts and conveying them to Staffs in the field.

Ultra was the product of breaking the most secret German machine cyphers used by the German armed services and some other bodies. The machine in question was called the Enigma machine. For.

thirty years after the war ended nothing was publicly known about this extraordinary feat. In the seventies the secret came out but even now new information crops up from time to time and some mysteries remain undisclosed.

In the last week of March 1941 Ultra began to give signs of movements of units of Fliegerkorps XI which, with its HQ in northern Germany, was the Luftwaffe's parachute arm commanded by General Student. There were also short Ultra messages ordering moves by individuals who were known to us from previous Ultra intelligence to be officers or men belonging to units of Fliegerkorps XI. Clearly something was in the wind and it involved a parachute operation, the first since the invasion of the Low Countries a year earlier. Another source was railway Enigma which in late April revealed reinforcements on the move to the south east when, in the absence of some new plan, they were no longer required. There was also a first direct reference to Crete (26 April) when the prinicipal Luftwaffe HQ in the Balkans asked for maps and photographs of the island. But there was still no clear indication of any objective. It might be Crete, or it might be the Dodecanese, or Cyprus, or Syria, or Iraq where the pro-German Rashid Ali was preparing his coup.

The growing probability that the Germans intended to attack Crete became a virtual certainty when the Luftwaffe was ordered to take care not to destroy its airfields and to conduct detailed aerial photography, and on 5 May Ultra removed any lingering doubts. On 6 May the Germans were shown to be expecting to be ready by 17 May and from then onwards Ultra provided blow coverage of the German preliminaries, including dropping areas for their parachutists. By 16 May the scale of the German attack could be worked out with considerable accuracy - it was slightly exaggerated.

General Freyberg VC arrived in Crete from Greece on 29 April and was appointed GOC - in - C that day. Wavell arrived from Cairo on the next day. After a conference Wavell took Freyberg aside and told him about Ultra and the restrictions on its operational use. Then he went back to Cairo. A few days later Freyberg received direct from Bletchley Park, British cryptographers' centre, a long signal which was a compendium of Ultra intelligence about the coming attack. This resumé reported, among other things, that on Day One Maleme, Candia and Retimo airfields would be the main targets of parachute landings and that on the same day about 100 dive bombers and 100 fighter aircraft would be transferred to Maleme and Candia and -still on Day One- that a seaborne contingent would arrive with anti-aircraft batteries, motor-cyclists, anti-tank units; the size of the force was put at 30-35,000 men, including 12,000 parachutists, and the air support was estimated at 150 long range bombers and 100 heavy fighter aircraft. Freyberg was stunned by this information. It showed that the deployment of his defences was all wrong. But he could not redeploy because the intelligence on which such a redeployment must rest was Ultra and only Ultra. Freyberg's son, Colonel Lord Freyberg, has told me that his father - who related these matters to him many years later when he felt that his life was ending - sent to Cairo to seek Wavell's permission to reorganize his defence but received no response, either because Wavell felt unable to change his orders or because he referred the matter to Churchill who reaffirmed the rule about not jeopardizing Ultra. From this point up to the eve of the attack Freyberg received 36 more Ultra signals from Bletchley Park which gave him an accurate picture of things that he could do little about. But not nothing. Although there was no saving Crete the defenders were able to inflict on the invaders far more serious losses than they had anticipated. Their own intelligence had seriously underestimated the strength of the forces opposed to them and, unknown to themselves, they were also put at risk by pre-invasion Enigma decodes and by the reading, during the operations of 20 May - I June, of non-Enigma cyphers of Fliegerkorps XI. The German parachutists were so badly mauled that they never again attempted a similar operation. So far from making a similar attack on Malta, as some feared, Fliegerkorps XI's units were converted into infantry. They ended the war as part of the garrison of Brest on the Atlantic coast of Brittany where they surrendered to the Americans in September 1944.

Peter Calvocoressi, England

The fear of compromising the secret

My father did know in advance about the German attack through "ULTRA", which was the system used to break the German coding. He was not allowed to make proper use of this knowledge for fear of compromising the secret.

Paul Freyberg, England

General Freyberg to General Wavell, Commander-in Chief, Middle East

1 May 1941

With reference to the War Office appreciation of the scale of attack on Crete. The forces at my disposal are totally inadequate to meet the attack envisaged. Unless the number of fighter aircraft is greatly increased and naval forces are made available to deal with a seaborne attack I cannot hope to hold out with land forces alone, which, as a result of the campaign in Greece, are now devoid of any artillery, have insufficient tools for digging, very little transport, and inadequate war reserves of equipment and ammunition. The force here can and will fight, but cannot hope to repel invasion without full support from the Navy and Air Force. If, for other reasons, these cannot be made available at once, I urge that the question of holding Crete should be reconsidered.

General Wavell to General Freyberg

2 May 1941

The Commander-in-Chief, Mediterranean, is prepared to support you if Crete is attacked.

I have most definite instructions from the War Cabinet to hold Crete and, even if the question were reconsidered, I am doubtful if the troops could be removed before the enemy attack.

The difficulties and dangers of your situation are fully realised, but I am confident that you and the magnificent troops at your disposal will be equal to the task. We have very anxious times ahead in the Middle East for the next few weeks.

Bullets wouldn't stop them

About mid April in 1941 we noticed that practically all the destroyers had left Alexandria, and the talk that they were evacuating the allied forces from Greece to Crete.

At the end of the month it came our turn (H.M.A.S. PERTH) in company with H.M.S. ORION - we left Alexandria and steamed towards Greece. After we were well at sea our captain spoke to us over the ship's loud speaker system.

"The German Army is in control in Greece. Most of the surviving allied forces have been evacuated to Crete. Tonight ORION and PERTH are to take off the remaining units fighting the rear guard action. At 11.30 tonight we are to be off shore at Salamis; we will be close to the enemy forces and it is known that they have torpedo boats stationed at Piraeus so absolute quiet must be maintained as we must not jeopardise this evacuation. The ship will be closed up at full action stations from 7 o'clock."

We were at our destination at the appointed time and as soon as we flashed the signal to shore scores of small boats came towards us. Soon we had hundreds of soldiers, to our surprise they were Australians, clambering up the nets and as they arrived on deck they were taken to the mess decks where they were given scalding tea and a hot meal.

We must have had some 400 soldiers on board when we left around 2 a.m. leaving H.M.S. ORION still there; and headed at full speed for Crete.

At 4 a.m. when I was relieved from my action station and entered the mess deck I saw soldiers everywhere, some sleeping and others talking. I joined a group and asked "how was it fellas?"

A corporal, a self - appointed spokesman for the group, said: "It was hell for the last month, we have been retreating from the Germans. We first struck them, or they struck us, around Larissa. First they bombed us unmercifully and we had no planes to stop them, then their armoured divisions, hundreds of tanks came through and all we could do was get out of their way; then came the footsloggers and you should have seen them. I reckon they must have been Hitler's crack Stormtroopers. Big fellows marching like machines in columns. Bullets wouldn't stop them, they just kept coming marching straight over their dead mates in front. The only time they broke ranks was when the Maoris got among them with bayonets - they don't like steel.

There were too many of them for us and we just had to fall back and that is all we have been doing retreating through the snow and the cold. I guess we have lost most of our regiment and most of the Kiwi regiment was wiped out around Lamia.

We were told that our forces were being evacuated to Crete and we are the last. We met up with the British forces at Mandra. The Scottish boys, The Black Watch, and us were selected to fight the rear guard action while most of the others were evacuated further down the coast. The Scotchmen are fighting the rear guard action for us and I suppose that other ship is there to take them off if they can make it. I hope to God they can."

We arrived at Suda Bay around 11 a.m. that day and watched the soldiers go ashore, at least they had rested for about 9 hours and eaten well and so were probably a little happier and ready to meet whatever awaited them.

Bill Bracht, Australia

Sunday 27th April 1941

0400   By this time we had embarked 1000 Australian A.I.F. and some Imperial forces. It was quite a lot of men to have aboard considering the wounded and everywhere was packed out. These men have been through hell and are exhausted and hungry, most of them haven't shaved for weeks and have not had water to even drink for days. They are all without kit and most of them only have a pair of trousers and shorts. They all show the signs of their privations but are still able to laugh and crack jokes. Everyone of them can show a bullet wound or two and one chap was complaining about his leg being sore so he was ushered into the sick bay. We were later told that he had five machine gun bullets in the leg above the knee and they had been there for seven days. That was one case and there were many others. When we had all the troops aboard we shoved off full speed for Suda Bay.

From J.K.E. Nelson's War Diary, Australia

Water cascades and high flames

25 April 1941

A sunny day, and we were sent to look for ships embarking British troops in the Athens, Corinth and Nauplion areas. As there seemed to be almost no more fighterplanes in those areas, each of us flew on his own. I took off in the early afternoon and I went to Cape Sunion first. No ships around there. So I flew to the Corinth area. No ships either. I turned south to investigate the Nauplion area, and on my way I tried to identify Mykene. I told my crew that we were passing over a territory which had seen at least 3000 years of Greek history. Wasn't this King Agamemnon's home down there?

My navigator, sitting right next to me, was more concerned about Argos airfield straight ahead of us. He expected Hurricane fighters to take off from there, if they weren't in the air already, and were waiting in the sun in order to put themselves into an advantageous position for a surprise attack. For a few moments we forgot the antique scenery around us, but after a while we found, that there were obviously no fighters in the air. So, at least my eyes were looking again to the ground. The villages and the little towns looked like a playground of white dots, as the houses were mostly plain white. The sun was pouring her mild afternoon light over the scenery of yellow-brown soil, blue sea and blue sky, and the "white dots" accumulated to a town along the border of the sea. From a small harbour the houses climbed up to a rocky hill, the entrance to the port was protected by a small island covered by the stonewalls of a small medieval fort. The map showed that this could only be Nauplion. We were not fired at by A.A. salvoes, at least I saw none. Everything looked peaceful and untouched. But there was something which made my heart beat faster.

Right in the middle between the jetty and the small island fort, there was a big ship. Two funnels, a high superstructure, a passenger liner. This was the first ship of this kind I had ever seen. It was a fascinating sight. There it was, motionless, no wake, and we were moving towards this unique target: "Switch the fuse box on, all bombs at once!" The navigator acted accordingly. I turned my Ju 88 a little in order to approach the target slightly diagonal. Cooler flaps shut, propellers back into the half-past-eight-position. Their rotation became slower and the noise became lower. The target down there slipped through the red stripe across the window below my feet. We now were in the 60 grade angle for diving. I pushed a little knob, the air brakes came out of the wings - and down we went with increasing speed. The ship, now in front of my nose, seemed to become bigger and bigger. I hardly felt my navigator's fist hammering on my knee. "Thousand!" he cried. I lifted the aircraft's nose a little and pushed the red button. The bombs went their way and the Ju 88 hers, flattening out her dive. This had been a text-book attack, and I brought the aircraft back to normal. I could not see whether the bombs had hit, but my radio-operator and my air-gunner, both looking to the rear, suddenly shouted simultaneously: We've hit her! Two full hits, two bombs nearmisses. Water cascades and high flames.

I risked a quick look back, and I saw what they had described. What did I feel?

Relief after maximal tension. Being proud, that a junior crew had been successful. Sorrow, that a beautiful ship was gone. Satisfaction, that she would no longer transport British Forces, and that was all that counted on this day.

Gerd Stamp, Germany

Alexandria
15 May 1941

Dear Mama,

Well, I don't know what news I can give you. We really had the hell of a time in Greece. It wasn't much fun taking on half the German Airforce with literally a handful of fighters. My machine was shot up quite a bit but I always managed to get back. The difficulty was to choose a time to land when the German fighters weren't ground strafing our aerodrome. Later on we hopped from place to place trying to cover the evacuation - hiding our planes in olive groves and covering them with olive branches in a fairly fruitless endeavour to prevent them being spotted by one or other of the swarms of aircraft overhead. Anyway I don't think anything as bad as that will happen again ...

The handful of pilots who survived the Grecian campaign were tremendously lucky. The odds were strongly against any of us coming out alive. The five who flew our remaining Hurricanes to Crete were to fight valiantly on the island when the Germans attacked a short time later with a massive airborne invasion.

Roald Dahl, GOING SOLO

The "Evrotas" on its way to Crete

When the German troops landed on Greek soil, the Greek army began to withdraw. The British troops which included Australians, New Zealanders and Cypriots retreated till they reached Gytheion in order to leave for Crete or Alexandria. There were many Greek civilians and Europeans who had reached Gytheion before the British, people who had abandoned all they owned in this world in order to flee before the arrival of the Germans. Gytheion was packed with foreigners. They were prepared to pay any amount for a means to escape. The Germans bombed all the ports as well as all means of transport, daily. Their aim was to stop the British troops from leaving Greece.

It was the day before Easter, I don't remember the exact date, April. I was about sixteen at the time. The ship on which I served, the "Evrotas", was chartered by foreigners who were in Gytheion. Those who were rich paid a lot, but they managed to guarantee themselves a place on the boat leaving for Crete. We left Gytheion on the Saturday afternoon before Easter. We were terrified the Germans might bomb us and had no idea if we would get to Crete. The weather was fine. We arrived at Kythira at nightfall and headed straight for Crete. Captain Vangelis Psarakis was in the boat together with the engineer Theodoros and us two sailors. The Captain ordered us to go up to the bow and sit down by turns, keeping an eye out for the mines (similar to the ones the Italians had dropped in various places). The passengers talked all night long, others who were afraid and desperate kept asking when we would arrive; where we were; if we were heading in the right direction and so on.

Daybreak - we were still in the Cretan Sea. We were in great danger because the German aircrafts had landed in Crete. The Germans had taken almost half of Greece. I could not recall if they had entered Athens. It was ten o'clock in the morning as we arrived at Castelli Kissamou in Crete. The passengers hurried to get off the ship with their belongings and find a way to leave.

That afternoon we left for Gytheion and when we arrived at the port, the British officers came and informed us that we were to follow orders. We had to take the British troops on board, but we didn't know where to.

The British piled on to the ship one after the other. The ship was full, there was no room left. "Stop, stop" I shouted at them, that was all I knew how to say. I untied the ropes with great difficulty, while the British clung onto the "Evrotas". Those who were not able to hang on to the ship, remained on shore. They began to swear and protest, as if it were my fault that there was no more room on the ship.

We were about 10 miles from Gytheion. We encountered a storm and as we continued on, it got worse. As the waves crashed onto the "Evrotas" the soldiers began to protest, there was water everywhere. They were swearing, but I don't know at whom. The Captain became irritated.

Suddenly we heard Theodoros Byrakos, the engineer, shouting at us. One of the engines was not functioning properly. The pump was unable to get rid of the water and so we were told to start using buckets. As I carried on getting the water out from the engine, the engineer asked me to tell the Captain that there was nothing we could do and that we ought to return to Gytheion to repair the engine.

I climbed up onto the bridge with great difficulty. We normally called the bridge "the steering wheel room" (timoniera). I told the Captain what the engineer had suggested. He started cursing the weather. He was in a desperate state. "How are we going to get back?" he asked. "The British will think we are trying to sabotage them or that we don't want to take them with us. They'll kill us".

The Captain was in a dilemma, he didn't know what to do. The Captain and the engineer consulted each other once again. The British were not aware that we were heading back. Everyone was tired, sleepy and dizzy. It was between two and three o'clock. We hoped to get to Gytheion by nightfall.

Daybreak. The soldiers began to recover from the hardship of the storm. They were immediately overcome by a sense of worry. We had changed direction at daylight and were still at sea, which meant we would have great difficulty avoiding the "stukas" (German bombers). One of the Cypriot soldiers who spoke Greek, informed the Captain that the General wanted to know where we were going; where we were at the moment and finally why we had turned back. We told him that there was something wrong with the engine and we were returning to Gytheion to repair it. We would be leaving again that same night. But the General was not convinced and threatened to kill the Captain, saying that he was collaborating with the Germans (5th column). The General approached the Captain and began to shout clutching his pistol. He made a variety of threats. Finally a Greek named Stathakos who spoke English, intervened. Stathakos had boarded the ship along with the British troops without being noticed. The Cypriot together with the Greek Stathakos, convinced the British General that the Captain was not a collaborator nor was anyone else. Furthermore they told him that this was the only ship transporting British troops.

At sunrise we were still at sea. The engine was still not functioning properly when we arrived at Gytheion between six and seven o'clock in the morning. The soldiers rushed out to get as far away from the

35

port as possible. The Cypriot informed the Captain that the General and his men were to return at ten o'clock that evening and that everything should be ready.

It was pitch dark. The British were returning. A Cypriot soldier together with a British were stationed at the entrance leading to the ship. They kept an eye on those who were boarding. Only the British were allowed to do so. They began to come and go freely. The engines were running and the Captain ordered me to untie the ropes. As I was doing so, I heard voices from outside:

"Hey boy, I am Kontopirakis, take me on board". I ran astern and tried to hoist him on board, but the British would not hear of it and I had trouble convincing them that he was my cousin. After much persuasion, I managed to get the Cretan on board.

There were many Cretan soldiers on shore, some begged us to take them on board, while others accused us of taking the British and leaving the Greeks behind. I untied the ropes and set the engines running. One of the Cretans was clinging onto the ladder and I had to pull him up with it. When the British saw this, they nearly killed him. I informed the Captain that all was clear astern and moved to the bow to lift the anchor so we could set off.

The Captain gave the order for us to get going and we began to sail out of the port of Gytheion heading for Kythira. The weather was mild, the sky was clear and the engine was functioning properly. The "Evrotas" set off in a hurry.

I was seated in the "steering wheel room". I kept an eye on the compass so that we would not change course. I looked ahead, I looked behind me, I even looked at the sky. The British who were close by, offered me biscuits and cigarettes. They talked to me. We were not able to understand each other when we spoke, so we used gestures. The only thing I understood was when they said my name. They called me Jimmy, everyone knew who I was by now and they all yelled: "Jimmy, Jimmy" and many other things I didn't understand. Everything was running smoothly up to now. The day was dawning and the island of Kythira was in sight. We rounded on the island's north eastern side and sailed into the small port of Avlemona.

The British were all on their feet, their guns and belongings by their side. Upon reaching the shore, they were instructed to disembark immediately and go and hide in the bushes. They were to remain there without moving a muscle. At nightfall we were to let them know what to do.

We cast anchor and ventured forth. The officers and troops disembarked as well as Captain Vangelis and Theodoros the engineer. I remained behind with a British soldier who was guarding the weapons and belongings the British had left on the ship.

Thinking that the "stukas" would bomb us sooner or later, I got off the ship and fell onto some rocks which resembled trenches. I lay on the rocks, while the British soldier stood near the ship's mast. I gestured to him to come on shore and hide, but he did not stir at all. Barely moments later, the "stukas" seemed to be returning in full force. I buried my head in the rocks and listened as the bombs whistled by. I was covered in stones and water. I froze. I thought the bombs had fallen directly on top of me. The bombs fell on the harbour, one on the beach, the other in the middle of the port. There were about fifteen ships of various sizes in the harbour. They had all been hit and were no longer seaworthy. The "Evrotas" was lucky and suffered no damage, neither did the British soldier who had not moved from his post.

The British soldiers who were hidden in the bushes dared not move. While all this was going on the "stukas" continued to drop bombs and circled the harbour possibly in order to drop more, or to survey the results or even to leave.

Suddenly we caught sight of a third aeroplane which began to fire and head off the "stukas", who in turn returned fire. Consequently a small scale airbattle erupted above our heads. The "stukas" withdrew straight away. The third aeroplane was a Hurricane which had come for us. The General who was the highest ranking officer among us, had already contacted the British base at Suda, Hania in Crete, and a plane had arrived with instructions. After the "stukas" had left the Hurricane returned to the harbour. It flew low. On catching sight of the plane, the British jumped out from behind the bushes and began shouting, as if they wanted to touch it with their own hands. All of a sudden the pilot threw out a small package, waved goodbye and left. The soldiers took the package to the General who opened it and read the message. We were to be ready by ten o'clock that night. The engine was to be switched on. A vessel would sail into the harbour and at the given signal (using a beacon) we were to follow it and nothing more.

We positioned ourselves in the middle of the harbour at ten o'clock exactly. A faint blue light appeared and flashed on and off like the morse code. The General told the Captain to follow the motorboat ahead of us. We followed the motorboat out of the harbour of Avlemona and continued on to the Cretan Sea. We didn't know where we were going.

We must have covered between five and ten miles. We met up with four large warships. As we drew near one of the warships, the British prepared to go on board. As I watched the British climbing on board, they shouted at me: "Come on Jimmy, come on". I got excited and told the Captain I would be leaving too. He began to yell. I started to climb up the ship's ladder while the Captain carried on shouting. On seing me leave, the engineer decided to come with me. The Captain began to weep. He begged us to stay with him. He would not be able to leave on his own. We felt very sorry for him and I got off the ship and back onto the "Evrotas".

Dimitrios Kontos, Piraeus

Bundesarchiv - Militärarchiv, Freiburg, Germany.

The maps of Crete

On the morning of May 17th 1941, a German car drew to a halt in the front yard of the Aspiotis-Elka factory which was situated in Vouliagmenis Street. In that factory the official documents of the State were printed and, as a representative, I surveyed their printing.

The German car was carrying a load of paper. The Germans disembarked from the car. They entered the factory and ordered the machines to be stopped in order to print their own maps.

With an incredible speed they removed from the car the paper and printing zincs they had ready. On some of the zincs the airport sites in Crete were engraved and on others the airport sites of Attica. The Germans ordered that the maps should be ready by 3 o'clock that afternoon.

As soon as the printing was over the Germans took the maps, their printing zincs and, with great care, they gathered the misprinted copies of the maps in sacks and left.

The printed maps had the sites of the Cretan airports on one side and the sites of the Attica airports on the other.

On May 20th 1941 the operation for the occupation of Crete had begun.

Anastasios Zavitsas, Ta Nea, Athens, 1-6-1984

Time of anxiety

On 19 May 1941 at 20:30 hrs, Naval Echelon-Maleme put out to sea from the port of Piraeus. The Reichenhall Mountain Troops battalion reinforced by some support elements under command attacks from other formations left the land on an assortment of scarcely seaworthy Greek coasting tramps and some larger rusty "death traps", to be disembarked in Maleme, Chania Bay, Crete after 300 km by sea.

As the enemy naval formation was moving in a semi-circle round Milos I decided to go on to Crete in fulfilment of my orders. As I was discussing our situation with Lindner, standing in the bows, the Greek crew left the ship and got into a boat. The German naval party-on-board did not interfere, only reporting the incident to me when the boat was already 100 metres away. My first reaction was to force them back to the ship by threatening them with my pistol but I abstained as I could continue without them relying on the naval personnel on board and on the specialists. In any case the unreliable Greek crew would only have been in the way. About two hours later the cylinder ring again burnt out and after this had been put right it was found that the compressed air container had not enough pressure left to start the motor. At this point in time the vessel was about 50 km off Cape Spatha. I had all sails set and continued on to Cape Spatha. The battle between enemy naval units and German aircraft came constantly near moving in the direction of Milos and the Peloponnese. Impacts and hits could be seen 'quite close. Anxiety that these ships might move in the direction of Crete was not proved right. With a fairly favourable wind we reached a point 5 km to the North East of Cape Spatha by 17:00 hours.

At that time a complete calm set in, and most unluckily for us. I was almost sure that enemy naval forces would attack during the night as the vessel had been lying a whole day now in full sight of Crete. I therefore ordered two raiding parties to be got together to make for the shore in two large rubber dingies and secure a landing place for the vessel. Flares were handed out for intercommunication and a detail of signals personnel joined them. I had also the two shipwrecked men we had fished out of the lifeboat and the two wounded men accompany the party to the land. They were in a poor state of morale, spiritually and physically. I briefed the landing party on my intention to join the units fighting in Maleme. The landing party was made up of one officer and thirty-six NCOs and privates with four MGs and several automatic rifles.

Two officers and 74 ORs remained on board. I ordered that all got ready for abandoning ship - this order to be given by me when the time for it had come. There were still four small inflatable dingies on board as safety equipment and I had rafts made from the planks of the ship.

Greek fishing boats tow-away
Germans in order to occupy the Greek islands.

Towards 18:00 hrs we got wind which brought us up to about 300 metres off the coast. Then a complete calm set in once more, and as there was a very strong current along the shore the ship was driven off a little to seaward. During the last four kilometres of our approach to the coast British warships were looking for us with their searchlights repeatedly passing very close by us but did not spot us. During this critical time the conduct of all on board was without reproach.

J. Horbach, News sheet of the Mountain
Troops Old Comrade Association, No 4/78
From the collection of Jean-Louis Roba, Belgium

At Tanagra airport

The first vertical assault "stukas" have arrived together with the "Messerschmitt" fighter planes.

Feverish preparations - something very serious is obviously being targeted against our islands.

Our anxiety and curiosity were heightened on seeing some wooden aircraft similar but smaller to standard aeroplanes functioning without engines. They were "gliders" used for transporting military forces. We had never seen them before.

These funny looking aircraft were being "towed" by the bombers

41

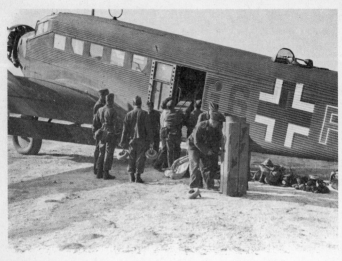

Bundesarchiv - Militärarchiv, Freiburg, Germany.

one by one and in twos. They came and went, landed and took off, transporting swarms of armed forces on to our soil.

In the beginning we thought it to be really funny - later on we saw some of them returning - their wings and fuselage riddled with bullets. We then realized that this bloody uproar was being borne by our heroic Crete. We grew serious and very sad. Gradually our hatred for them began to intensify.

Many of the "Heinkels" and "Messerschmitts" returned from their missions seriously damaged or utterly destroyed. There were many wounded.

The infantry and the parachutists began to feel disheartened, they refused to board these "hearses". Over a bottle of raki, they'd confess to us locals their worst fears. Some were punished and soon these "hearses" disappeared and the Tanagra airport sank into oblivion.

Yiannis M. Vassilas, Athens

German parachutists listing their personal belongings and placing them in boxes before departing for Crete, so that in case they are killed these may be returned to their families.
From the Jean-Louis Roda collection, - Belgium.

Adventure and fate alike

41° in the shade! Though it was late in the afternoon the sun was still scorching mercilessly. Tents stood in the half shadow cast by the sparse, small leaves of gnarled olive trees. The hard grass had been crushed underfoot and reddish yellow dust came up with every step.

All weapons were checked. Where the grass was still thicker long parachute strips were being packed into plump bundles which for all of us meant adventure and fate alike. Bodies stripped to the waist bent in the sun over red, yellow and white weapons containers. Markings and rings painted in bright colours were the last visible expression of the complicated organisation for a parachute troops operation of this kind. It had begun at home, somewhere in Germany; all of this had been moved up over thousands of rail kilometres, mainly by a detour to Constanza, then flown over rugged mountains or taken by ship to Piraeus.

Now we were prepared for action. It was the 19th of May 1941.

My jeep - booty from Corinth - passed slowly through the dive grove followed by a dense cloud of smoke.

"Hello, Lieutenant, Sir!" It was my old sergeant Simon. He jumped on my jeep and gave me a questioning look under his captured pith-helmet. "Crete? - bit dicey, still only afternoon and time for a second wave!" "What? - second wave when it's all over?" "Yes, and what's more there's lots of stones there and damned all else, no grub either! But let the boss tell you - here he comes."

I waved to Lt. Jahnke as he drew up in the truck, shook Simon's hand. I was not to see either again ...

The picture was the same in my company area. As I came up men busy with the containers rose to their feet, let the parachutes lie and crowded round me. They knew that we were to go into action, but where? There was talk of Crete, there had been something about it in the press - that Crete was next!

Every parachute troops operation succeeds or fails by keeping things under one's hat, and it was still too early to tell them what I had heard at the battalion ops. briefing. It was all too easy for Greeks on the road to catch a word or other while bargaining with our chaps over a pound of cherries.

Crete! I had as yet no idea of how this name was to be linked with memories of sweat and blood, hunger and thirst, cruelty and toughness.

I had the map and aereal pictures of our operationed sector at Rethymnon (Retimo). Some lines, arrows and symbols indicated what Captain Kroh had just briefed his company commanders on. There was still a little time left before the written order for action would come.

"Sergeant-Major Amm!"

"Yes, Sir!"

"Call the platoon commanders."

"Very well, Sir!"

He did not have to call them. The lot of them had already come as though 'quite by chance' they had some work to do nearby.

"Lt. Wenzlaff, Lt. Schulze, Sgt. Major Barutzki, be seated." They sat down, full of curiosity, around the grey officer's box serving as a table. The maps and photos for the operation lay on that box: Crete!

Anton von Roon, "Parachute troops operation - Crete" MEN OF ACTION

Blinding Greek dust helped defeat Hitler

Dust turned the tide of the Second World War by delaying the capture of Crete by Hitler's crack paratroops and forcing him to postpone his attack on Russia.

Retired Lieutenant-Colonel Josef Neuhaus, a Luftwaffe fighter pilot aged 24 during the German thrust against Yugoslavia and Greece in 1941, said that 500 Ju 52 transport planes taking the parachutists to Crete from improvised airfields in southern Greece could not take off in rapid sequence because of the dust.

"The clouds of dust whipped up by the first take-offs blinded the other pilots, with the result that by the time the transports reached their destination, our fighters and bombers providing the air cover had to dash back to refuel," he said.

Mario Modiano, THE TIMES, London, 22-10-1987

What kind of hell they are flying

The 20th of May is a brilliant sunny day. The inhabitants of the small town of Megara are listening with surprise to the sound of aircraft engines reaching them from the military airstrip near their town because that sound is continuous and louder by far than ever before. Then they see it happen as one browny three-engined Junker 52 after another, like links in a chain, are taking off the dusty runway pulling behind them by rope transport gliders looking like clumsy silent birds.

There are about nine to eleven men squatting in such "crates". They are bunched up close together astride a pole stretched along the contraption. They carry heavy packs with weapons and other equipment, also life-jackets as the flight is over the sea.

Lieutenant Genz, aged 25, OC 1 Company, 1 Battalion of the Parachute Assault Regiment still stands by the glider in which he is to fly and is about to board it as the last to do so when a messenger is seen racing across the airstrip towards his glider. He hands an Order to the company commander who looks at the date and is surprised because according to the date the Order should have reached him two days ago. Then he reads the Order. Colonel (Ret'd) Genz still remembers this moment and says: "I did get cold feet when I read it because item 1, and this was in those days always the so-called enemy item, read: "Contrary to previous assumption of enemy strength on the island one will have to reckon not with about 12000 but with about 48000 men". No wonder that the Lieutenant felt queasy. He knows, of course, as Company Commander only his own and his neighbouring units' battle tasks but not the entire operational plan, but he does know that just about 4000 paratroops are to touch down in Crete. 4000 of them lightly armed with pistols, machine-guns, hand-grenades and light mortars are to engage an enemy with a tenfold superiority in numbers, well entrenched in fortified positions and supported by artillery and armour ....

"Come on in, Sir, it's our turn now!" yells No 1 Company Sergeant Major from the glider.

It is not only Lieutenant Genz's boys but most of the scarcely 4000 strong force who have no idea towards what kind of hell they are flying. True they are, everyone of them, volunteers, splendidly trained for dicey special commitments. They are also fully aware that in their way of fighting they are nearer death than other soldiers. What they do not know is that only every second one of them will see to - morrow's dawn.

Der Zweite Weltkrieg, Heft 29

Last minute preparations

We were coming down from the North Epirus front, through Western Greece, on the tragic days of the third-fourth week of April 1941, by two trucks of our unit. We were among others, eight reserve officers, lieutenants and second lieutenants and we were discussing what would be the best to do upon arriving home, since we knew that the Germans would very soon enter Athens. The conclusion we all reached was that we ought to find a way to pursue the fight in whichever way possible. On our arrival in Athens at dawn, we separated. We fixed a meeting for that evening at Syntagma on the condition that each of us, spending no more than a few minutes with our families, would try to find a solution so that we might be able to leave for Crete or even Egypt, the soonest possible. We did not as yet know whether there were any Germans in Crete or not.

So I ran home where I found out that the King and Government had just left for Crete and that the British troops that were still in Athens were leaving and noone knew where they were heading. I was told by the Greek garrison commander's office to go home, take off my uniform and wait for any developments because nobody, at this time, was able to give any concrete information. I then tried to find out where the British units' offices were situated. The few I finally succeeded in finding, were either vacant or the officers and armed soldiers were in a hurry to gather whatever they could and leave; so they sent me away. Finally somebody told me that the British headquarters could be found at the Acropole Hotel in Patission Street. There, they were also in a hurry to leave but after much pleading and argument, an officer phoned his Commanding officer on one of the top floors and I was sent there. The Commander, a brave English Captain, heard that we were eight new officers with no other wish but to fight with all our strength for our country and that it was impossible for the Allied forces not to be in need of people like us. The Commander replied that, yes, he was convinced but on the other hand could do nothing. "I will give you a confidential piece of information", he said "that may be of use to you. Tonight at midnight a coal-carrier ship called GEORGE POTAMIANOS will sail out from Keratsini. She is going to Crete and you will be able to get on board without difficulty".

I hurried home and as it was still too early for my appointment with the other seven men, I got a suitcase packed with my most necessary belongings and left to meet them at Syntagma Square. I was happy because I was about to tell them that an immediate solution had been found. As they arrived one by one I gave them the good news enthusiastically. It was only when I told the last man, that I became aware that this enthusiasm was not mutually shared. Each of them were prevented by either their wife, mother or sister and could not leave just then.

I kissed my loved ones goodbye and went down to Keratsini by myself. The cargo ship had in fact already docked. Nobody stopped me from getting on board. I searched for a long time in the dark to find someone to ask. I was met with silence or one-word replies. At some point I noticed a dim light and distinguished two figures in soldiers' caps. I drew near and saw two middle-aged majors, one of them - Anastasios Dalipis- whom I happened to know. He introduced me to the other one, who was Captain Pavlis Gyparis, the well known "pallikari" and right hand of the late Eleftherios Venizelos. Both had been dismissed in the 1935 coup d'état, I think; but they were called back a few months before to rejoin the army with the rank they had held at the time of their dismissal. They were the ones who told me that, apart from coal, the ship was carrying wounded Cretans who were able to walk. In the ship there were others, non-wounded officers and infantry soldiers, also some in civilian clothes.

The ship set out a little after midnight and cast anchor, before sunrise, in a deserted little port the name of which I was unable to ascertain. Our aim was not to be seen by the German planes since we were completely unarmed. Indeed, some planes which we caught sight of in the distance, did not approach us. On the second night the ship sailed out again and arrived in Suda after daybreak. As we found out later, we were relatively safe from the planes because a fair amount of anti-aircraft units had settled around the bay of Suda. There were, however, some sunken ships in the bay.

In Suda we were met by a small military group who told the badly wounded to go to their homes by any means of transportation and the rest to present themselves to the Military Headquarters at Chania, about 4-5 kilometres away.

On our arrival we found out that there was a Greek Military Command for the whole of Crete. Its commander was Major-General Constantinos Vassos, descendant of a very well known military family. The Chief-of-Staff, a Cretan I think, was a wonderful officer and man whose name I am sorry to say escapes me. The only organized military forces were British, independent of the Greek

Command but in "open-hearted" contact with them.

The Military Command was trying to establish a fighting unit for the defence of the island made up of volunteers like us who presented themselves there and a number of infantry soldiers- mostly Cretans who were already there- organising the few staff and personnel, trying to find a way to arm them and form a commissariat for its needs.

In the meantime the government which had settled somewhere in Crete, with the Cretan Emmanuel Tsouderos as Prime Minister, decided it would be better to replace the Military Commander with a Cretan Major-General. That was done.

In the few weeks that followed, a defence plan was drawn up, guard posts were set up in dominating strategical points, telephone lines were installed in from the Military Command to the guard posts, improvised fortified positions were established etc. Next to the Military Command at the bottom of a dam, an underground galley in the shape of a Π, with two protective walls in front of its entrances, was constructed in order to be used as a shelter against possible air raids.

Amid the feverish preparations, those of us who were posted in Chania, had our "entertainment". A local fellow combatant informed us that in the narrow streets of the market place, there was a small confectioner's shop, whose owner made two trays of "galaktoboureko" every afternoon, with the scarce sugar he managed to get hold of. At a certain time early in the afternoon, he served the desert piping hot. Both trays lasted one hour at the most. Whenever we were able to steal a few minutes at the right time, we ran to the confectioner for a piece of "galaktoboureko" and if we managed to deceive him, we got a second piece and some of us a third. Whoever hasn't been to the front will probably not understand this great pleasure. But if the only sugar their body received in 6 or 7 months was from a handful of raisins once or twice a week, they would understand. (To be honest, when we found ourselves near Aghioi Saranta and we happened to send a truck with suppliers over there, we used to buy "halva" of which there were large quantities in the Italian warehouses.)

During the second week of May, a few trucks came- I don't know from where- full of guns, to the Military Command. They must have

49

been about 5,000. As far as bullets were concerned they were sent without being counted. Our eyes sparkled with joy. Each man in our force could be given at least a gun and there would be quite a few left over. Our joy though was short-lived. Our new Military Commander, assuming that there was no time to organise a regular force, thought the guns would bring a better result in the hands of the civilians who came to ask for one, without listing it or noting down the receiver's credentials and without unloading them and counting them first. This was justified by the fact that it was an emergency in view of the expected German attack and maybe the much talked about and unrivalled bravery of the Cretan population.

We were thus obliged to share the guns out, taking them from the trucks as they had come, also giving each man a handful of bullets. We had many customers because they had all been properly briefed. As we were sharing out the guns we understood that not all arms were the

The War Illustrated, London, 13.6.1941.

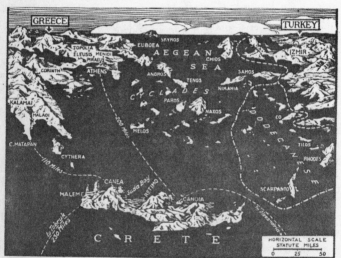

THE ISLAND OF CRETE, invaded by Nazi air-borne troops on May 20, lies at the southern end of the Aegean Sea and has an area of 3,195 square miles. (England has an area of 50,874 sq. miles). There are no railways, and few good roads. Heraklion (Candia) on the north coast is the largest city, with a population of some 34,000. The only other modern towns are Canea (27,000) and Retimo (9,000).
Specially drawn for The War Illustrated *by Felix Gardon*

same, but it was too late for our urgent orders to be changed. We were left with a small number of guns and a little pile of cartridges. As we were putting the remaining guns in order, we noticed there were some Mauzer, Manliher, St. Etienne, Gra and Enfield. The various cartridges were not suited to the guns. We ended up giving out to each man (including the officers) a gun, a few usable cartridges and a few reserves.

Vassilios Emke, Athens

The Minotaur

THE "ISLE OF DOOM"

Before the battle

In their uneven fight against the Germans on mainland Greece, in April 1941, the Greeks were assisted by two and a half divisions and two to three battalions of Allied troops, composed of English, Australians and New Zealanders, known as the "British Expeditionary Corps". Fifty thousand men in all. A front was created along the Aliakmon river, but soon the British and Allied forces were ordered to fall back to Thermopylae. The legendary pass was the last attempt to create a front. However, after three days of brave fighting, the Greeks and British were finally obliged to withdraw southward, through delayed action.

While the battle was raging around Corinth, the British succeeded in blowing up the Isthmus. By this time the greatest bulk of the "British Expeditionary Corps" had already crossed the Corinth Canal and was safe on the Peloponnese. From there, as well as from the beaches of Attica, the British Navy successfully evacuated forty-three thousand British soldiers, about half of which were taken to Crete.

These men, shattered by hardships and exhaustion, yet never demoralized, took part together with the Greeks in the last minute preparations for the imminent German invasion. Here it must be mentioned that the Greek forces in Crete were limited at the time of the battle, as the tough and fearless 5th Cretan Division was not on the island, as having taken part in the epic fight against Mussolini's armies and the Germans. The Greeks had been assured that the defence of the island would be covered by the British. Moreover, the locals themselves, those brave and proud warriors, had hardly any weapons, as the Metaxas regime had practically confiscated them with the outbreak of war. Armoured with all sorts of antiquated guns, they stood by the side of their Allies, ready to face the imminent danger.

Not arms but much courage

I was evacuated from Greece aboard H.M.S. "Glendyle" and landed at Suda Bay on Anzac day 25 April 1941. I was then Intelligence Sgt. for 22 Battalion and we were in defence positions at Maleme. Prior to the battle I was instructed by Colonel Andrew V.C. to travel northwards up the coast toward Kolimbari to search for personnel from the Royal Military College from Athens who were reported to have sailed for that area. The purpose of my search was to locate their positions, find out their condition, what arms and ammunition they had, and in general to inform them of the impending invasion by the Germans and tell them of the general battle plan, and information. Along with Corporal Tom de Lisle we located the party at the Monastery at Kolimbari, under command of a Greek Brigadier. We had a friendly and pleasant visit and I was shown their very meagre supply of ancient arms and ammunition. I clearly remember the Brigadier saying: "We have not much arms, but we have much courage". We explained that they could expect little support in the matter of supplies and that their nearest support was the Greek Regiment at Kastelli who they should contact. I believe that history states that these brave people at Kolimbari were subsequently executed in reprisals for acts in the battle at Kastelli.

Frank Twigg, New Zealand

Waiting for a meal

The "Ack-Ack Cruise Phoebus" sailed into the port of Suda-Bay Crete. We disembarked, and we were informed to take the road west and we would come to an olive-field cook-station. This was a couple of miles. Along the main road on the left, there was the open cook-house and a queue snake-like and thousands of troops waiting to get a meal. I was among hundreds who got nothing and just as I, had joined other troops making our further way along the road to another open cook-house. There was none. And it was dusk, I slept on a wooden form inside the door-way of a monastery. And my first encounter with the Cretans was a priest or monk who woke me up and gave me some oranges. And I left to be on my way again westward with stragglers who like myself were looking for the camp and cook-house from the previous day. I came to the area where there were thousands of troops, British, Australian and New Zealanders and found a botch of Royal Army Ordnance Corp lads who I had been attached to in Greece. So I joined them, they rallied round with their meagre rations of bread and tin-food, and I got a cold meal sharing with them my three oranges I had from the Greek priest or monk who had given them to me and I had eaten one. I spent about a week in this area sleeping out in the open, and each morning collecting dry rations. And as I was still with my rifle and ammunition I had to take on guard-duty at night, as the talk going around that Crete would be invaded by the Germans and by paratroops.

Edward Carracher, Scotland

No boots, no rifle

Everybody was relieved to be out of Greece and we hadn't been bombed or sunk on the way, that wouldn't have been exciting, and there we were. And there was the local "raki" well, there wasn't much food. So, I think that morale was all right. I remember Freyberg asked one pertinent question to Vasey, who was a Senior Australian officer that was our Brigade Commander. And he said to Vasey: "How many men have you got who haven't any weapons?" And Vasey told him approximately, I think, several hundred who had no rifles. Freyberg said, "Mm, as much as that?" He was surprised about it. But he said that the Germans would land on the twentieth of May and we believed him. But we thought they'd come by sea, we hadn't heard about the parachute drop in Corinth. Nobody told us about that. One battalion or half a battalion landed with no boots at all. Their ship had been torpedoed, a cruiser had come alongside, they were told to jump, "take your boots off, leave your rifle behind and jump". And they jumped. So they arrived in Crete, no boots, no rifle. So, you see, we were not really very well equiped. We had, I think, four or five guns, 75mm., French guns, and you looked through the barrel and there were no instruments to go with it.

Verbal testimony of Ray Sandover, Australia

Attack on a hospital ship

Arrived in Canea, we stretcher patients were hoisted on to a caique which took us out to the hospital ship ABA 534, standing off the harbour. Then into clean hospital cots below decks. Soon we were visited by General Freyberg, who chatted to each patient, with particular attention to New Zealanders. Going ashore, his boat was (I think) attacked by an aircraft.

ABA set sail, around the western end of Crete so far as I recall, then headed towards Palestine. My recollection of time is hazy, but I believe it was the same day that we came under air attack. It was a notable action, in which a determined effort was made to sink the ship, and one bomb exploded close enough to seemingly lift the ship bodily, piercing the hull in a number of places and, so far as I recall, killing a patient in his cot. It was an uncomfortable experience, and there was some panic on board among patients who may well have already been shell shocked. The Navy arrived to defend us, and the action, during which a Navy helmsman earned a posthumous V.C., was notable enough to form the subject of a painting by an official war artist, published years later in Picture Post. The skirmish ended, the Navy and the Luftwaffe both departed, and we continued our undeviating way towards Haifa. Quiet, but uncanny, steaming through the night with lights blazing and floodlights illuminating the red crosses on the ship's side. I spent much of the night speculating on whether some U-boat commander might be lining us up in his sights ....

This attack on a hospital ship was not unusual, and I believe that ABA may later have shared the fate of others which went to the bottom.

On this occasion, however, I have always felt that the fault is shared by both sides. It is a personal opinion, and perhaps only a German war diary would confirm or confound it ....

Before the attack occurred, soon after leaving Canea, the order was given by O.C. Troops that men capable of walking could go on to the upper deck provided they wore greatcoats and helmets. This seemed an innocuous procedure at the time.

Very soon, however, we were spotted by a German plane, a Heinkel I believe, which did not attack but flew round us several times, very close and in a tight circle. So close, in fact, that through the porthole beside my cot, I could see the heads of the aircrew. Did they, I wonder, report that apparently unwounded troops were being evacuated on the hospital ship? If so, it would account for a good deal of what shortly happened.

Testimony of an N.C.O in the R.A.M.C.

"Lie down aeroplanes!"

My first memories of Crete are of limping into Suda Bay on a bright afternoon late in April 1941, on board a small Greek cargo vessel. Part of the evacuation of Piraeus and originally scheduled for Alexandria, we were a missed bag of Australian and Cypriot troops, together with "Doc" Stephanides (so well beloved of the Durrell family) and a British Consul and his wife and small baby.

It did not take the stukas long to find us, and we had, as a sole target, to put up with some intensive bombing: it still amazes me how we escaped being sent to the bottom. One very near missed started some plates, and reduced our speed to one and a half knots - which put paid to the idea of going to Alexandria. I have vague memories of our anchoring for the night off Anti-Kythera.

Two things about the trip remain very vivid to me: the weird noise made by hundreds of ammunition boots scraping on the iron decks as we took notional cover from the dive-bombers and the calm generated by Doctor (Captain) Stephanides, the British family and by the quite imperturbable Greek captain of the ship.

Our company of Cypriot pioneers, mostly Greek, in which I was an "anthypolochagós" (second lieutenant) after camping out in some orange groves near the harbour, settled into more permanent quarters in and around a farm on the road to Khania. We were soon hard at work on the quayside at Suda Bay- digging slit trenches, stevedoring and being generally useful.

The period leading up to the airborne invasion was characterised by almost incessant air raids, and our Cypriots were in great demand

57

as air sentries -for some reason they could detect the approach of enemy aircraft very quickly, and their cries of "katse khamo, aeroplana" (ie. lie down aeroplanes) were generally well in advance of the official air-raid warning. One quickly got used to diving into a slit trench to avoid the sting in the tails of the Dornier "flying pencils" as they flew low over the olive groves.

The absence of a language barrier made life more interesting- one of our sergeants was liturgically minded and sang in the neighbouring Orthodox Church (when duty permitted).

G.W. Stow, England

Hitler's Isle of Doom

Here I sit on the Isle of Crete
Bludging on my blistered feet

I sailed to Greece to win the war
We marched and groaned beneath our load
Whilst Jerry bombed us off the road
He chased us here he chased us there
The bastards chased us everywhere
And whilst he dropped his load of death
We cursed the bloody R.A.F.
Yet the R.A.F. was there in force
They left a few at home of course?
We saw the entire force one day
When a Hurricane hurried the other way
And then we heard the wireless news
When portly Winston aired his views
The R.A.F. are now in Greece
Fighting hard to win the peace
We scratched our heads and said "pig's arse"
For this to us was just a farce
For if in Greece the airforce be
Then where the bloody hell are we?!!!
The bullets whizzed, the big guns roared

We hawled for ships to get aboard
At last they came and on we got
And sailed away from that cursed spot
Then the navy landed us on Crete
The army marched us off our bloody feet
The food was light the water crook
I got fed up and slung my hook ...

And now it looks like even betting
A man will soon become a Cretan
And spend his days in blackest gloom
On Adolf Hiltler's isle of gloom.

Author unknown   Contributed by T.F. Beel, New Zealand

Lord Haw-Haw

At this period of the war the infamous Lord Haw-Haw was continually broadcasting propaganda from Germany. One day in my rounds at Maleme a group who had a radio informed my section that Haw-Haw had warned the New Zealanders that the Luftwaffe had a bullet for every leaf and a bomb for every olive tree in Crete.

Frank Twigg, New Zealand

No newspapers, rumours only

As a 2nd Lieutenant in the New Zealand army on Crete in May, 1941, I was called from my unit and instructed to start an English newspaper on the island within, if possible, a week or ten days time. General Freyberg, who was commanding the troops who were awaiting the Nazi attack on Crete, was greatly concerned about the complete lack of any reliable news service for the troops. Most of us on Crete had been hastily evacuated after the collapse of Greece and were as isolated as if the island had suddenly been lifted up and suspended as a separate planet above the earth. Such few radio sets as the fighting units possessed had been smashed before leaving Greece. There was no English newspaper on Crete and the number of officers and men who could have translated the skimpy Greek papers numbered at most half a dozen, and they were already employed on full time intelligence work. It was the ideal soil for rumour, and rumour flourished accordingly.

General Freyberg decided that the only way to counter this was to produce not just a cyclostyled news sheet but a proper newspaper. And so one afternoon early in May, 1941, I found myself facing him across a rough wooden table in his dugout headquarters in a quarry above Canea town. His orders were very plain. They were to produce an English newspaper - something that looked as normal and reliable as possible.

Imperial War Museum, London.

I gathered in three fellow New-Zealanders - two reporters and a printer.

The printing press consisted of a small dark semi-underground shop with a staff consisting of one over-worked Greek called Nico and two girls. The entire type had to be set by hand and though the Greek girls were charming (for what Greek girls are not charming?) neither they nor Nico spoke a word of English - a drawback, I am sure you will agree, in someone about to set up type in our language. However, we set to work and disced the French type from the boxes, got ourselves an editorial office in a villa in Canea used for contact by the underground movement on the Greek mainland, and a radio capable of bringing in the B.B.C. Equipped, we settled down to prepare our first number.

Geoffrey Cox, "The Crete News"
Inky Way Annual, London, December 1951

Chania, before the battle

We were on the alert twenty four hours a day. On call continuously. No one could do anything, you could not wash, nor eat, nor cook. Shelter, shelter, shelter.

With the fall of Athens and of Mainland Greece, around the beginning of May, Crete became the free state. Government and embassy officials began to move to the city. Houses were converted into ministries and embassies. Their value shot up. People were running through the streets, searching for a place to sleep. We were young and it was a fascinating experience for us then. We fed, washed and generally took care of as many people as we could.

Verbal testimony of Loula Manousaki-Schlauer, Chania

Nailed to the ground and waiting for death

Word had falsely gone round that planes were equipped with

The harbour of Chania, capital of Crete.
The Weekly News, Auckland, New Zealand, 14.5.1941.

reconnaissance mechanisms directly connected to automatic machine guns, which fired automatically. Every time someone moved they would be a target for the yellow tipped planes.

I recall one such plane coming straight at us and firing all over the place. The stones began to throw out sparks one after the other. We had all fallen flat on our stomachs and quick as a flash my grandmother had flung herself on top of me to protect me from the shellfire.

We grew frightened as we realized that at any moment one of those "steel birds", hovering over the olive trees and houses, would lose balance and fall on top of us. That feeling of fear remained with me for many years after the war.

The piercing whistle of a bomb being dropped was enough to nail you to the ground. Once there you waited for death. Then you heard the blast and the earth's tremor rocking you. The closer the bomb fell, the louder and shriller the whistle. You consoled yourself with the fact that another one had gone. When they threw a bunch of them, however, which was normally about six, you lost count and concentration and left yourself at God's mercy.

We were then told that during the bombings, we should keep our mouths open to avoid bursting our eardrums.

Marcos Polioudakis, THE BATTLE OF CRETE AT RETHYMNON

The last piece of free Greek soil

On May the 7th I arranged to have the whole morning free to go to Canea, as there were many things I wanted to buy, including a change of underclothes, as I still had only the clothes in which I had left Piraeus.

I noticed that the people were very calm and paid very little attention to the sirens. Either they were a tough lot or they had not yet experienced a real bombing. The alert only lasted for about half an hour, however, and we only heard some distant gunfire from the direction of Suda.

I bought one of the local daily papers, and saw that it was on the whole very optimistic. The editorial stressed that Crete could and would defend itself and that this last piece of free Greek soil must be held to the very last.

Theodore Stephanides, CLIMAX IN CRETE

British tanks are being blessed by Bishop Agathangelos Xirouchakis. Imperial War Museum, London.

*British troops pause to chat to a Greek dressed in the
traditional Crete manner.*
Imperial War Museum, London.

General Freyberg to General Wavell

16 May 1941

My plans for the defence of Crete have been completed, and I have
just returned from a final tour of the defences. The visits have
encouraged me greatly. Everywhere all ranks are fit and morale is now
high. All the defences have been strengthened and the positions wired
as much as possible. We have forty-five field guns in action with
adequate ammunition dumped. There are two infantry tanks at each
aerodrome. Carriers and transport are still being unloaded and
delivered. The 2nd Battalion, Leicesters, have arrived and will make
Heraklion stronger. Although I do not wish to seem over-confident, I
feel that at least we will give an excellent account of ourselves, and
with the help of the Royal Navy I trust that Crete will be held.

The guns at the Dapia warehouses

The following episode occurred during the period of intensive German bombings when I was serving at a branch of B. Freyberg's British Headquarters. This particular branch was also the seat of the Staff Officer heading the British mission. We were positioned on high ground built from superposed rows of stones which resembled "sills". They had dug several identical-looking trenches and, moments before I arrived, a wave of German bombers flew over them, and sent all those working in the buildings, diving into the trenches. The enormous Admiral Turnbull and the relatively tiny Sir Harold Caccia were among them. Turnbull's backside protruded visibly due to lack of space, whereas Caccia could not be seen at all. This unfortunately resulted in irreparable damage to that special spot of the Admiral's uniform, brought upon by the hot air from the nearest explosion. Caccia, on the other hand, was covered in dust -from head to toe- as if he had been buried in a moist grave. Both were unhurt. The Admiral sat motionless in his office waiting for spare trousers. As I recall, ten minutes later, they were both drinking a spot of whisky with that indomitable and well known British phlegm. Please note that the cellar at Headquarters was the deepest and safest trench of all.

I was surprised at how many Cretan men and women of all ages were frantically demanding weapons, and how intensely upset I was when I attempted in vain, to make good use of this marvellous display of conviction. I was liaison officer to Commander Jasper Scawent Blunt, one time head of the British Military Mission. I was aware that there were 400 Lee Enfield 303 infantry rifles hidden in the vaulted warehouses in the Venetian dockyards on the quay at Chania. About a week at least before the German attack, I did everything in my power to make sure that these guns and ammunition were distributed to those Cretans. I managed to approach the narrow-minded English bureaucracy which had had no precedent of this kind. Generals Skoulas and Tzanakakis who were the representatives of the Greek Government at the time, were unapproachable. The late St. Dimitrakakis, Military Attaché to the temporary Government, could not find the time to get involved, despite his promise to do so. There were guns left over since the British, the New Zealanders and the

Australians etc. had had to leave the mainland for Crete and had already been re-armed upon their arrival on the 13th-14th of May.

Thus, in the Chania area there were 400 unarmed Cretans with the result that within a week 150-200 exhausted and encircled German parachutists succeeded in keeping control of Maleme airstrip all night long until reinforcements on board gliders arrived in the morning, as there were no more parachutists left. That night there were not even two Allied companies available to stage a night attack, to obliterate this enemy "pocket". However, the presence of 400 local Cretans, who knew the area well, would have achieved a different turn of events. But the British did not wish to entrust the regular army guns to non regimented Cretans.

All those Cretans who possessed old "gra" weapons or hunting rifles, fought at Maleme as well as other places. The outcome of the Battle of Crete is well known. As far as I know, the said guns fell into the hands of the Germans, exactly as they were, unused, in the warehouses of Dapia.

George Xen. Pavlidis, Athens

THE SPEAR-POINT
OF THE NAZI LANCE

The first airborne invasion in history

Tuesday, 20th May, 1941. Early, shortly after 8 a.m., an "earthquake bombardement" shook the entire island. That was the beginning of the first full-scale airborne invasion in history.

The first wave of the attack sent by General Student comprised a tremendous combined force of 280 bombers, 150 dive bombers and 180 fighters, followed by 500 transport aircraft and 70 to 80 ghost troop-carrying gliders towed by Junkers 52. His plan was to neutralise first the anti-aircraft batteries at the principal airports and then launch the first wave of airborne troops: six thousand parachutists. The first drop in the morning was on Maleme airport, followed by two more drops in the afternoon, on Rethymnon and Heraclion airstrips. The battle, which was to be described by Churchill as a "head-on collision with the very spear-point of the Nazi lance", had started.

Where Daedalus and Icarus flew

"20 May 1941. It is early dawn. The haze of the night still spreads like a veil over land and sea. A red sun hovers over the horizon, and suddenly there is something like a vibration perceptible over the Aegean Sea. The coast over which Daedalus and Icarus made mankind's first flight is witnessing an air offensive on a vast scale. Flanked and escorted by fighters and bombers hundreds of transport aircraft roar over the sea. While fire from German aircraft weapons is unleashed penetrating British defence positions, bombs shatter trenches, tents and buildings, an equally formidable load drops from the Junker aircraft - they are German parachute troops. They were born in times of want and endurance following the First World War and were trained and hardened for self-sacrifice. They are Germany's most daring of her very best troops.

The fiercest struggle that any German formation had ever had to face begins now on the hot soil of Crete. The decision to form such a corps was daring enough and the launching of such an operation for the capture of Crete is as daring as the spirit of those engaged in this struggle.

The morse signals being flashed through the close knit signals net of the island tell it and beyond it to the world: "Hitler dared! German paratroops in Crete!"

From the book by Air Force General Student
Bernhard Ramcke, VOM SCHIFFSJUNGEN ZUM FALLSCHIRMJÄGER-GENERAL

In close wing formations

The First Parachute Operation in the morning of 20 May 1941.

Jump time over the objective was set for 0700, 20 May 1941. As had been arranged between the air unit commanders and the ground forces, the parachute troops were enplaned early enough during the night of 19 - 20 May 1941 to allow the start to take place on schedule in the manner above mentioned.

The two wings commanded by the air task force commander Gen. Conrad, executed the mission simultaneously and met the previously arranged timetable.

The principal targets for the 2nd Air Transport Wing (Special Purpose) were MALEMES airfield and the area to the south. The bulk of the towed gliders, each carrying 120 paratroops, also landed at those points.

The airplanes approached Crete in closed wing formation.

Skimming the water along the east coast of the Peloponnesos, they headed toward the western part of Crete, then turned east, crossed the mountains on the west coast of Crete, and descended toward the targets. Reducing its speed over the targets, the wing dropped the parachute units from a height of 120 m., then headed northward and again skimmed over the sea back to its bases.

Shortly before the wing arrived with the parachute troops, the Stukas and bombers of VIII Air Corps executed an attack on the prospective targets.

The approach flight of the wing proceeded without enemy interference. Only after it had reached the targets did enemy ground defences open strong anti-aircraft fire from machine guns and 20-mm. Flak. The casualty rate among the parachute troops and the personnel of the wing was extremely high. A number of airplanes were shot down in flames; a few made emergency landings or plunged into the sea.

No further enemy interference was encountered on the return flight. As had been expected, long intervals of time separated the components of the wing as they landed at the auxiliary airfields. Despite those long intervals, however, the dust clouds were so dense that the landings presented the most serious difficulties and collisions could not be avoided.

Rüdiger von Heyking, from the U.S. Archives "Studies"
Contributed by Jean-Louis Roba, Belgium

"Get ready, Crete!"

"Battalion! Get ready!" Only three words, yet it is no more and no less than: The Assault on Crete.

The aircraft rises slowly. The engines hum evenly, and the airfield goes on shrinking. Comrades down there wave to us for the last time. The bird turns away to the South-East.

The pilot looks over his shoulder from the cockpit to where we are sitting. "All O.K.?" He raises his hand: "Good!" We are sitting in two rows facing each other, with steel helmets under our seats, gripping our rifles. Our packs, light machine guns and ammunition are stowed behind the commander's seat on the level of the wings.

Light reaches us through the windows in sharp beams. We nod to each other. My neighbour, a tower of a man, woodlogger, dairyman and cart builder by profession whose fist almost seems to be crushing the stock of his rifle, is clumsily folding a piece of paper. Who knows - better is best. One clever chap has a huge paper bag between his knees with "battalion vomit bag" written on it. A fellow with a sense of humour has pressed it into his head; he looks after it like after a treasure.

About half of the men have dozed off straight away - from the heat. Below us Attica is spread out like a map. Fields in the valleys and on the plateau are already empty. There are dark dots all over them. They are flocks of sheep. And now our motors are roaring over the capital of the country. People are knocking into each other, getting in each other's way in the overcrowded main streets of the city. An NCO points downward saying something but we can't hear anything in the noise from the engines. We can guess what he is trying to say to us. The Temple of Zeus, and not far from it, looking tiny, the Temple of Theseus. Now the shadow of JU, for fractions of seconds, glides over the huge ruins of the Acropolis whose pillars and towers glow in red-golden hues.

The sight of this vast fortress and temple has a deep effect on us. We feel or rather are palpably aware that we too are helping to build great times and that only toughness can look history in the face.

For this we are flying!

We are now a full hour on the way when all of a sudden the pilot pushes the nose of our Junker down. We are roaring a few metres over the water on meeting a British naval formation and take full cover this way. The six big naval vessels can be seen quite well and the white wash left by them in their wake as they zig-zagged wildly on their course. Clouds from AA guns lay over the ships and are billowing up. They grow, concentrating narrowly, then draw away without, so it seems, any plan. Beyond, over there, only a few kilometres from us there is fierce fighting. Some of our fighter escorts turn away to join in the fray.

With little space to spare three aircraft roar over our clumsy Junker. We see youthful, laughing faces, from under the protecting cover of their cockpits, waving to us: "Good luck to you, Comrades!" Who knows what is in store for us? But it is something great, unknown and like an adventure. Body and soul are totally committed, yet there is still something left for our folk at home to whom we owe both life and its joys. They are the ones who for each one of us make up the great community on whose behalf we carry arms. This bidding farewell in silence is interrupted by the call from the aircraft radio operator: "Get ready, Crete!"

A huge blue silhouette rises from the sea. Steep mountain peaks, jutting promontories, dark blue eroded ravines. Our planes plunge towards the island like iron shavings drawn by a magnet. To our right a long and deeply fissured peninsula reaches out for the blue sea. Flying at an altitude half that of the mountains our JU follows the coast line. The pilot has pushed the aircraft down as much as possible not to present a target to the British. Machine gun bursts skim the water below us- but fall far too short.

"Hold tight!" Suddenly the ground is over us with buildings, a strip of shore, vineyards and spray from the sea. There is nowhere to touch down, and once more the JU lifts itself and floats in a wide curve over the water. Brown fountains erupt and cover the transport aircraft already landed with earth, smoke and dust.

"It's Ascension Day, isn't it?" says one of us, and we shout into each other's ears: "Once we're down this opportunity has been missed for good and all!"

Once again the pilot makes an attempt to land, this time he tries it on a stretch of pebbles along the gently curving bay, but the terrain could scarcely be more unscrutable. It consists of an uneven high and narrow strip along the shore which to make things even worse is crossed by boggy brooks with densely matted reed islands and a wrecked German aircraft thrown in for good measure.

The terrain seems bewitched. What about another go for the airfield? No, that won't do either! Continuous impacts from enemy shelling with British and German aircraft lying about in motley array

71

on the runway. In spite of all this chaos some Junkers still manage to land men, weapons, munition and then take off in dense smoke from bursting shells.

The pilot must decide now. It will be a hard choice to make and we are fully aware of this, yet we observe all that is going on as though it were merely a game. We seem to be detached from ourselves watching ourselves like bystanders. Our pilot curses. He has to touch down but is determined to return his aircraft to base. "Damn bloody Crete!"

Well, well - have things come to this? MG bullets pierce the right wing. Now he grits his teeth. To hell with it- the bird must land. The JU just manages to jump over a vine, touches ground, rears up and digs with one wing into the ground. Grinding under the huge pressure it breaks asunder in the middle and rips the fuselage half a turn to the left.

Men, packs, life jackets, ammunition are thrown forward, torn and squeezed tightly. No use holding on to anything. For some seconds we have lost every bit of control over our bodies. Then the JU comes to a halt half standing on its head. But we still grip our rifles. None have been hurt.

"Out!" someone calls.

Only two hours ago we were lying under the shade of our planes on the mainland and now we are being fired on from everywhere. We plunged into one of the most important British strongholds.

Now suddenly we become fully aware of the importance and of every kind of consequences imaginable of being on Crete, one of the cornerstones of Britain's rule over the Mediterranean. The British had only one thing in mind: The island must be held-and held at any cost. We, too, have but one order: The island must be taken. These and similar thoughts flash by while already running over the narrow strip of ground by the sea to get away from enemy fire. Slowly and carefully captured trucks pass by with wounded mountain troops on the way to the first aid stations.

Kurt Neher, Germany
VON SERBIEN BIS KRETA

Song of the Paratroops

Red shines the sun, stand by, it may not smile for us tomorrow.
Start up the motors, let them have it full,
Get going now, lift off against the foe.
There's no way back, Comrade, no way back.
Dark clouds ahead, far to the West.
Come then, say nothing, - come!

Engines athunder, in thoughts alone,
In thoughts of dear ones left at home.
Now lads it's time to jump
And we are floating to the foe
Quick we are landing now.
There's no way back, Comrade, no way back
(Repeat refrain from verse I).

We are but few yet our blood is wild!
Dread neither foe nor death.
One thing we know - for Germany in need - we care!
We fight, we win, we die
To arms, to arms!
There's no way back, no way back
(Repeat refrain from verse I).

20 May, 1941, Crete, Maleme, Height 107

Crete is in sight. Stand by! We are still about 180 metres above ground; we'll be dangling from our 'chutes too bloody long! A splattering against the fuselage, and the fellow behind me collapses unconscious - or dead? No time to think about it. Now's the moment! Get my cycle out, have to grip the respirator with one hand, as I can't squeeze it into its container because of my Leica camera. Here I go, the first to jump. As the 'chute opens, I hear whistling in the air, all around me. It's bullets! The British are ready for us and greet us. In no time I become aware of floating over a British position. Six Tommies are standing firing at me. Bloody bastards! Wait till I touch down! I unstrap myself but still hang from the thigh belts and get my pistol ready.

From the War Diary of Helmut Wenzel, Germany

Unfere Fallfdirmjäger

Gleich Adlern stoßen fie erdenwärts,
Im Sturz in die Tiefe, dem Feinde ins Herz,
Verkrallt, mit ftählernen Fängen,
Die Stellung des Gegners zu fprengen.

*"Like steel-fanged eagles plunging earthward
to shatter enemy defences".*
Der Stürmer, Nürnberg, 12.6.1941

Paratroops tell of their experiences

The first to jump was a Major, recounts a paratroop NCO from Dortmund, a cheerful 21 years old despatch rider. I jumped sixth after the staff bugler. I can still see him clearly in front of me making his way to the door with his full load on him, holding in his left hand the recognition mark for airmen and his respirator and bugle dangling from his chest. Seconds later he jumped with me like a Stuka following him. My chute had not yet opened when I heard the bugle sounding quite close to me.

Po-ta-toe soup- Po-ta-toe soup - all day long po-ta-toe soup - Po-ta-toe soo-oo-oop!!!

I turned round in my belt and saw Ernst floating in front of me, his head inclined slightly back and his bugle to his lips, tightly gripping his recognition mark for airmen. In my utter amazement I nearly forgot all about landing. I managed in the nick of time to bring my legs together for, after all, one drops at the rate of 4 metres a second when jumping, and this despite the chute, and when one has forgotten to close one's legs it's "Kingdom Come!"

Well, I had a bumpy landing and said "amen". I shed my belt at once and had a good look round at what was going on. Quite close to me stood a tethered donkey with its saddle close by. Our CO had told us before the start to look out for animals to carry loads. Hence I crept up to brother donkey and said to him: "Follow me in the name of Law", and mounted him. We had scarcely gone twenty paces when I fell off. Then I tightened the saddle. We soon found a weapons container and I took a machine carbine from it and loaded the rest on my friend. I met wounded comrades, bandaged them and soon after joined my group.

Kurt Pauli, VON SERBIEN BIS KRETA

Baron von der Heydte remembers

Being dropped in battle is always a wonderful experience. You are, of course, anxious but still you feel you are over the enemy - I can't describe it otherwise because you're coming from heaven. And the enemy is on the ground and this gives you a sort of strength, a feeling of strength. This feeling, however, disappears the moment you are on the ground. The moment you are on the ground you feel very weak, because you have to free yourself from the parachute, you have to look

PK — Zeichnung: Baltz.

for your weapons, and you are shot, or, if not shot, you are in the line of fire.

We did not meet much resistance where we were dropped. My battalion was dropped in the Prison Valley. We had been the first battalion of our regiment and I was the first to be dropped, and therefore I was dropped, I would say, in a valley of peace. It was still peaceful because the enemy who was on the hills didn't realize what happened in the first moment - and then suddenly battle went on-from one minute to the other.

In the first few hours we felt all the horror of a modern warfare. To give you an example, the two hours after the dropping, a fifteen year old boy came to our lines. He had his hand on his belt. I thought he brought me something, but no, he was wounded, and all his entrails, his inside, was open and he was holding it so that it would not fall out.

We had been very well equipped, but the equipment was not yet proved, because the first paratroopers' attack had been at Narvik and in quite different circumstances. We had the same equipment, the same uniforms, the same food as in Narvik, but of course the temperature we had here, and also the enemy situation, were quite different. So, I would say that the equipment was good but it was not appropriate for the kind of fighting we had to fight in Crete.

The feeling after the landing is quite different from the feeling of a normal soldier, because the normal soldier goes slowly into the battle but the paratrooper comes from peace-time into the battle in one minute. And then the normal soldier has a front line, the normal soldier knows where the enemy is. The paratrooper has an enemy everywhere, and especially in Crete because in Crete we hadn't got only the enemy soldiers against us but also the whole population. It was really "la vie en masse', and I must say that the Greek population fought in a wonderful way.

Baron von der Heydte, Germany

Transcripts of interviews conducted for the documentary film 'TOUCH AND GO - THE BATTLE FOR CRETE, MAY 1941' written and directed by Tom Steel and produced by Jeremy Isaacs Productions for the New Zealand Broadcasting Corporation.

Utter chaos

The sky was pitch black. You couldn't see anything anymore, just those monstrous things which terrified you. You could hear the animals, the dogs and pigeons moaning and screeching with fear. There was utter chaos. Even the animals could sense the danger that awaited us then. Later, the parachutists began to drop.

Verbal testimony of Mrs. Vourexaki-Nikoloudaki, Chania
Contributed by Tassos Nollas, Athens

It dropped like a stone

You should have seen the parachutes dropping here, the parachutists falling from the sky. If you made a hole in his parachute, he'd shoot down to the ground like a stone and get killed. Then you'd grab his gun.

Verbal testimony of Stamatis Borakis, Samaria Gorge

Like balls of flame

The sky was lit up by German parachutists who became balls of flame as they leapt from aeroplanes set on fire by anti-aircraft fire. Many were burnt to death as they fell.

Testimony of a British soldier
The Christchurch Star-Sun, New Zealand, 28-5-1941

A cloud of coloured parachutes

At about 9 o'clock the steady drone of heavier aircraft could be heard. It was a beautifully clear day and from where I stood I could see easily to Maleme though it was some eight miles away. All at once, as it seemed, there appeared over Maleme and between there and Canea a close formation of heavy, black-painted aircraft and no sooner had they crossed the coast line than a cloud of many coloured parachutes blossomed underneath them. It was a sparkling and stirring sight. George Beamish, who was crouching beside me, stood up in unabashed professional jealousy. At least I think that was what he was feeling; what he actually said was: "What a remarkable sight - looks like the end of the world".

David Hunt, A DON AT WAR

Sketch by Alex. Droudakis, Chania.

Umbrellas, umbrellas

On Tuesday morning, the 20th of May, the maid came shouting: "Madam, come and see umbrellas, umbrellas!" The parachutists are here. My goodness, it was a sight I'll not forget.

But they weren't that near. We were right in the city of Chania and they were landing in Aghyia, about 6-7 kilometres away. But we saw all the carnage. We saw the "stukas" attack, then planes would fly over us and start bombing and machine - gun firing. Then the parachutists would drop out. The villagers got their own back then. Bodies hung up on trees like grapes. It was awful.

Verbal testimony of Marika Markantonaki, Chania

He killed him with his cane

I remember a time when a couple of parachutists landed in my uncle's yard, right outside his house in fact. He killed one of them outright with his cane, because as they were landing they carried both a pistol and a revolver. Most of the time they were dizzy or they would land on a tree. They would fall everywhere, some even fell on the roofs.

Verbal testimony of Michalis Doulakis, Maleme

Encounter with the British
in the Second World War

Just before my parachute landing, and at the moment when I raise my arms for the forward roll, a bullet grazes me across the chest, passes through the right arm pit and leaves close to the neck artery. No time to bother. Braces, tunic, camouflage, overalls and binocular strap have been shot through, and the Leica carrying strap is torn. I make a very soft landing in a vineyard less than thirty metres from the British MG position. Straight away I fire at two Tommies with my pistol, they fall over, the others - dumbfounded - take cover. This gives

me the chance to free myself of my 'chute. But now they are turning their MG on me. I squeeze into a small hollow in the ground; but haversack and water bottle, still showing, get riddled. Tommy thinks me dead and stops firing. I creep on, tightly pressed to the ground. Where is my platoon? Must collect it! I am desperate, get up and shout as loud as I can: "3 Platoon, this way, to me!" No sooner said and done, when a shot from quite close by grazes my head, this time, however, better aimed than on Fort Eben Emael in Belgium! The bullet went right through my steel helmet, tore the scalp injuring the skull bone. I felt the blow, there was ringing in my head, black and red spots went round and round. I had to gather every ounce of willpower not to faint and I succeeded. My call had been heard! Four parachutists came crawling along towards me. They were: Corporal Engel, Gloerfeld, Primbke and Mospak. Gloerfeld bandaged me up and I rubbed earth on the bandage so as not to become conspicuous. Then we formed a "hedgehog". Bullets were whistling close around us, and one of them tore up my boot and passed through the ankle bone tissue. Then the British went into the attack but were driven back by our hand grenades. They didn't come too close as they weren't sure how many there were of us defending. The worst of it was that we couldn't get at our weapon containers. There was one of them quite close. We crept there only to find that it was the battalion signals container! However, there was one rifle and one machine gun in it. Better than nothing as hitherto we had only pistols and grenades to defend ourselves with. Out of frustration, an NCO smashed the signals apparatus.

German stukas, bombers and fighters were circling over us throughout the day without being much use to us because we and the enemy were lying about all mixed up together; moreover, the enemy had the identifying marks for our airmen and swastika flags as well, and some of our weapons too. No front could be made out.

The heat was awful and our clothes were much too warm. We would have given everything for a bottle of water! Thus we chewed leaves from the vines, they tasted rather bitter. The idea of surrender never crossed our minds. It was Mosbach above all who showed a hell of a lot of guts. There we lay all day long anxiously observing an enemy AA battery on height 107 firing at our aircraft. If only we could get at them there. It was only towards the evening that our Air Force captains pinpointed this dangerous position and attacked. It blew up. This was my first happy moment in Crete.

. I constantly had to fight against fainting. A nauseating smell came from my collar opening. My chest wound had not yet been bandaged. The right arm was getting increasingly numb, and then night came, which happens very quickly here. Here, there is almost no dusk as in Germany. To avoid capture now was the time to vanish off the scene, and off we went crawling towards the airfield; I, in the lead with pistol in hand, the others following. I suddenly heard a sound in front of me. Friend or foe? I cocked the pistol and passed a sign to the chaps in my wake to keep still. It must have been an Englishman approaching us in the vineyard because I heard the same sounds to the left of us. After a while, flares went up behind us - on that hill where we lay - and then there was an awful lot of firing - I think that the Tommies were having a go at each other. We found the nest empty. Thus, we went on crawling all night long over thorns and thistles, through muck and over stones always in danger of bumping into the British. I wanted us to reach the village, missed the direction and, creeping down a steep incline, found ourselves on the western edge of the airfield.

From the War Diary of Helmut Wenzel, Germany

Survival of the luckiest

Whichever side they are on, observers of the Battle of Crete will have respect for the courage, but not envy for the task, of the men in a glider. Taking off in a tow is a risky business. When they cut adrift and sail down into the unknown, over mountainous country, with very speculative landing places (the choice places for welcome parties) glider troops must feel that man and nature are both against them, and it is a case of the survival of the luckiest.

Japan Times and Advertiser, Tokyo, 22-5-1941

Strange men from the skies

Almost simultaneously with the awareness of a heavy droning in the distance, I noticed one of our number frantically pointing out to sea, and agitatedly drawing our attention to something which at first I could not discern.

Automatically the sound of droning engines caused me to look toward the unfriendly skies, but I quickly noted that my comrade's finger was not indicating anything skywards, but rather something toward the far horizon of the encircling sea.

My momentary fears were of an invasion by sea, and I half expected to see an armada of invasion ships approaching our shores, but what I saw was probably unprecedented in any previous operation of war.

I saw them crawling like noisome giants towards us, their undercarriage appearing almost to be sweeping the placid sea.

They were coming in waves, the blackness of them added the sinister to the fantastic, they were easily the largest planes that we had ever seen.

I felt myself muttering the two fatal words through my clenched teeth, "troop carriers", it was quite obvious to all of us now that the invasion of our short-lived sanctuary was to be made from the air.

Very slowly the great heavily laden troop carriers drew ever closer to the island, every eye was glued onto them like a cat would watch a mouse, but then there was a difference, for they were the cats and we were the mice.

Instinctively rifles and machine guns were in our hands, spare bandoliers of ammunition were thrown over our shoulders, the strange fight with these men from the skies was about to begin.

Then the signal for the big drop took place. It was a magnesium flare that suddenly appeared, and even in the bright sunlit morning sky, the super brightness of it as it slowly floated toward the earth, left us in no doubt at all that the battle was on.

The paratroops must have jumped at the first show of the flare, but it seemed a while before the mushroom-shaped parachutes began to

How the Nazis Used Gliders in Crete

1, A German plane towing three troop-carrying gliders, or air trailers. The rear one is attached by cable to the tail unit of the towing plane; the others to the engine nacelles. Rudder bias holds the outer trailers in correct formation. Two, three and four-engined planes were used, including the Ju 52.

2, Dual control. If one glider pilot is shot, the other takes command.

A number of trailers in line astern (3) on a single cable demands a long take-off and presents control difficulties. As many as 10 on one aeroplane were observed over Crete. One trailer may lose height and so drag down the tail of the preceding one (4). In line astern with fuselage attachment (5) and (6), if one glider rides high it may foul the tail unit of the preceding glider with its control lines. These formations were observed by an Australian correspondent in use in Crete. Gliders of varied sizes were employed, some carrying 6 men, others carrying 6 men, others 12 or even 26. All were of simple construction with skylights instead of windows. *Specially drawn for* THE WAR ILLUS-TRATED *by War Artists, Ltd.*

The War Illustrated, July 1941.

appear all over the sky. In actual fact it was only a matter of seconds. It was a revelation in modern warfare, but for those who were guarding that land strip it must have been a most demoralizing experience. There were men and equipment falling everywhere. The sky was alive with the descending attackers.

The glider troops trying desperately to get their heavy machine gun into action, and our new rifles so hot with rapid fire that little warm rivulets of grease were running all over our hands and bare arms. I remember too a pathetic looking German trying to drag his bullet-riddled body behind the glider for a refuge which it could not offer and a field grey uniformed arm which kept managing to raise itself a few inches from the ground to wave a white handkerchief - a token of surrender.

...There was one man still alive. We were about to continue to the glider way down to our left (the one which had shown most fight) when we heard a most agonizing voice panting over and over again, "shotten, shotten", which translated into English means, "shoot me, shoot me".

We moved into the direction of the voice, and we found him, he had crawled into a little grassy hollow a few yards away from his comrades. I don't know how he had got so far, for half his hip was shot away, he had been hit with the heavy calibre bullet of the anti-tank rifle.

I gazed down into his tormented countenance and felt great compassion. A short while before he had been a fine specimen of manhood, as of course were all these airborne troops, all specially chosen men with a high standard of physical fitness, and now here he lay at my feet pleading with me to put an end to his horrible suffering and wasted life.

More however was I touched when I stood over one of the grotesque shapes of the dead German soldiers and examined the photographs which had been taken from him. I saw him in civilian clothes in what looked like a German park or garden, a smart young man smiling at what appeared to be his two children picking flowers. I could not help looking down at his horribly distorted form, and wondering if maybe tomorrow someone else would be standing over me gazing at the few photographs which I carried. It was a sobering thought and it didn't cheer me up at all.

Arnold Richard Ashworth, England

THE ACHILLES' HEEL

First operations in Western Crete

New Zealand Major-General Bernard Freyberg was chosen by General Wavell to command the Allied and Greek forces in Crete, where he arrived on the 29th April 1941 after being evacuated from Mainland Greece. A man of great courage and military experience, six foot tall, with wide shoulders, incapable of fear, eleven times wounded in his career as a soldier, he seemed ideal for the task.

Freyberg, as we are aware, knew well in advance the German intention to conquer Crete thanks to ULTRA Intelligence, but for fear of compromising the secret he was not allowed to make proper use of this knowledge. Therefore he did not alter his defence plan which he knew as being initially wrong. Besides he was expecting a massive invasion from the sea.

For the German part, General Kurt Student, an officer of the highest calibre, although he underestimated the strength of the Greek and Allied forces in Crete because of bad German Intelligence, he had the insight to concentrate his assault on the only foothold in Crete, the "Achilles' heel" of Cretan defence. "I decided", as he wrote later, "to concentrate all our forces against one spot. We selected Maleme airport because here, at least, we could see a glimmer of light."

Thus Maleme and its surrounding area in the western part of Crete, became the focal point of the epic battle.

Those responsible for the war

The head of the Royal Airforce in Crete happened to be a school-friend of mine, from when I was in England. I remained at his Head-

Bundesarchiv - Militärarchiv, Freiburg, Germany.

quarters as a liaison officer and spent my time running here and there, watching the Battle of Crete at close hand.

The following account comes from rough notes I had taken before arriving in Cairo. We heard the gliders landing and the machine-gun fire at Akrotiri in Chania. I was stationed at RAF Headquarters in a tent high up on St. Mathew's hills, near Akrotiri. We had a small regiment of Scottish soldiers to protect us. The battle however was being decided at Maleme and Heraclion. I went to Akrotiri to find out exactly what the situation was, at the request of my old schoolfriend and head of the RAF squadron, Beamish. From what I could tell, a couple of gliders had made crash landings and most of those on board had died. Those who survived attempted to protect and defend themselves as best they could. We were in no danger but I was moved by what I saw. As I drew near one of the aeroplanes I saw 10-12 blond god-like youngsters, no more than 18-20 years old, lying dead in a row. Who knows how many mothers and fathers would mourn them on learning of their plight. Further away I could hear someone weeping and wailing. A young Cretan woman, clasping two youngsters in her arms, was mourning her dead husband pitifully, outside their isolated hut. I learnt that her husband had rushed out to protect his country and his family, with an axe in hand, but was shot in the head by a German bullet, probably someone's who had escaped death and had hidden himself somewhere.

On my return to Headquarters the officer in charge of our squadron "Blackwatch" and I, agreed to send a few men to round up the remainders.

The German bombers, known as the "stukas" obliterated the city. It was horrendous watching them massacre the innocent and defenceless population. They had already silenced the last of the sparse anti-aircraft artillery.

"If I had a German here I'd strangle him on the spot", I seethed at Dalson. "Take your air-rifle and come with me", said Dalson. He led me to the Blackwatch camp. A Scottish soldier was guarding a German hostage, probably someone he'd captured at Akrotiri. The hostage was facing the wall and had his hands in the air. "Kill him", said Dalson "to satisfy your hatred".

Returning to our camp we agreed that the war didn't make you hate your fellowman but rather those responsible for making you go to war.

Verbal testimony of George Tzanetakis, Athens

He had a sword one metre long, tied to his belt

I had been a priest for five years, when on that doomed day, early in the morning, the parachutists began their descent. Within ten minutes I was ready to go where duty called. I stole my uncle's rifle and raced to the church cemetery which was very near by. I sounded the bell and within half an hour all those who were able-bodied and possessed guns, had gathered about me.

Crowds from all of Selino rushed to get to Anovo-Floria and Messavlia to forestall the descent on Kandanos ...

As the sun set, our numbers grew as we carried on in the darkness. We were all fighters with a common cause...

As we headed on into the darkness our song and laughter was disturbed by a strange sound which ruined the splendour of the night. It was a metallic sound commonly known as "grinding".

I was in the middle of our group and stopped to see where on earth this "grinding" was coming from.

I asked a young man of about 16-17 years old who was standing nearby and he answered my question. "This piece of iron that's making the grinding sound belongs to me, Father Stylianos". He lifted his arm to show me. It was a Turkish sword, about a metre in length, known as a "gra" (those of us who are older remember them well). He had the sword tied at the hilt on to his belt using a flimsy rope, so that he wouldn't get tired of holding it in his hand .... however due to its size and weight, it dragged along the ground and the metal made this "grinding" sound ....

When I asked him "Where are you going my lad?", he answered: "The same place as you, Father". "Yes," I answered "but we are not going off to celebrate, we're going off to war and if anything should happen to you we'll have to answer to your father". The boy drew near and said: "Let me kill one of them too, Father .... My mother has sent me .... I don't have a father .... My mother gave me this sword that I might fight with you."

Testimony of Stylianos Frantzeskakis, Archimandrite of Palaiochora, and extracts from his book UNENSLAVED

The free-range marksmen of the Rodopos Peninsula

On May 20th 1941, the day of the German invasion of Crete, the First Attack Regiment of the 7th German Parachutists' Division landed between the Rodopos Peninsula and Maleme airport.

At the same time behind the Double Company of the Greek army, groups of armed local volunteers appeared, asking to take part in the defence of the area.

These armed inhabitants were children and older men; the real fighting people were away with their 5th Division of Cretans in Epirus. They were armed with whatever oddity one could imagine ranging

Paleochora, 1941.
The officiating priest Stylianos Frantzeskakis.

91

Stukas
KRETA, SIEG DER KÜNSTEN.

from knives, hunting rifles and war guns of different kinds. This bore witness to the source from which the equipment came and the completely voluntary arrival of the people. Truly I wonder where, faced with the machine-gun fire of 1380 airplanes, did these simple islanders find this courage, when everything normally would have been paralyzed?

The Cretan's struggle for his freedom and his every moment's readiness for a heroic deed, comes from his family upbringing. He is taught this at home during the very first moments of his life. He learns and sings it, it becomes a way of life. The state just helps by offering him the means to do so.

During the afternoon hours pressure from the Germans upon the Double Company of the Greeks was intense. They aimed to join the parachutists who had landed behind the Double Company in Castelli at Kissamos. At that time the free range marksmen of the Rodopos

Peninsula slipped with admirable agility through passages only they knew, behind the Germans and the results were almost immediate.

At dusk the German pressure, upon the Double Company which had by now reached a point of separation, was beginning to subside. This fact allowed the Greeks to withdraw during the night hours of the 20th - 21st May 1941 from Rodopos and settle themselves in defensive positions at Deliana. By this time they had managed during the whole day of the 20th May, to prevent the German parachutists of Tavronitis and Castelli from joining. They managed to widen the bridge which was the basic objective of the first day's undertakings.

The resistance of the inhabitants of Rodopos was not a unique phenomenon. A similar reaction and heroic disposition was evident in the people of the whole island. This had been a totally unheard of occurrence in those days during the Second World War. Nowhere had there been such a manifestation of mass mobilization by a people determined to display total resistance against the German occupation of their country.

This is why, and rightly so, the battle of Crete is known as the first resistance battle of the Second World War.

Dimitrios Provatas, Athens

The battle rages at Castelli in Kissamos

On the morning of May 20th 1941, I was at my village -Herethiana of Kissamos -which is situated on a hill, 7 kilometres southeast of the Castelli plain.

A few days earlier, I had returned by a small boat along the south coast of the Peloponnese, from the Albanian front.

I presented myself at the Military headquarters in Chania and they posted me as reserve assistant surgeon of the cadets' battalion at Castelli. Every morning I used to go to my office at Castelli, in civilian clothes, and returned to my village and family when it was time to rest.

That morning, a little after 7, a loud roar was heard from afar, from the Peloponnese. A few moments later, some small

93

reconnaissance aircraft dashed towards Chania followed by numerous large transport aeroplanes surrounded by fighters.

All the villagers gathered in the main road, under trees. As the plain and the sea could not be seen, some climbed up the northern hill. At around 8 a.m. three fighter planes descended and bombed the area from Castelli to Drapania and soon after some transport aircraft which were visible, descended and dropped parachutes which looked like umbrellas. We then realized that parachutists with their supplies were dropping onto Castelli plain.

My 60 year old father, dug up a long Manliher gun which he had not handed in during the Metaxas arms requisition. He too wanted to go and fight. It was only when I told him that I too had to enlist, even without a weapon, that he gave it to me. Clutching both my doctor's kit and the gun in one hand, I put 20-25 bullets in my jacket pocket. I was not even sure that they were unused.

As I was coming down towards the plain, alone, I hid under a tree because three fighter aircraft were flying low. I wanted to try out the bullets so I shot at the last one twice. They then turned around from afar, headed towards me and shot at the trees around me. Luckily I hid myself in time under the trunk of a big oak tree.

I crossed the rivers Tiflo and Kakoperato on the south side of the plain. There I met 5-6 villagers from Potamida, some others from Kaloudiana and two soldiers of the cadet battalion which had its head - quarters under an olive mill. They soon disappeared. In a few minutes we had entered the battle, each of us protected by the trunk of a small olive tree.

We began to surround the parachutists soon after their descent. First came just a few civilians and gradually more civilians and soldiers gathered around them.

About 40 civilians came from the eastern side, about 25 from the south and more from the west together with soldiers and the British. The men from the eastern side marched faster than us. They shot sparingly as we had. The Germans answered with more frequent shots which decreased little by little. Suddenly I heard a machine-gun "clucking" near the civilians. It was Costis Xanthoudakis who- as I found out two hours later- had found a German machine-gun and had immediately learnt how to use it.

94

They were the first to arrive in the middle of the plain. The western front was the largest in terms of manpower and organized attacks. By I o'clock all the Germans had been wiped out.

I made sure that all the wounded- Greeks and Germans- were transported to Castelli's Primary School where there were two of our doctors. Unfortunately I din't have many bandages on hand. The first German I bandaged, I myself had shot. He had leapt backwards at a distance of 14-15 metres in front of me. As soon as I wounded him he put up his hands but did not throw his gun. He left it beside him. I leapt towards him, grabbed his gun and just as I was examining his wound (right through his thigh), I saw someone I knew getting ready to execute him. I did not let him.

·Most of the wounded were transported by the assistant driver George Stephanakis on his own, in a small bus. Today he owns many coaches in Athens.

Theoharis Mylonakis, Chania

At Maleme

The most fierce battle was fought at Maleme. Maleme witnessed the greatest combat and the biggest slaughter of parachutists. It was said that many parachutists had refused to board aeroplanes because of what was happening at Maleme. They had been informed from Athens about the massacre. The Germans in Athens executed all those who refused to go.

Verbal testimony of Stylianos Koundouros, Agios Nikolaos

A 19 year old Maori remembers

Our bayonets terrified the Germans, said the sergeant. We asked for no quarter and got none. We lay all day at the mercy of hundreds of dive-bombers. When nightfall came, we fixed bayonets and charged, fighting until each dawn in the bloodiest, most inhuman battles.

We lay on open ground, watching until our eyes ached, shower on shower of parachutists floating down. We lay behind rocks and in drains - anything which gave us shelter from the relentless hail of bombs and bullets. We had to keep our bayonets sheathed and stay motionless while the sun shone so as not to betray our positions.

We shouted Haka (the Maori war-cry) as we charged in the dark. Our main obstacle the first night was a solid line of machine gun-nests, but we quickly overran it and annihilated practically every German within reach.

The Mercury, New Zealand, 2-6-1941

The battle for Maleme "drome"

The Maori battalion pushed forward on our left flank, charging into the enemy with blood thirsty cries and much shouting. On approaching a small group of stone houses we met with a withering fire from machine-gun positions in upper and lower floors of the houses. These we attacked with fierce determination and succeeded in wiping them out. One house in particular put up a stubborn resistance and was causing many casualties on our men. Lieutenant Maxwell, our platoon officer, called for hand grenades. I was the only one in the platoon that had one, this he took from me and called on us to give him covering fire whilst he dashed forward and flung the grenade at the door of the house. With an earsplitting blast the door blew off its hinges, whilst we kept up a steady fire through all the shuttered windows. This had the desired effect, about six to eight Germans emerged with arms raised. These were taken prisoner and moved back under guard.

The advance continued and on our right now was the beach, the sight that met our eyes was one of violent destruction and carnage, scores of gliders lay scattered everywhere the whole length of the beach where they crash landed ploughing into one another in a tangled mass of wreckage, some were still burning. Again we came under fire apparently from one of the crashed aircraft, with one concerted charge at the point of the bayonet we overrun the Germans wiping out six or seven. Before moving off we entered one of the gliders, noticing a large

96

T.F. Beel, New Zealand, among two Greek soldiers.

urn with a tap fixed to the fuselage, we turned on the tap and dark brown ersatz coffee ran out - still warm. The sky was now turning grey heralding the pre-dawn. We were well behind schedule.

Finally we fought our way to the perimeter of the airfield which was like a platoon in front of us, on slightly higher ground, we advanced to the edge of the "drome" shielded by the raised ground in front of us from fire from the airfield. Once we were in position we were told by our officer that this was to be the final assault on the "drome".

At his command we rose as one man and stormed up the slope. I had just gained the higher ground in full view of the aerodrome and with bren gun at hip when I felt a tremendous blow to my left shoulder which flung me backwards down the slope I had just surmounted, at the same instant that I came to rest a mortar bomb exploded with a terrific blast several yards from me and I felt another blow in my right arm, this blast momentarily stunned me and when I eventually clambered to my feet I felt a numbing sensation in my arm and realized I had been hit by a splinter from the bomb. I had difficulty in carrying the heavy bren gun but at this moment a soldier passed me and I exchanged the bren for his much lighter rifle.

As I was making up my mind as to what I should do, a medical officer approached me and asked if I was all right; having told him of my wounds he set to work and applied field dressings, then tying a "wounded" label on my battle dress blouse he told me to make my way back to the first aid post - about a mile back. As he was telling me this a German fighter plane skimmed over us at tree top level machine gunning, one soldier had been caught in the hail of bullets, he ran past me screaming holding his intestines in his hands, my last glimpse of him was the medical officer had thrown him to the ground and was doing what he could for the soldier.

......

En route we were passing a large clump of canes when we heard a slight rattling coming from the clump. We quickly unslung our rifles and called out "who is in there? come out"; to our surprise three Germans emerged with hands in the air, we took a look into the canes to make sure no more Germans were in there; in doing so we found a rifle and two Tommy guns discarded on the ground. It was then we realized just how lucky we were, the Germans must have heard us coming and could have cut us all down. It appears these Germans had been missed in the advance and passed over and they were only too happy to surrender to us.

I was badly shaken and was relieved to be told that I along with a number of other wounded were being taken by truck to the 2/7 General Hospital. When we arrived there the hospital was packed with both British and German wounded. During our short stay there we had ample opportunity to mix and talk with the German paratroopers and the atmosphere was very amicable and friendly. We played games together like snakes and ladders and ludo. Most Germans, particularly the paratroopers, spoke good English. One remark that a young blond German made I have never forgotten: "Why are we fighting one another, two of the finest fighting nations on earth; together we could conquer the world!"

The comparative quiet of the hospital was suddenly shattered by the roar of aircraft, strafing with cannon and machine gun fire, we rushed outside (British and German) to witness three or four fighters making strafing runs over the hospital grounds. We turned to the Germans and said "why? this is a hospital and your pilots are violating the Geneva Convention". "Because, said one German, there are British troops walking around out there with combat helmets on and bearing arms". We had to admit he was right. The Germans gathered up a white sheet and tore strips from a red blanket; these they hastily laid out on the ground in front of the hospital to form a large red cross, they calmly stood around the red cross and waved their arms frantically above their heads warning the fighters off. It seemed to work for the planes pulled off and disappeared.

Tom F. Beel, New Zealand.

I was frightened all the time

A few years ago I was back in Crete, and an extraordinary thing happened: I was talking to a German, who was about my age, and he said that he'd been a sergeant major in the paratroopers. And he'd landed about twenty yards from where we were standing. So I said "how did you feel?" He said "I was frightened the whole time". I said "so was I, that makes two of us!"

Verbal testimony by Kenneth Stalder, England

"We shall get him out"
An Air Transport Command airman remembers Crete

Depressing rumours were circulating about huge losses by our paratroops and it was even said that operation "Merkur" might have to be abandoned.

As I knew the frequency and code of the Maleme paratroop group I sat down at the JU radio receiver as soon as it became dark and wrote down the radio messages coming in from Maleme. There was repeated mention that ammunition was running out and then came the following message: "Severely wounded General Meindl must be moved to mainland at earliest opportunity." Koenitz and I were of one mind: "We'll get him out!"

We immediately asked our wing commander Wilke for permission to fly before dawn. His reply was: "Permission from me not given, but if you start on this without being specially tasked then I was unable to stop you."

This was all we needed. We had our aircraft loaded with ammunition crates and started with a new flight mechanic while it was still dark.

While approaching the bay of Rodopos peninsula Koenitz put the aircraft to a steep climb of 250 metres but nothing stirred when we came over the airfield. We saw German flag markers at its eastern edge.

"We'll land behind the airfield near the shore to the West of Tavronitis".

We had to glide in from the East over the British positions with all that explosive freight of ours. Koenitz made a masterly landing on the narrow beach steeply sloping to the sea, even though the beach was strewn with stones, some of them as much as 20cm in diametre. This

100

was an outstanding piece of work. As soon as we had switched off the engines, two paratroops came running up: "Have you ammunition?" - "Two and a half tons of it" - we replied. This was greeted with shouts of delight. More paratroops came running up and unloaded our splendid JU. I had myself taken to the first aid post. It was as hot as hell. The casualties were lying under trees. The badly wounded General Meindl had a grazed heart and a shot through the arm.

He opened his eyes for a moment in a semi-delirious state, recognised me and whispered: "Things, my dear fellow, look pretty bad, there's snow, much snow". Eight of the badly wounded were taken on stretchers to the beach.

Some paratroops had cleared away the larger stones from the "runway" but even so the aircraft did not reach the required speed; finally Koenitz simply pulled the Kite up sharply - it pancaked but still had enough speed to lift itself off - but only just.

After a long banking turn we set course for Athens. We flew low over the sea till Koenitz rose to 500 metres at the southern tip of the Peloponnese. I put out the aerial and switched on the transmitter to report to Athens our e.t.a. and whom we had on board. When we had touched down in Phaleron I saw a number of ambulances coming towards us: - We had made it.

From an article by Dr. Steinweg, for a special publication of the Comrades Association of Former Airmen
Contributed by Jean-Louis Roba, Belgium

General Student recounts to Raymond Cartier

On the night of the 20th May, I waited with my pistol continuously by my side, ready to use it on myself, if the worse came to the worst. If they had launched a counter attack (which they did not) from high ground 107 overlooking Maleme, then the situation would have been critical for us. We would have been overthrown.

Kathimerini, Athens, 2-6-1985

General Student.

THE RETURN OF "MERCURY"

First operations east of Chania

In the afternoon of May 20th a second airborne assault took place over the cities of Heraclion and Rethymnon and their respective airfields. The seizure of Heraclion had been assigned to the First Regiment, commanded by Colonel Bräuer. The Second Parachute Regiment under the command of Colonel Sturm was to capture Rethymnon.

The first day of assault, however, was far from successful for the Germans. In fact, it almost turned to disaster. The German parachutists, that flower of Hitler's army, as feared by the Führer himself, was almost decimated. Thanks to the bravery and savage fight for freedom of the entire Cretan population, -men, women, children, priests-, also thanks to the strenuous and valiant Allied resistance, that valuable weapon, the paratroopers, had suffered severe losses. In the late evening and night of the 20th May at the German Headquarters at the Hotel Grande Bretagne in Athens, General Student was extremely worried to the point of panic. At Maleme airport the situation was grave; in Rethymnon hopeless; in Heraclion vague. On that day the casualties suffered by the 7th Parachute Division were greater than the total Wehrmacht killed in the war to date. Having almost imposed his plan to the Führer, Student knows that his whole military reputation is at risk. Hitler orders Goebbels to conceal the invasion from the German people.

A cloudless day

My pleasant life in Crete came to an abrupt end on 20th May, a cloudless and warm day. Although for some weeks, since the Germans had occupied mainland Greece, we had been expecting an early invasion, it was still something of a surprise when it happened. Proceedings began during the afternoon with some heavy bombing of the airfield area, two to three miles east of the town, but also of the harbour. Then, around 5 p.m., we saw the troop-carriers and the first parachutists. I was in the western part of the city and so saw only those who descended some distance beyond the western entrance to the city, known as the Chania Gate. But a total of some two thousand German troops were landed on this first day, of whom at least half were wiped out by the end of it. They had, it seems, expected to capture the town and the airfield at once and without difficulty, but their Intelligence must have been very poor, since Brigadier Chappel's British force consisted of 4,000 men, and there were also quite a large number of Greek troops plus many armed civilians, from elderly to very young men, who fought most valiantly and effectively. The Germans failed to take the airfield that day, and never did take it until after the evacuation; they did occupy the Greek barracks immediately to the south of the airfield, and they forced their way through the town to the harbour. But from both these areas they were driven out in the next day or two.

Ralph Stockbridge, England

Bravery on both sides

We were made to embus, and move to the Military airfield, which, I think, was Dopolia. As I Regiment was generally first to go into action, we could spend some time in our tents, till the return of the Junkers. At midday, we were ordered to get into our 'chutes and wait at the edge of the airfield.

There were chaps from a fresh intake with us and their morale had to be kept up as well as our own. Then we heard and saw the first Junker making a very unsteady touch-down. We rejoiced in the thought that it had downed an aircraft, but then spotted that it had no under-carriage and large holes were visible in the wings. Everybody's face dropped. The crew climbed out and told us of street fighting and

104

of bravery on both sides, but it was only when the Junker captain saw the Narvik badges on several sleeves that he knew that we would measure up to our task. The Lieutenant was to command the squadron of our three Junkers. He was a highly experienced airman and those of our platoon who survived owe their lives to him.

When the three Junkers took off in line from the airfield, we flew very low towards Iraklion. We sat looking grim till someone began singing "Red shines the sun". While still singing, we heard the captain calling out "land", but at this very moment the aircraft was pulled up steeply and all of us slid backwards and rolled forward to regain equilibrium. We saw the airfield where we were to be landed, but the aircraft vanished behind a mountain and now came the order to jump - there was a rush and we were floating in the air.

A farmer and his little girl were in a ploughed field. I came down at her feet. She was scared out of her wits and I think nothing made sense to her anymore. When I had disentangled myself from my "umbrella", I went over to her, picked her up and hinted to her to run home, but she wouldn't go without her father.

As dad had a donkey with him, the thought struck me of confiscating it and to tell both to make off for home. Now, however, the artillery had started firing and father and daughter left for home. I took the donkey and loaded it up with the explosive charges entrusted to me. Lt. Col. Bräuer (later to become General) ordered us to assemble on the road and march in the direction of Iraklion. Officers of our Battalion HQ led the march and I led my donkey. Suddenly, a staff sergeant, either Bayer, or the chap who was later in charge of our reinforcements by sea, hoisted the swastika flag to show that we are Germans, and then it all started up because of the enemy. I let my donkey run away with the explosive charges and it trotted off unhesitatingly in the direction of the Battalion HQ Company. A Mc H. 11 was our luck, the British turned off the heat and peace and quiet returned.

On our march forward we came across a corpse of a shepherd and hoped that no-one would say that we had killed him. We advanced only as far as the house on the left side of the road. Daddy Bräuer was standing there erect with a cigarette in a holder in his mouth in the midst of a hail of whistling bullets, and directed soldiers who had come

105

singly to their positions. When I came up I saw Alfred Schreiermann, second in command of our squad, lying at the feet of Lt. Colonel Bräuer, digging himself in, and at that moment I heard him yell with pain, having been hit in the hollow of the knee. Our General, Herr Bräuer, immediately called for a medical orderly and I did not have to help as a specialist had come. I asked Herr General at least to take cover behind the house and this he did, and said with his dry humour: "I think those fellows wanted to knock my cigarette out of my mouth". When Herr General became aware that he and I were the only ones lying down under cover of the house, he called for Major Walter; well, I won't repeat what he said. During the night, I went over to the other side of the road and dug myself in the field near a well, behind which Schmidt, my squad commander, and my pal Helmut Bardeke were also digging in.

Thomas Mikfeld, Germany

Paratroopers and Airborne troops in the shade of tall cactus-bushes await further orders.
Bundesarchiv - Militärarchiv, Freiburg, Germany.

106

One fought as best one could

As we were about to leave Aghia Ekaterini square at Heraclion, we heard shouting: "The parachutists have fallen". "Where have they fallen?" we said. "Outside Chanioporta". We ran to the warehouse next door to Chanioporta where the guns were stored, broke down the door, took the weapons and stood guard outside, waiting for the aircraft. Upon their arrival we opened fire.

The Germans who dropped down onto this area, were too numerous to mention and they fired continuously at us daily. We, of course, killed as many as possible. They opened fire at Yophirakia and Liophita. We just shot them as they came down from the sky. The local police were also there, led by their Captain, Kalaphotakis. The battle was being fought on three fronts; by the civilians, by the police and by the military. The army was well organized, but eventually split up into groups and fought as best and wherever they could.

When the word got round that we were fighting along with many others, our numbers increased as people left their villages to join us. The women brought us food and water and fought along with us. We were not very organised naturally but followed anyone who showed more courage and zeal than the rest. The battle lasted six days. Heraclion surrendered on the eighth day.

Verbal testimony of Christos Bantouvas, Heraclion
Contributed by Dim. Melas, Heraclion

The women carried sickles and sticks

You should have seen the womenfolk carrying the cartridge belts folded round their waists. The women emerged in Chersonissos carrying sickles, sticks and virtually anything they could lay their hands on. The Germans suffered extensive losses at the hands of these women. When we heard that the parachutists had fallen on flat ground here at Lassithi, my wife said to me calmly: "Take your gun and run." A teacher from our village with a three metre long stick also ran to go with me. People were suffering tremendously here. The parachutists fell from both Chersonissos and Heraclion and massacred many people. God, however, destroyed them too. These people had no fear whatsoever.

Verbal testimony of Ioannis Spanakis, Aghios Georgios, Lassithi
Contributed by Katerina Spanaki

Maximos Sivetides, THE BATTLE OF CRETE CONTINUES.

Georgina Anyfantis

Women played a dramatic role in the Battle of Crete. The story of Georgina Anyfantis has already become a Cretan legend. Georgina, twenty-two years old, fled from the mainland after all her family had been killed in the Nazi blitzkrieg, and asked an opportunity to fight with the army defending Crete. She was given a uniform and assigned to a machine-gun post on the edge of a landing field. The post was attacked by Nazi bombers, and only Georgina survived. Later in the day German troop carriers approached, flying low. She manned the gun, waited until the aircraft were close then fired point blank. Two planes, each carrying twenty men, crashed. Georgina escaped from the field before it was captured by the Nazis, and evacuated with the main British forces to Egypt. She is now serving as a volunteer in the South African Women's Air Force.

Betty Wason, MIRACLE IN HELLAS - THE GREEKS FIGHT ON

Women of Crete in uniform

The courage of the Cretan women, some of whom fought side by side with their menfolk in defence of their homes, makes a glorious chapter in itself. Ten of them, wearing Greek uniforms and fully armed, were taken prisoner by the Germans. They were shipped to Athens, and then on Hitler's orders sent to Berlin, the Fuehrer having expressed a wish to see them. A more ominous note was struck by the report that the Nazis had been given orders to examine the shoulders of the Cretan women and girls to see if there were any tell-tale marks of rifle-butts.

The War Illustrated, London 4-7-1941

Telegrams in Brief

The Greek Legation states that 500 CRETAN women have been deported to Germany for taking part in the defence of their native island.

THE TIMES, London, 28-7-1941

The second Parachute Operation in the afternoon of 20 May 1941 - Rethymnon

Following the first commitment of paratroops and the landing of the wing at Topolia and Megara, preparations began immediately for the take-off scheduled for the afternoon of the same day.

The wing followed the same take-off procedure it had observed in the morning of that day. This time the planes headed directly toward Crete. The objective was Rethymnon aerodrome.

When the wing reached the objective it found itself without combat aviation support by VIII Air Corps, because the corps had never reached a decision on the postponement of the take-off. The paratroops jumped without the least bit of protection into a hail of enemy fire -- fire which was all the more intense because the enemy had been forewarned and counted on more parachute landings that day. The losses of the wing were extremly high.

Rüdiger von Heyking, from the U.S. Archives "Studies"
Contributed by Jean-Louis Roba, Belgium

Being shot like ducks

It was a warm still day and a group of us were playing cards under the shade of an olive tree. As I played my cards I could see a small group of men on the beach while just to the right of me was an elderly Cretan peasant working in his vineyard, when we all heard on that sultry May afternoon the sound of distant aircraft.

We could tell by the growing volume of sound, that this was going to be something more than the usual nuisance raids and we all hurried to our pits. Soon we saw a vast number of planes flying fairly low approaching from the east.

The planes were transport planes and were accompanied by a heavy escort of fighters (Messerschmitt).

Then for a moment I watched spellbound with awe as paratroops began to spill out of the planes and I thought surely this must be the greatest number of planes I have ever seen.

As the men who issued from them were swiftly descending to earth, they were greeted by the crackle of rifle fire, which increased with intensity with every second. Some paratroops had their chutes caught in the fuselage of the planes and I saw one plummet to earth; his parachute having failed to open.

The platoon officer ordered me to report to Battalion Head-quarters that paratroops were landing east of the landing field. Before I reached Headquarters the planes were overhead and German paratroops were landing just below our positions.

I had no sooner given my message to the Commanding Officer when a transport plane belching smoke, fire and paratroops was flying overhead, perhaps fifty feet above the olive trees. The men that jumped from that doomed aircraft were either killed in descent or shot on landing.

After delivering my message I returned to my position to participate in the battle which was in progress.

Paratroops who had landed safely were being shot while others were being shot like so many ducks as they made their swift descent. For the remainder of the afternoon the battle raged with pockets of Germans successfully finding cover in the vineyards ridges and any place which offered shelter from view.

These three hundred or so Germans had consolidated in a little village about two miles east of Retimo. It was these Germans who determinedly with the support of their Luftwaffe resisted our Battalion's (2/11) efforts to dislodge them and caused our heavy losses.

Only two of the men that were on the beach managed to reach our lines, as far as I know. The old man who was working in his vineyard didn't get a chance to escape from the battle that enveloped him in awful suddenness and was subsequently killed.

I can recall with some amusement an indignant German paratroop prisoner who reproached us about the unfair manner that we conducted war.

"You should not shoot us while we are descending" he said in perfect English. "You must wait until we have landed and formed into our units".

W.J. Thornton, Australia
From his letter to Mr. Stockton, dated 22.10.1965

In close combat it is kill or be killed

At about 4 p.m. on 20th May the hum of many approaching planes could be heard and preceded by two Dorniers (I think) which dropped smoke flares to indicate landing areas flights of Junker 52 troop carrier planes (about 18 in each group) and say 8-9 flights in all, three to four minutes apart, came across the sea from Greece 3/4 miles east of our positions and then turned west at coast and dropped parachutists (20 or so per plane) from the olive oil factory (to east at Stavromenos) over air strip and on to Perivolia. I think 1.600 in all were dropped at 200 feet, and it was rather frightening.

I was in an observation post slit trench on east side of Hill, known later as Hill A with the telephone linked to Brigade Headquarters and after reporting the sighting of the incoming flights and numbers, I shook hands with my signaller and said: "We may have five or six minutes to live but we will get a few before we die". We did, at close range, and having captured a few of their light automatic weapons and cleared those in immediate vicinity of guns the real action commenced. In all 253 parachutists were killed in and around Hill A for 29 of ours. Apart from Lieutenant Faulkner killed by a sniper on nearby knoll, we lost Sergeant Jack Washer and 11 other men. Three

112

infantries with us shot ten / eleven Germans as they landed which helped and provided extra weapons.

In the late evening of the 20th May some few hours after the landing and in the darkness the Germans had gathered in strength on the East side and North of Hill A. And when it became apparent that we gunners could not hold on without supporting infantry and small arms (a few 1st Battalion were with us) we arranged that firing pins be removed from each 75mm gun and hidden nearby individually but in front of every gun crew member so that enemy could not use guns against us when Hill was evacuated and on recapture in day light at least some of each crew alive would know where pins were buried and guns could quickly be put back into action.

Next morning at dawn Major Ian Campbell (o/c of forces) brought us a company of 1st Battalion plus a company of Greek Infantry on flank and with Don Troop Gunners assisting from the Waddi Trash to west of Hill A. The Hill was retaken and with guns quickly back into action many Germans retreating towards olive oil factory to east were killed. The Germans had brought together a circular next of four heavy machine guns facing the attack, but fortunately for us two of their planes that came at dawn from Greece had difficulty in deciding who held which areas as our forces had placed captured swastika flags in and around us and they dropped two bombs direct hits on their men manning the machine guns just as our attack started. When I reached their guns eight or nine men were really smashed to pieces but one survived and when I got him to stand he was a mess - with shock and calmly walked back down the Hill in direction I pointed. It is thought the attack would not have succeeded if machine guns had opened up as it was pretty heavy going as it was with a number of ours killed and wounded ... War is really horrible but once in close combat it is kill or be killed.

On 21st and 22nd May, when we were burying the dead, I looked at a little wallet of the first man I shot, a parachute Hauptmann - (Captain), and in it was a photo of his wife and five year-old daughter. I thought things could have been in reverse, as I also had a photo of my wife and daughter in my wallet.

George K., Australia

The legend of Max Schmeling - world heavyweight boxing champion

By the late 1930s, Schmeling became very unpopular in the United States and elsewhere because of his adherence to Adolf Hitler and the German race myth. Later he turned against the Nazi government, which, for punishment, assigned him to parachute forces in 1941. He was wounded during the German airborne invasion of Crete in that year.

From the ENCYCLOPAEDIA BRITANNICA, Vol. III

Max's contribution to the war

"... Right after the Parachute - Fall I got wounded. I was taken to the Military hospital, and from there I was sent straight back to Germany. This is how my contribution to the war events came to an end."

Max Schmeling, Germany
From his letter to the authors dated 30-1-1985

Mystery of Max Schmeling

BERLIN, Friday.
The German News Agency claims that Max Schmeling the boxer, is alive.

SOUTH WALES ECHO, 30-5-1941

'Max Schmeling Shot Dead'

TRIED TO ESCAPE FROM ESCORT

Max Schmeling, former world heavy-weight boxing champion, has been killed in the fighting in Crete, the British United Press correspondent learns from New Zealand sources in Alexandria.

EVENING STANDARD, London, 29-5-1941

Poor Max....

In my fourth company, the mortar company, I had a famous boxer called Max Schmeling, and the poor man became ill. He felt ill in the first hours before he could use his mortar, and he was sent to Athens with the first plane because it was a rather difficult problem for the doctors ...

Baron von der Heydte, Germany

Transcripts of interviews conducted for the documentary film 'TOUCH AND GO - THE BATTLE FOR CRETE, MAY 1941' written and directed by Tom Steel and produced by Jeremy Isaacs Productions for the New Zealand Broadcasting Corporation.

Max Schmeling taken prisoner

The first night, the parachutists gathered at an old house situated at the branch of the main road leading to the village of Pyrghi.

On the morning of the 21st of May 1941, Greek and Australian soldiers under the command of sublieutenant I. Tratseas, combed the area around the house and took thirty-five parachutists as prisoners. Among those captured was Germany's champion boxer Max Schmeling.

Marcos Polioudakis, THE BATTLE OF CRETE AT RETHYMNON

Gaolbirds against soldiers!

The group in which Max Schmeling fought was dropped with the task to secure the road along the coast and to occupy a prison in that sector. On arrival and during the drop the paratroopers were met by intensive firing. Rifle and machine gun shots whipped at men from all directions. The snipers were sitting on treetops, in gardens and houses. Even so the paratroops landed with only slight losses. But what kind of enemy was this? The lot of them were civilian snipers with only a few British officers around who apparently had taken over the leadership of this lot.

Not one British soldier was in sight.

After taking some of these prisoners - the rest ran away. The paratroops took the prison whose inmates had all been set free by the British, apparently with the object to arm them or to equip them with the weapons of the paratroops to attack the Germans. Gaolbirds against soldiers!

KRETA, SIEG DER KÜNSTEN

In the toughly fought engagements where personal combat was not unusual Schmeling found himself separated from his group and had to fight for half of a day through the Cretan wilderness till he found some others who had also lost contact with the group. Carefully and constantly on the look out for the British and civilian snipers the small party stalked along on the quiet through the difficult terrain. In the evening they met a larger German group of paratroopers and with these they carried on the struggle for dominating the important road. Here too they took British prisoners. Schmeling had the impression that the Tommies appeared to be content that the fighting had come to an end for them at last. In any case they made no effort to escape although they were aware of our difficullt situation.

Asked about how the British had fought, Max Schmeling said that they had fought with determination but had never defended themselves to the last round. Usually they withdrew at nightfall to occupy a new position or else they surrendered to the boldly attacking paratroopers.

"We don't want to generalise, said Max Schmeling. Many of the British behaved in a soldierly way and also treated our prisoners decently. Thus I saw a British medical officer whom we had captured helping in our forward casualty centre. This, however, is exceptional, and does not alter the fact that the disregard of the Laws of War by the British commanders and troops, and above all by inciting the Cretan population to dastardly and underhanded guerilla warfare had cost many a German his life.

War Reporter Siegfried Kappe
Völkischer Beobachter, Munich, 31-5-1941

Max's American English

I was an N.C.O. in the 2/1st Battalion which with the 2/11th Battalion (West Australians) defended Rethymnon, or Retimo as we called it, the centre airstrip of the island. The 2/11th defended the town, and the 2/1st the airstrip. I was on the forward 'A' Ridge in good position camouflaged by grape vines.

The first German paratroops dropped on us at 3.30 p.m. in bright sunshine, but missed their objective and were cut to pieces. They didn't have a chance; by nightfall we had 623 prisoners in the cage at Piji, including Max Schmeling, who had previous to the outbreak of war been Boxing Heavyweight Champion of the World. He was older than most, a Sergeant; most of the Germans were aged 19 to 21 years, very fit. He spoke good American English and told us "In ten days time you will be in here and I'll be free'. "Why?" "The other end of the island has fallen, Maleme, and Heraklion is evacuated by the British Fleet". How right he was!

A.S. Young, Australia

General Freyberg to General Wavell

20 May 1941

Today has been a hard one. We have been hard pressed. I believe that so far we hold the aerodrome at Maleme, Heraklion, and Retimo and the two harbours. The margin by which we hold them is a bare one and it would be wrong of me to paint an optimistic picture. The fighting has been heavy and large numbers of Germans have been killed. Communications are most difficult. The scale of air attack upon us has been severe. Everybody here realises the vital issue and we will fight it out.

Later: A German operation order with most ambitious objectives, all of which failed, has just been captured.

LUFTWAFFE VERSUS ROYAL NAVY

Three fatal days: May 21st, 22nd and 23rd 1941

"Thursday 22nd May 1941", as recorded by one historian, *was a day of tragedy for the Mediterranean fleet; for the Luftwaffe it was a day of rejoicing."* In fact, that day marked the culmination of a gigantic duel between two equally redoubtable war leaders: Admiral Andrew Cunningham, Commander-in-Chief of the British Mediterranean Fleet, and Air-General Wolfram von Richthofen, commanding Luftflotte VIII. The main objective of Cunningham's warships was initially the prevention of a seaborne invasion of Crete. Actually, during the night of the 21st to 22nd May he succeeds in completely destroying a German convoy trying to invade Crete near Chania. Richthofen's aim with a massive air fleet at his disposal was one and only: the annihilation of the British fleet, pride of the Empire.

And the inevitable happened. On the 22nd and 23rd May and subsequent days no less than eleven British warships were lost with more than 2.000 naval personnel killed or missing. On the 23rd May Cunningham cables to the Admiralty a dark picture of the naval situation in Crete: *"I am afraid that in the coastal area we have to admit defeat and accept the fact that losses are too great to justify us in trying to prevent seaborne attacks on Crete. This is a melancholy conclusion, but it must be faced. As I have always feared, enemy command of the air unchallenged by our own airforce, and in these restricted waters, with Mediterranean weather, is too great odds for us to take on."*

Any hope of a victory of naval force over air power had faded away. Richthofen without warships proved stronger than Cunningham without airforce.

Crucial day in war

(Rec. 6.30 p.m.) LONDON, May 21.

"The Navy is participating in the Crete operations", said the
First Lord of the Admiralty, Mr. A. V. Alexander, in a speech in
London. "There once more it is doing what it can. Today is
perhaps the most crucial of the war."

The Southland Times,
Invercargill, New Zealand, 23-5-1941

"Stukaritis", a war disease...

AJAX probably had the best morale of any ship in the fleet,
because it had the reputation of the River Plate. And a lot of the men
who'd been on the River Plate signed on for the next commission
which was the one I was in. And we had a lot of battle experience and
we had a very good captain called McCarthy who later became an
admiral. And our morale was as high as anybody's.

After the evacuation from Greece, however, when we were nearly
sunk, we had thirty men with breakdowns out of eight hundred. We
called it "stukaritis"! I named it, I called it that! And interestingly
enough it was the strongest men who went first. We had our
commander who was second in command to the captain. He was a
naval boxing champion. He was the first to go. The second man to go
was the physical training instructor. He was the chief petty officer.
Very strong, extravert. And one midship man went, because he was an
only child and his mother was a widow, and he worried that she'd be
worried about him. It was natural. And, as I say, another twenty seven
men. They couldn't go on. They cried and cried. These people were
treated as sick, and they went back to fight, later on. They probably
went to Cairo, to the military hospital. And one of the best men of the
ship, who was a leading seaman, who was on the bridge with me, as we
got into Alexandria we were tidying up; the ship had anchored and
things were a bit tidier, and he turned around and said to me: "If the
old man (which is a sailor's euphemism of the captain), if the old man

120

tells us we are going back to Crete, we bloody well aren't going." That was unprecedented. And everyone jumped if the door shut. And we were all biting our nails. We were in exhaustion for a long time. We lived on bully beef, which is corn beef, and ships biscuits, which they still issued them. They were used in Nelson's time and they still were. You could dip them in cocoa and they were delicious. They withdrew them after or before the Korean War, I think, from the rations. There was nothing wrong with them.

Verbal testimony of Michael Milburn, England

With the Navy off Crete
How enemy convoys were broken up

CEASELESS AIR ATTACKS

When the battle for Crete began, British naval forces, because of the lack of all fighter air support, had to fight their way along the northern coast of Crete relying entirely on their own anti-aircraft fire, while the sky was filled with German aircraft of every type (says Reuter's correspondent in a message from Alexandria).

On the morning of May 20, when the airborne invasion took place, our naval forces entered the Aegean Sea to cover the beaches in the regions of Canea and Candia; but they withdrew when there were no signs of enemy ships. During the night of May 20 about eight E-boats attacked our forces, but they were easily repelled and at least three of them were sunk. During the withdrawal through the Straits of Kaso, between the eastern end of Crete and the Dodecanese groups, H.M. destroyer Juno was hit by a stick of bombs and sank immediately, but our other units were undamaged.

During the night of May 21 reconnaissance reports indicated an attempt at a seaborne invasion had started and it was this convoy of caiques which was completely broken up, as announced by Mr. Churchill in the House of Commons on

Thursday. An enemy destroyer escorting the convoy was sunk. Meanwhile other units which had found the shores at Candia all quiet during the night continued at dawn to search northwards towards the island of Melos to the north of Crete.

The Times, London, 28-5-1941

The "Argonaut Venture"

While the landing from the air succeeded on the Maleme airfield in the face of very great difficulties the fate of the "light ships flotilla" was being sealed on the coast.

Lieutenant S.R. of U regiment tells the story:

"When the sun was setting for the third time the sea which up to then had been very calm began to stir. The small cutters of the van of our flotilla began to pitch. Their motors were weak, they carried a heavy freight and were slow. The Italian torpedo boat guarding its flock ahead, then on our flanks and then from the rear, was skipping water over her deck. Thus the convoy was making its way towards Crete.

The morale on all ships was excellent. The "England Song" could be heard repeatedly. Musicians had settled below the yards, performing on their concertinas. One of them had brought a guitar. Mountain troops, paratroopers and a few sailors were lying on deck in suspense as one does when one is faced by the unknown.

The CO of the Mountain Troops was sitting at a table with some of his officers in the mess. The duty officer joined them to report that all is well on board. The smoking lamp swings in its gimbal over the table with the movement of the ship and dimly lights up the faces of the almost silent officers. A clock is ticking on the wall. It now rings 10 o'clock.

Almost at the same moment a huge explosion shatters the silence of the room. A hard jolt lifts the ship for seconds which seem to be the beginning of an absurd infinity. Senior Lt. P. and Lt. Sch. rush up on deck. The ship's sails stand out white like a magnesium torch lit up by a beam from a searchlight. For a moment that painful light is switched off. Black shadows glide by to port. Once again the arm of that searchlight has us in its grip. This is followed by a broadside. Shells come screaming at us; - there are hits, steel splinters, wrecked timbers, yells from the wounded.

Lt. P. jumps below deck and is met by bitter, biting smoke in the dark hold. "All to the deck!" Men come rushing up from the hold. Dinghies and life boats are got ready for launching. Everybody is going all out to get the wounded off the vessel. The man at the helm has turned the ship on an opposite course.

A fresh hit sets the ship alight. Some men are flung overboard by the blast from the detonation. Some had already jumped. They managed to reach a life boat and two dinghies. The ship sinks with a huge tongue of flame.

MOUNTAIN TROOPS IN CRETE, edited by Major Flecker

War at Sea.

They must have blocked out the sun on Crete that day

During the night the fleet regrouped into two sections to patrol the ocean of Crete. The cruisers PERTH and NAIAD, the anti-aircraft ships CARLISLE and CALCUTTA and destroyers NUBIAN, KANDEHAR and KINGSTON formed one group and further east the cruisers ORION, AJAX and DIDO (the FIJI had been sunk) destroyers JANUS, HASTY, HEREWARD and KIMBERLEY formed another group, and still further east the cruisers GLOUCESTER and PHOEBE and remaining destroyers GREYHOUND, KELLY and KASHMIR formed the other group.

We on the PERTH remained closed up all night at our Action Stations. Shortly after midnight we heard and saw gunfire from the centre group which contained our sister ship AJAX (PERTH and AJAX had been nicknamed the "Terrible Twins" being the same class and always together). We were advised by our captain that this section of the fleet had been attacked by Italian motor torpedo boats.

Shortly before dawn our surface radar picked up ships, on went our searchlights, there in the beams, about 8000 yards away were a mass of small boats, low Greek caiques, their decks crammed with men. All ships switched on searchlights and opened fire. It was a horrible massacre of defenceless men and boats, it had to be done. Soldiers jumped overboard and others were blown to kingdom come by murderous gunfire. The destroyers raced across the area churning the sea into a cauldron. It was soon over and once more the ocean was strewn with burning debris, patches of oil and dead men.

"Inhuman" you say! War is inhuman and when a man has seen his comrades killed before his eyes he is apt to let instinct overcome reason.

At approximately 6 a.m. on May 21st we saw the invasion armada, an air armada, high in the sky to the north-west, hundreds of them like a swarm of locusts; it seemed that every German and Italian plane that could carry a bomb was headed for Crete.

This was the spearhead and we could do nothing to stop them, they were well outside the range of the Fleet's guns. Nothing could stop them, there wasn't a single allied aircraft in the air around Crete that day.

For approximately an hour in a never ending line the bombers with their loads of death dealing destruction flew on towards the Island of Crete, a faint sound, like the buzz of angry wasps, the sound of their engines reached us, we felt sorry for the inhabitants of Crete.

At about 7 a.m. came the real invasion force, another armada, literally thousands of giant troop carrying planes Junkers 54's and Wulf transports, there were that many of them that they must have blocked out the sun on Crete that day. This surely must have been the greatest airborne invasion the world had ever known, an invading armada that encountered no opposition.

We were still patrolling the Sea of Crete, for the moment we were as supreme on the water as the Luftwaffe was in the sky.

At 8.30 a.m. the Captain's voice was heard over the loud speaker system. "The Germans are endeavouring to supplement the invasion by sea, hundreds of small boats loaded with soldiers are making their way from Greece to Crete - (Dunkirk in reverse). The fleet must stop them at all costs if Crete is to have any chance of survival."

Bill Bracht, Australia

Men were dying there ....

Paratrooper Joseph Wuerz witnessed the tragedy at sea in the glare of exploding flares: "Shortly before the attack the Greek crew blew up the engine of the vessel we were on. Sabotage! We could neither shoot nor help; we just stood by looking on in helpless rage. One of my dearest friends was found dead after 16 hours floating in the sea. Sixty of my company drowned. The survivors were brought back to Athens, then we were flown to Crete where we took part in the mopping up operations in the final stages."

The Germans had to depend on supplies from the air right to the end of the Battle of Crete as the British Fleet fighting valiantly on in the downpour of bombs from German "Stukas" prevented all reinforcements reaching the island by sea. For their suicidal action the

British paid a heavy price with the loss of three cruisers and six destroyers. Three battleships were damaged as well as one aircraft carrier, six cruisers, five destroyers and 2.000 sailors perished at sea.

People in Germany were at this time unaware of what was going on in Crete. It was only on 25 May, five days after the battle had begun, that the Defence Forces Bulletin announced for the first time that there was fighting on this Mediterranean island and that men were dying there.

Günter Stein, "Arms of World War II, Special Issue"

If only we'd lost all our ships

We lost seven of our finest ships in Cretan waters. We lost another four in the waters round Sphakia during the evacuation. If only we'd lost all of them, then we would have had to stay in Crete and fight.

Extract from a written account by Brigadier Inglis to Lieutenant-Colonel Ch. Stavroulakis, in Egypt after the battle.

Yiannis Stratigakis, PAGES OF CRETAN GLORY

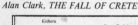

Alan Clark, THE FALL OF CRETE

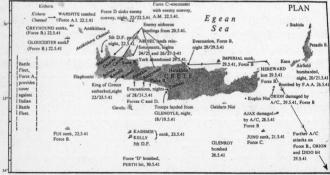

126

22 May 1941

News from VIII Fliegerkorps say, that there is a formation of warships on their way from Crete to Milos Island. This we have orders to attack.

Ju 88s of our entire wing, three squadrons, are on the way to intercept the British vessels. We fly in formation, however not too close, and the pilots do not have to have eyes only for their immediate neighbour. This gives me a good chance to look down to the sea myself. We have a heavy bombload at our racks, and the engines have to work hard to get us 3000 meters high. There are islands passing on our portside, Milos ahead, and "water only" after Milos. Crete's skyline emerges from the horizon ahead, and there, suddenly, are flat clouds lower to us. They are transparent but the sea underneath looks rather dark and empty. Then I see white traces, the unmistakable mark of ships. According to the trace the ships must be rather big and rather fast moving.

When we executed our wide turn in order to get in diving position, I saw more traces of more ships, all making for the West on an 270 degrees heading. We now approached the vessels from easterly direction. Sometimes I saw one or more ships, sometimes they were almost hidden below the thin clouds. Then they started firing at us. I saw the gunfire and they sent rather a barrage upwards. Bursts with black-brownish smoke exploded within our formation, and one never knew whether the next salvo would hit an aircraft or detonate close enough for assuring damage. One could not see the millions of splinters, but I knew that they were there. So our only means was to practice evasive flying by zig-zagging every now and then.

I saw the Ju 88s ahead of me diving down now, and a big ship was coming my way. I saw her now clearly on top of her wake. So far I had seen more or less the wakes only, now a considerable warship came closer to the red line across the window at my feet. A final look to the instruments and I shouted "Ready for diving". My crew members replied affirmative, and down we went.

I had the vessel now in my aiming objective. From bows to the stern she filled the circle, and then with decreasing distance she seemed to grow fast. This was not a destroyer, this was a cruiser, and now I saw two more of them in line ahead. This was something I had never seen before.

This seemed to be a complete cruiser squadron with destroyers in company. "My" cruiser now shot at me with every gunbarrel, and her speed was so fast that she forced me to flatten my dive. This, I felt, might lead to wrong aiming. My navigator struck my knee for the third time: Thousand Meters, he shouted, and I drew my control stick a little more than normal allowing for the ship's unexpected speed. I pushed the button, immediately turning to starboard, and the bombs dropped. I was now in easy reach of the light guns, and the tracers, the "red Privates" as we used to call them, were everywhere. I could catch them with my hands, but I preferred to give full throttle and limp away. I would have given a fortune for more speed to get out of reach of these gunners. All of a sudden there were cascades of water coming up my way. They shot at me with heavy artillery planting water-trees straight into my course. Any collision with them might have lead to crashing into the sea. I began to dance what I will circumscribe with an "A.A.-valse", turn and turn, upward and downward, using the three dimensions. It was no fun, however. I felt that there were professionals firing at me. Good Lord, this was my first encounter with British cruisers, I said to myself, and I am still alive, still flying, to the North now, home to Eleusis. The bombs had hit the wake.

A cloud of smoke ahead made my navigator shout: Turn and pass on the left hand side. We could not figure out what it might be. Coming closer fast I discovered small ships behind the smokescreen, and a small destroyer in company. This vessel produced a lot of smoke and enveloped a considerable number of small sailing ships with that smoke. We saw people waving to us, German Army soldiers in their grey uniforms. The destroyer showed the Italian flag. How did they come here? Nobody had told us, that our own troops were on the seaway to Crete. What if we had mistaken them for British troops leaving Milos Island? I felt utterly disgusted to see them engaged by British cruisers which we had just left. These caiques had no arms, except for the light handweapons of the soldiers. And the single Italian destroyer, what would she be able to do against British cruisers? I felt weak in my stomach thinking it over.

At Eleusis I reported what I had seen. My Ju 88 was taken care of, bombs were reloaded, fuel was enough, we straightaway got prepared for a next raid. From now on we flew in smaller formation. The atmosphere in Eleusis was hectic. The ground crews were working without any rest, the air crews jumped into their planes as soon as 2 or 3 Ju 88s were ready for take-off. None of us had ever attacked cruisers before, and there they were, lots of them, as West of Crete there were even more than we had seen South of Milos Island. The situation was rather confused, for the reports of sightings were manifold and diverging.

The battle was going on. At the briefing we were told that a whole Air Armada was in action. Do 17s of KG 2 made highlevel attacks, He 111s of KG 26 made lowlevel attacks with torpedoes, Ju 87s of Stuka 2 and Ju 88s of LG 1 and KG 30 made diving attacks. Elements of fighter groups made gliding attacks with bombs. This was a day of historical meaning: Sailors only in battle against aircrews only, focused on one day and on one spot.

Lieutenant Gerhard Brenner of Ludwigsburg near Stuttgart was our senior and most experienced pilot. He took me and two more pilots to our second raid on that day. We knew where to go, so we took off and set course for the Suda Bay area. The British cruisers were supposed to have reached that area at the time of our arrival. The flight was uneventful until we saw bursts in the air ahead. So we had no problems of finding the cruisers. This time I dived at a steeper angle for a cruiser, again. I was right to do so, and the bombs were almost direct hits on both sides of the vessel.

When my Ju 88 flattened out I had to go through the fire-shower again. There was no way out, and then came the ominous WAPP-WAPP-WAPP-WAPP. We were hit.

The steering was O.K., the engines sang their song. We carefully watched the instruments for oil-pressure, no slackening. Everything seemed to be normal. The sun was shining lovely, the sea was blue and so were the skies. The rocky mountains of the Peloponnese Peninsula were on our portside, we were still flying and we felt that we had done our bit. The A.A. hits seemed to have done no harm to our Ju 88, and half-an-hour later we were approaching Eleusis again.

I decreased the speed, and I moved the handle to put the landing flaps in proper position. No reaction, nothing. There was no pressure in the hydraulic system. I tried to get the wheels out. Nothing. No pressure. This then is the hour of our airgunner. His muscles have to pump the emergency system by hand. Thank heavens, it worked, however slowly, and this process was irreversible. We could by no means retract the undercarriage, we had to land. No touch and go, nothing. I had to produce an efficient touch-down. Fortunately enough the runway was solid, and it was long enough. But still, I had not done this kind of landing before and I knew of no one who had. Everything looked fine so far, and I asked my navigator to fire red signals. This would tell the ground crews to get everybody and everything out of my way, as an "emergency" was coming in. Over Salamis Island my airgunner started pumping. The undercarriage came out, but I was not sure whether the wheels would stand the touch-down. Now the landing flaps moved into position. We now crossed the beach and I was grateful the runway was long enough to allow a late touch-down. Within seconds we were on the ground now. Would the undercarriage hold? Yes, it did, and I felt relieved. A stone fell from my heart.

"We are burning" shouted the radio-operator! "I see flames below the tail!" He was so exited. "Do you see flames or sparks?" He seemed to have forgotten that the tail-wheel was not coming out when pumped by hand. So the tail was a steel-bow, and as we had landed on a macadam-runway, the steel tail was a sparking end.

I parked my Ju 88 and we jumped out. What a relief. We saw a number of hits rather substantial holes in our portside wing. Oil was leaking from them, Hydraulic Oil. My L1+NK was gone for the time being. But she had us taken home safely. We caressed her. She had done a fine job.

The situation room was a bees nest. Brenner reported what we had done, and our A2 officer asked for what we wished to add. No comment, all clear. We prepared for raid number three. The runway looked like a rush-hour, a constant flow of aircraft coming and going. The briefing officer had told us, to fly to Kythera Island. There and West of the Kythera Straits we would find enough targets, amongst them two battleships.

We took off early in the afternoon. Again these scenic views and this overwhelming blue, now cloudless. It was an Aegean day. We had no losses up to now, and we were on our way for the third raid on this day. We made a wide turn around the Kythera area, and we tried to find out what all these vessels were doing. They were zigzagging all the time, a few close to the Islands of Kythera and Antikythera, the majority more to the West. And there I saw two majestic ships, giants vis-a-vis their destroyer escorts. They put up a tremendous fire barrage, this could only be battleships. We were all bowing our heads downward to look at this performance. None of us had ever seen battleships before. It seemed as if they were firing all their guns simultaneously, becoming invisible by a cloud of dark smoke for seconds. They made for the open sea southwest of Crete, their wakes were those of considerable speed. They had left two cruisers near Kythera and we assumed that they were to go to Crete and bombard the area where our parachutists had been dropped two days ago. So we concentrated our efforts to prevent them going there. One was sunk a few miles from the southern end of Kythera Island. She had been burning and the pile of black smoke could be seen from far away. Brenner and I attacked the other cruiser close to Antikythera. Near misses only, and Brenner was furious at himself.

When we were back at Eleusis, we screened handbooks etc. for a particular shape of a stern. The rear end of this ship was different from other cruisers, it looked like a square. There was only one ship similar to what we had seen, so it looked as if we had seen H.M.S. FIJI.

Brenner prepared for a fourth raid. Secretly he took off, all by himself. Later he told me, that he had found the cruiser flying along an oiltrace, which revealed the course the vessel had taken to the South. He had hit her; shortly after his final blow she sank. When he left her, she had a heavy list and no more speed. One year later, Brenner was shot down by a cruiser south of Crete. He and his men fought for their lives in a rubber-dinghy.

In vain. The sea was stronger.

Two more Ju 88s we lost on that 22 May 1941. A young officer, son of a Luftwaffe General officer, was missing. His radio-operator later was found dead at a beach. One Ju 88 had attacked the cruiser south of Antikythera. The aircraft was hit by A.A. fire, it ditched into the sea close to the rocks north of Monemvasia. The crew was helped out of the water by a Greek civilian who ran down the rocks to rescue his enemies. He and his wife looked after the wet strangers whose compatriots had occupied his country.

An act of humanity was done by an elderly Greek couple.

Gerd Stamp, Germany

AUSTRALIAN CRUISER'S IN ENEMY AIR ATTACK
Perth Bears Battle Scars

From JOHN HETHERINGTON, Special Correspondent of The Herald with the A.I.F.

ALEXANDRIA, Tuesday. — I have just been examining the bullet-riddled ensign which flew from the gaff of the Australian cruiser Perth throughout the all-day strafe of British warships by the Luftwaffe in the Aegean Sea on May 22. The ship is scarred by bomb splinters and bullets from the German planes, which showered down missiles almost ceaselessly for 13 hours, but every plate is sound, and only five men suffered minor wounds.

The captain whose cabin wall was pierced by a shell from an air cannon, told me: "It was the liveliest day I have ever spent and I do not particularly want to repeat it. Still, it is something to have come through what must be a unique experience in the history of warfare."

The Sun, 28-5-1941
Contributed by J.K.E. Nelson, Australia

Tuesday 20th May

German parachute troops landed in Cania this morning. We are stopping convoys from reinforcing them. 21.00 we entered E Boat Alley and encountered several E Boats before midnight. We all opened fire. This morning 1700 troops landed in Candia wearing N.Z. battledress. 20.00 aircraft attack. Two torpedoes dropped but missed

132

Wednesday 21st May

We are patrolling the Crete coast off Cania to intercept German troopships. Battles are in Western end. 06.30 a.m. attacked by single ... 3 more attempts were made on us before 09.00. Attacked by waves of bombs all day. Had over 20 bombs... Alongside the destroyer JUNO. Later sunk. 13.00. Attacked while picking up survivors.

From the War Diary of J.K.E. Nelson, Australia on board HMAS PERTH.

ΜΑΊΟΣ – MAY

20 Τρίτη Niilad r u desii
Tuesday

German Parachute Troops landed in Cania This morning we are Stopping Convoys from reinforcing Them.

2100 We entered E Boat Alley and encounte several E boats before midnight we all opened fire This morning 1700 Troop land in Candia wearing N.Z. Battle dress. 2000 Aircraft attack Two Torpedoes dropped but missed. 1st degree Frost 2100 - 0900:

21 Τετάρτη Κωνσταντίνου καὶ Ἐλένης
Wednesday

We are Patrolling the Crete Coast off Cani To intercept German Troop ships. Battlers are u Western End. 0630 Attacked by Single 1 3 more attempts were made on us before 09 Attacked y waves of bombs all day had over 2 bombs land alongside the destroyer "Juno" later sur ... 1300. Attacked while picking up survivors. 1

Thursday 22nd May

06.00 Four Raid .... Raided all day and had over 60 bombs dropped around us. Dive bombers attacked every 5 minutes of the day up till 20.00. 08.00 we sunk two vessels carrying German troops to Crete. We ran into a German convoy and score hits on a destroyer. 13.00 Assistance was .... by meeting the Fleet. Destroyer GREYHOUND was hit and sunk 5 minutes later ... 11.00 CARLISLE was hit but got control over damage. 17.00 GLOUCESTER was sunk. Waves of planes came at us all day. 19.00 FIJI sunk. 13.00 WARSPITE hit.

Friday 23rd May

Only a few raids today. NAIAD is hit and can only make 12 knots. We are holed forward but under control. KASHMIR (1690 tons) blown in halves and sunk. HMS KELLY also sunk.

From the War Diary of J.K.E. Nelson, Australia, on board H.M.A.S PERTH

The Germans were diving into the water

According to my diary the event took place 8 a.m. approximately. on Thursday May 22nd 1941.

H.M.A.S. PERTH was engaged in patrolling the Aegean Sea, seeking to destroy German seaborne forces landing on the coast of Crete to reinforce airborne troops already landed.

Our day started off with air attacks at 6 a.m. and these carried on throughout the day at five minute intervals non stop until 8 p.m. and it was recorded that the dive bombers had dropped sixty bombs around us as near misses.

At 8 a.m. we sighted two caiques flying swastika flags. We sank one and fired a warning shot at the other and the Germans in reply ram up a white flag and lowered the swastika indicating that they were abandoning ship.

Boats were lowered and a number of soldiers boarded them. However, as the number was comparatively small according to the caiques' carrying capacity, we opened fire with pom poms. This resulted in many more soldiers swarming on deck and diving into the sea.

"We opened fire on a caique with pom poms and it was like pouring boiling water into an ants' nest. The Germans came pouring from below and scrambled into boats or dived into the water", as the Yeoman of signals remembers.

PERTH then steamed around the caique and fired a four-inch gun and I recall seeing a German soldier clinging to the side of the forward mast riggings when the second shell hit. After the smoke cleared he had disappeared.

The caique then began to settle by the stern and sank rapidly. PERTH was savagely attacked by dive bombers after the sinking of the caique and although the German aircraft had been overhead the whole time, the pilots were evidently unwilling to attack because of the danger of killing or wounding the Germans in the water.

J. K.E. Nelson, Australia

The caique hit by HMAS PERTH and on fire. Looking closely at the photograph, one can see what appears to be the German soldier whom I saw clinging to the rigging.
J.K.E. Nelson Austrtalia.

The sinking of H.M.S. FIJI, 22nd May, 1941

Written on board EMPRESS OF AUSTRALIA by Ted Gardner who was a journalist before the war.

Our ship, H.M.S. FIJI (8,631 tons), one of Britain's fastest and most powerful cruisers, relentlessly dive-bombed from dawn to dusk, until her shell rooms were emptied of A. A. ammunition, lay in the sea, still floating, her propellers turned to the clouds, motionless. We could just see one dim, lonely figure sitting on one of the starboard screws.

A moment later, a cry broke out all round. "They're coming back". We strained our eyes. Above the waves, hardly recognisable at first, we saw the thin lines of their foremasts, then their funnels, and lastly, pushing cautiously through the water, their bows. "Up the Navy!"

The destroyers KINGSTON and KANDAHAR, themselves perilously short of ammunition and fuel, had waited for the safety of night to return. They withdrew out of bomber range shortly after we had been fatally hit. Their action saved us from further machine gun attacks. A few of our men had been wounded by bullets from a low-flying bomber. Now, hidden by darkness, nearly 600 out of a complement of 800 were safely picked up.

The attack began at dawn. We needed rest. The night we had spent patrolling the Greek coast, and air defence the previous day had depleted our ammunition.

Just after six o'clock as the sun rose above the snowtopped mountains of Kithera Strait, the first formation, 16 JU 87's appeared flying high against the hot, blue sky. A fierce barrage met their dives. Their bombs went wide.

Half an hour later, a second formation closed over us, one plane swooping so low that we could see the tyres on its landing wheels turning with the force of the dive. The noise of our guns was too great for us to hear its engines.

We saw the bombs, small and black at first, falling, increasing prodigiously, now with fins that turned the air into a shriek. We crouched. The explosions rocked the ship. One bomb threw up a wave that drenched the bridge personnel with black water.

All about us, the sea gave up fountains of water sparkling in the sunlight. One bomb splinter cut through seven bulkheads. Brilliant manoeuvring was saving us from direct hits.

We had 15 minutes to recover before the next attack. Again we eluded the bombs.

For two hours they left us alone. We believed the worst was over. By nine o'clock we were safely out of Kithera Strait, the narrow, rock-bound passage to the Aegean, and had joined the fleet.

At mid-day, the ship was startled by a bugle call to "Action Stations". We had been ordered back to Kithera Strait. H.M.S. CARLISLE, running the gauntlet we had survived earlier in the morning, was reported in difficulties. We were to assist her. CARLISLE, however, was able to get away under her own power. We returned to the fleet.

Meanwhile a caique, attempting to run German troops to Crete, was lighting the horizon with flames. She had been hit by shells from the destroyer GREYHOUND.

A moment later, GREYHOUND disappeared in a wreath of smoke. She sank in less than five minutes, victim of a furious counter attack from the air.

Destroyers KINGSTON and KANDAHAR were sent to rescue survivors. We and the cruiser GLOUCESTER were detached to give support.

Almost as soon as we gained full view of the Strait again, the bombers came out to meet us, and within a few minutes we were singled out as target.

The bombs exploded amidships, tearing down the foremast, the yellow air raid warning flag flying at the yard arm - we had had no time to hoist the red.

FIJI heeled over to 45 degrees. We left her turning over slowly. It was very cold.

H.M.S. FIJI - A MISCELLANY
Edited by D.W.H. Freer, England

HMS FIJI - A MISCELLANY
Edited by D.W.H. Freer, England.

Shipwrecked

I was in the water swimming and then the KINGSTON and one or two other ships came in to try and pick us up. But then they started getting bombed and their machine guns were lost in the water. They stayed for a few moments and there was bombing and so they left saying "we're going and we'll come back later on in the dark." So I had to keep swimming. I was in there for I suppose just about six hours. Oh, it was very cold. That's what killed a lot of the men.

We swam around there, and I saw a lot of my friends die, just hanging there in their life boats, their inflated ones. The water was so choppy in the Mediterranean. People always think of it as a blue expanse, but it can be wicked. Well, I am a good swimmer, but you don't swim really; you watch the waves and you invariably get caped up with salt.

It was just after midnight, I suppose, when we saw these two black shapes, destroyers, you came back on a wave, you were on, you looked around and down again you went, then up again you saw these two destroyers gradually decreasing circles. They came in and they pulled all those nets at the side, and picked us up. My tongue was hanging out there, solid salt. You were looking up the side of the ship, and you were bouncing, and all these ropes hanging and everything. The rope comes over and you are a desperate man, and they just pull you out of the sea. You landed on the deck and you laid there for minutes. Just like a fish being brought out of water. We were just like a heap of lead, you see, very heavy from all the water we had swallowed. So they just left you there until you'd coughed up. They gave us warm rum, Nelson's blood. Even the boys, fourteen year old lads. Then they said, "make your way there and the boys opened their lockers and gave us their spare clothing, and I got a towel and a pair of slippers."

Verbal testimony of Dennis Kelly, England, survivor of H.M.S. FIJI

The sinking of the KELLY

The last time anyone saw Mountbatten before the sinking of the KELLY was on the bridge. He was leaning against his favourite spot in order not to be swept overboard before he had judged it was the right time for him to be separated from his ship.

"I felt I had to be the last to abandon my ship", he told Patricia. "I abandoned ship rather late, because the bridge capsized and I became trapped in the raging waters. Fortunately I was wearing my helmet which due to its weight, enabled me to sink further down and break free from the bridge's plating. It was however most unpleasant to have to sink even further into the water in order to free oneself. I then began to swallow water. I knew I'd be dead at any minute if I did not stop doing so. I therefore put my left hand over my nose and mouth and forced them shut. Then I thought my lungs would burst. Finally I began to see the light of day. I shot out of the water like a cork popping out of a bottle."

Naftiki Hellas, Athens, February 1986

"Abandon ship!"

23 May 1941. 03.15 hrs. All of a sudden about 100 metres to the west of us two enemy warships hove into view.

I think there was one torpedo boat and one destroyer. They pinpointed us with their searchlights and immediately fired a broadside at the ship but only shredding the sails. I then gave the order: "Abandon ship!" Without any sign of panic the entire ship's company jumped overboard onto the previously finished contraptions. Three of the small inflated rafts were thrown over the side. The fourth with several wounded casualties in it had been taken in tow from the onset of darkness.

Everyone swam according to orders as quickly as they could towards the shore. The destroyer and the torpedo boat fired at the vessel with all their weapons for a quarter of an hour near enough. Then all was quiet for a while. The warships then steered off eastward, but then they turned their searchlights again on the ship and continued firing at it. They were joint in this by a light cruiser. S 14 began burning, firing ceased, searchlights were switched off and the enemy departed eastward. They briefly bombarded some targets on shore half-way between Khania and Maleme.

After swimming for about an hour I came upon a small inflated raft which was already occupied and ten men swimming round it. In spite of all our efforts it was quite out of question due to the strong current to reach the shore about 1 km away.

I ordered that the ten men swimming near the raft take it in turn to swim, cling to the raft and rest on it. We had to let ourselves drift with the current eastward. At about 0615 the first Ju 52 came over from Crete followed in close succession by other aircraft. The seventh of them dropped a raft and the others did likewise.

At about 0830 a sea rescue plane came on the scene picking up other shipwrecked personnel drifting without rubber dinghies further to the East.

At about 3 km East of Cape Spatha I managed by shouts and with gestures to bring the rafts together which had drifted apart somewhat.

140

I ordered the occupants of three rubber dinghies which I passed on the way to where the other rubber dinghies had concentrated to row into Maleme Bay and to reach land from there. This seemed the only way of avoiding the current.

However when I had swum to where the rubber dinghies had gathered I was told that the commander of the sea rescue aircraft had ordered not to make for the bay and avoid it if possible as we would be picked up. Three dinghies had already paddled into the bay, and could no longer be informed.

About 1230 the sea rescue plane arrived and took all 27 men and the wounded on board and the rest were lifted from the sea at 1600 hrs. Meanwhile the occupants of the three rubber dinghies were taken on board a small coaster which came out of Maleme Bay.

J. Horbach, News sheet of the Mountain Troops Old Comrade Association No 4/78
Contributed by Jean-Louis Roba, Belgium

HMS FIJI - A MISCELLANY
Edited by D.W.H. Freer, England.

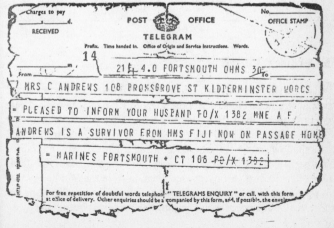

The cruiser YORK

The YORK was a British cruiser that had taken part in the naval battle at Rio de la Plata, where the VON SPEE had been sunk. There were three ships, the YORK, the AJAX and I don't know which other one. The YORK had been bombed and sunk by the German "stukas" in the shallow waters of the harbour at Suda. The Germans attempted to set her afloat again in order to use her for their own needs, the needs of war. The British sent over some dinghies from the Middle East for this purpose, along with a naval commander whom we called Cane but whose real name was Case. The job, however, had been done by an agent working for the British, a Greek named Byron, who had got there first. That is how I met him. He spoke to me in fluent "Katharevousa", old Greek. Then I lost him and never saw him again. I found out from the late Bantouvamanolis that he was a formidable British spy, who, however, did not survive the war. He had been able to infiltrate the German diving crew and instead of refloating the YORK, they sank her further still. After that she was useless. This occured after the battle. The YORK had been bombed during the naval battle, because the British fleet had been ordered by Cunningham to withdraw from Crete on the fourth day of the battle, thus leaving Freyberg unprotected from the sea. The YORK was hit during the battle outside the harbour at Suda. The British sank her and thinking that they would not leave, did not tow her ashore and repair her. It was at that point that the Germans tried again to refloat her, but spies working for the British prevented them from doing so.

Verbal testimony of Zacharias K. Bantouvas, Heraclion

Many Greek and British warships and merchant vessels lie in Suda Bay.
They were sunk by German bomb attacks.
Bundesarchiv - Militärarchiv, Freiburg, Germany.

The blackest week

It was the blackest week for the Royal Navy in the whole of World War II ... perhaps even of all time.

Douglas W.H. Freer, England, survivor of H.M.S. FIJI

In the Suda Bay, Crete
Signal, Germany, July 1941.
From the ELIA archives, Athens, Greece.

HOLD BACK THE DAWN

The battle goes on

On the second day of the invasion, in a desperate attack, General Student's airborne troops succeeded in securing the position which controlled the airport. Despite the ferocity of the defenders, for lack of communications due to shortage of wireless equipment and broken telephone lines, also due to the subsequent wrong decision not to counter-attack on time, this small and insignificant airstrip opened wide the gates to Nazi victory.

For the Allies this was the beginning of the end. After the capture of Maleme the island was at the mercy of the formidable Nazi war machine. Hitler's imperialist Eagle spread its wings over the "Isle of Doom", as labelled by the Berlin Radio Broadcast, its claws ready to seize its prey. Hour after hour, day after day, the concerted warfare of the Nazis poured on the island. The Greek and Allied heroic fighters had only the short nights to find some respite. Daybreak was the terrifying awakening of more airborne death and destruction. The soldiers' night prayer was: "My God, my God, hold back the dawn."

Great flashes lit up the skies

Another night passed in the cornfield under my solitary blanket but the nights were warm, and this particular one was further warmed by the naval battle which we heard and saw, seemingly for several hours. Great flashes lit up the skies, followed by the boom of naval guns. But never did the battle approach the northern shore. As we learned later, the early intelligence from Greece had meant that the

Royal Navy had lain in wait for the sea-borne invasion of picked German troops which had set out for Crete. Only one boatload of survivors landed on the promontory by Suda Bay a few miles to our east, and they were promptly rounded up by an especially vigilant beach-guard. So this huge force never reached the island; which meant that the sole point of entry for the invader was by parachute or through the disputed Maleme aerodrome.

J.D. Fraser, New Zealand

21 May 1941 (Wednesday)

... We attack Crete with airborne troops. A dangerous project. But it has been prepared. We hope to God that it succeeds. In this initial stage, however, everything is still secret. But London will soon make an announcement ...

THE GOEBBELS DIARIES, 1939-41

The German descent over Alikianos
(21st May 1941)

Today the sky grows black, today is woeful
the Germans land on Kairiti's plain
The sky is thick with aeroplanes
the sky rumbles, the earth trembles, the machine guns shriek.
Today the battle has begun, one on one.
The plain has blossomed, the canons roar
men run with their weapons, the elders with their sticks;
they run towards the gunfire and they do not fear death
nor Charon; they do not fear the bombshells but
fearlessly enter battle like red-breasted eagles.
They kill the Germans and take their weapons,
and leave the ground strewn with bodies.
The Rizites arrive, wings on their feet,

carrying their cartridges and clenching their teeth.
They chase the Germans like wild beasts towards Aghyia
thrashing them with frenzy, with fury.
Crete, my beautiful island, the harbours that surround you are like
golden garlands that crown your beauty.

Alikianos Kydonias
comp. Georgis Apothikianos
edit. G.D. Kapsomenos, 1945

We fought the hardest battles in Crete

We, the mountaineers, went to reinforce the parachutists. To begin
with they took us to Crete in Italian warships. On the way there we
were ordered to return to mainland Greece because the British fleet
had sailed from Suda and we'd fall in the midst of them. We then
returned to mainland Greece with the Italian warships and early the
next morning we left for Crete with the JU52, I think.

We landed at Maleme airport and advanced fighting all the way
towards Suda Bay. We stayed in Crete for about eight days. The
fighting was so swift that the population either fled or hid
underground. So we did not see any locals. We fought the Maoris,
(Newzealanders) and they were very tough. No, I never heard their
"Haka" war cry. We would hear various cries, but nothing was clear
because everything was happening so quickly.

Life at war cannot be compared to life on the home front. There is
no anxiety during battle. You just have to defend yourself. You just
have to be stronger than your adversary. Courage and anguish do not
exist here. Here it is a matter of life and death. You do not have time to
think clearly, because you are just trying to avoid getting killed.

The Junkers 52 carried between eight to twelve men, usually
twelve. We landed on this sandy beach and advanced. The JU 52s
returned as the British were firing at them with their artillery. It is
difficult to describe what you feel during battle. You have to make
split second decisions.

During the Second World War I fought first in Poland, then France, mainland Greece, Crete, Norway (the Ice front) and finally in Africa, Tunisia. We fought the hardest battles in Crete.

Happy times go by and bad memories gradually lose their intensity. There is nothing pleasant about war. No, the soldier does not have the sense of victory as, for example, a footballer has. A soldier's only purpose is to accomplish his mission. After that he knows he must go and fight somewhere else again. It is a hard life being a soldier.

Verbal testimony of Johann Pfefferkorn, Austria

Unable to distinguish friend from foe

The struggle for the airstrip raged to and fro. We could not seize it, nor was Tommy able to drive us into the sea. Our situation grew ever more critical as the hours passed. On the very first day the leaders of 2 and 4 Company had fallen. They were Jahnke and Morawetz. The next day the CO of 14 Company was also killed. The regimental HQ which had dropped right in the midst of the enemy had been overpowered after a hard fight and colonel Sturm, the CO, had been taken prisoner.

With this we lost all contact in the days following with higher command HQs. Our signals found no reception and we were out of range for signals with the mainland. General Student received no messages from our sector, nor were we able to put our airmen in the picture on the situation as our identification signs would have disclosed our positions to the British up in the mountains from where they had a good view of the terrain. Our identification marks for guiding our airmen had been captured by the enemy and were displayed by them for their own safety. They skillfully misled our flyers. Fighter aircraft sent by General von Richthofen in support of ground operations were thus unable to distinguish friend from foe; they turned away and helped our people elsewhere.

On one occasion a couple of Dorniers 17 threw their bombs on us resulting in particularly tragic losses. At several locations ammunition was nearly used up. We had left our rations with our tunics somewhere or other because of the heat. Water was to be had only in the adjoining factory. On the third day we found wine in the cellar of a hut. I had it rationed out in sips, otherwise men would have got drunk instantly through exhaustion and the awful thirst. To assuage hunger we cut ears of corn and chewed the grains. An ownerless goat which strayed to us was slaughtered on the spot and was cooked in MG boxes in sea water. Everyone received a tough, match box sized morsel tasting of oil!

Anton von Roon, "Parachute troops operation - Crete", MEN OF ACTION

"That man saved your life"

21 May 1941

We crawled last night for about 1 to 2 kilometres. It was here, on the edge of the airfield that I gave up, I couldn't manage further; I was about to faint. Mospak and Gloerfeld climbed down the steep slope into a dry water course, a "wadi" to look for water. We had to drag them out of there because they were too exhausted - there was no water in spite of digging for it. It was only now, that I had a look at my chest wound. The shirt was full of blood right up to the belt and smelled terribly of sweat and clotted blood. Must have lost much blood because the arm felt almost dead. Gloerfeld and Mospak bandaged me up the best they could. I got rid of my haversack, water bottle; the lot had in any case been shot. Blood stained the Leica container. Then, we again got ready for defence. Gloerfeld and Mospak kept a look-out to the left and half left, Engel ahead and I to the right. We heard several people approaching along the defile, and we were crazy enough to call for the pass-word!!! Engel, lying shoulder to shoulder with me was to observe ahead and, very likely, did not look too closely out for a moment. I only heard the shot and how his steel helmet hit against his rifle lying in front of him. I then saw his blood dripping from beneath his helmet. He died without uttering a word.

Now, we were once again spotted and right among the tommies.

149

Surrender? Never! I heard German troops approaching from the West, but certainly about half a kilometre away. I thought things out and then said to my chaps: "I'm off to our lines, if you want follow me, if not - stay put and fight for it here!" They tried to stop me from this 'dicey do', but I insisted. During a pause in the firing, I jumped up and ran down the defile towards the West, then over a wide unobstructed terrain, followed by firing on me. I saw them standing up and blazing away at me; like a hare chase it was! I, too, ran like a hare zig-zagging. At times, bullets hit the ground in front and behind me. It was not surprising that while I ran for my life, I failed to notice a dry water course. Suddenly, the ground gave way under me and I plunged down head over heels but got up at once only to see a tommy not more than 15 metres from me jump behind a tree raising his rifle on me. I jumped behind the nearest olive tree and pointed my pistol at him. We stood there facing each other and did not fire. Then I had enough of it and gestured to him to lose himself and I made it clear that I would not fire. He got the message, and he made off at speed.

I ran through the "wadi", which I think was about 50 metres across, saw more British, however, apparently withdrawing, and climbed up the bank. I was immediately met by a hail of bullets, but this time from our own machine guns. It took damned long before they stopped this outburst. Next to arrive were Primbkę and Mospak - good lads! I then joined the leading group and was able to give them a precise description of the terrain and told them where to find the tommies. We found ourselves again at the "wadi" but here I was done; I broke down and remembered nothing. I don't know how long I lay there unconscious. I woke up for a moment because someone was doing something to my head. I shall never forget this: An Englishman with large scissors was kneeling over me (he was just about to cut the hair over my head wound). A crowd of Englishmen was standing about. I asked horrified: "Am I a prisoner?" "No, no", says a small German parachutist. "They are our prisoners!" This was my salvation! And I relapsed into unconsciousness.

When I woke at the forward field ambulance at Malemes airfield the German M.D. asked me: "Who bandaged you? Well, fellow, that man saved your life! We've got nothing left" - he did not replace the bandage.

And I am still looking, for this British MO who, on 21st May, 1941, bandaged me on height 107, near Malemes, to say "thank you".

From the War Diary of Helmut Wenzel, Germany

On the death of a Military Press Photographer

The picture! The great events of war!
He stands while others lie in cover
And faces fire. Yet his picture comes out well
And records the great moment for posterity.
But while light penetrated his camera, enemy lead struck him down.
He, whose joy was to record in pictures laid down his life.
This then is the price claimed by time in flight from him
Who snatched the picture from it.
The picture was to vanish into darkness—
But, lo, behold it now shining in immortality.

Joseph Barth
VON SERBIEN BIS KRETA

Caring for the wounded enemies

On May 23rd 1941, I accepted a party of 70 wounded German paratroops from the German force still holding out in the olive-oil factory at Stavromenos. Very fortunately my battalion medical officer on Crete, Doctor Alan Carter, has given me some facts and detailed information. He was directly involved in my decision to care for the wounded German paratroops in 1941.

I will try now to explain as briefly as I can at 84 what actually happened at Rethymnon and you will note that our first move to give medical aid was on 21st May 1941. It was during the morning of 21st May that we drove the paratroops off and to the east of the vital Hill 'A', which guarded the eastern end of the airstrip. About midday, when I was at my Headquarters just south of the western end of the airstrip, I received a message from my Medical Officer (Captain Carter) asking permission for him to try to arrange a three-hour truce with the Germans at Stavromenos so that he could organise the collection of our wounded and also the German wounded who were lying in the flatish coastal strip between our right flank on Hill 'A' and the Germans who had retreated from Hill 'A' to the olive-oil factory at Stavromenos. (I will refer in future to this factory as "factory").

As soon as we had recaptured Hill 'A' and the country to its west, Captain Carter and his stretcher bearers had moved east of Hill 'A' down onto the flat narrow coastal strip 800 yards across which to the east stood the factory! I agreed Captain Carter try to arrange a truce with the Germans, so that our own and the paratroop wounded could be cared for. Captain Carter, under a white flag, then walked east to the factory and arranged a three hour truce. He then returned west towards our Hill 'A' and joined up with a paratroop medical post located in an isolated two roomed shack 300 yards east of Hill 'A'. This German medical post consisted of two German doctors and their staff. Captain Carter arranged, with the German doctors to work together as our prisoners. They decided to evacuate those well enough to be moved to our Medical Hospital at Adhele, but to keep the remaining wounded at their location. You will appreciate that during the 3-hour truce all the wounded (theirs and ours) had been collected at this ex-German Aid Post.

Captain Carter remained with the Germans at their Aid Post in the two room shack until 29 May on which day it was closed down and the remaining wounded (theirs and ours) were moved to Adhele.

On the evening of 21st May when the first convoy of German and our wounded were being transported in ambulances to Adhele, the column was attacked by the German Air Force and the German doctor with the column was one of those killed. This left one German doctor and he remained with Captain Carter until the medical post was closed down on 29th May.

Some of the German medical orderlies, etc. accompanied their wounded to Adhele where they joined in with our Australian Staff at our hospital. I only had time to visit this combined hospital once during the battle. The German NCOs and orderlies worked in well with our Australians and the German supply of drugs and medical

Street in Adele near Rethymnon
Marcos G. Polioudakis, THE BATTLE OF CRETE IN RETHYMNON

equipment was much appreciated at Adhele, as we were short of stores etc., as a result of losses during the withdrawal through Greece. The German and our own staff shared the same rations as our men (Australians). Everything was shared equally. Of course our hospital at Adhele also cared for the few-if any-captured paratroops, from the 10 day battles on my western front around Perivolia (western suburb of Rethymnon), but there could not have been many because the paratroop force in that area was never captured or overrun.

On the afternoon of 23rd May, a force of 70 paratroops (wounded) marched out of the factory to surrender to us, as they could not be cared for by the Germans in the factory apparently. We (Captain Carter) accepted them and they were sent on from the ex-German Aid Post by Carter to Adhele. We captured the factory on the morning of 26th May and we found that most of the paratroops had fled during the previous night leaving a small fit guard and about 40 more wounded to surrender to us.

The paratroops were the finest looking group of young men I have ever met. Hand-picked. They fought bravely and fairly. We had 500 of them as prisoners of war, so I saw a lot of them.

As you can see from my above story, there was really no alternative my troops and I could take in caring for the German wounded. An unsuccessful parachute landing will always end up with the defenders (us) having to care for the wounded paratroops in any curlige warfare.

Ian Campbell, Australia

He gave his life to save mine

I was about twelve, I had been fishing near the harbour. Suddenly in an instant everything was completely changed; it was unreal. There I was in the midst of a battle. I was frantic, terrified. A German paratrooper took me under his protection and reassured and comforted me. When a certain calm was restored and things had quietened a bit, he insisted that it was all right for me to go home. He gave me a bar of chocolate, or something just as nice, and said he

Weekly News, Auckland, New Zealand, 11-6-1941.

would cross the road with me to protect me. We had gone only a few metres when he lay dead before me, streaming with blood. He had a red flag with him which I took and which I still have today. I can never lose the feeling that he gave his life to save mine.

Manolis, Crete
"Sie gewannen die Herzen - die Kreter und die Deutschenheute"
Contributed by Adolf Strauch, Germany

The unpleasant Commander

On the second day of the battle we captured Commander Sturm. You see, Sturm landed in front of us. Now, when we went to this defensive Hill B, in Rethymno, or Perivolia, anyway near Rethymno airfield, we had sent occasionally a couple of chaps down to swim. A few at a time, because there was no soap anyway, you must get in the sea. And when they came out of the sea, they tried to filter through the vineyards and get back to our positions, overlooking the vineyards, to see whether we could see them or whether we couldn't. So we thought if people land on this beach and try to filter forward we know every inch of this beach. But there was one place that we couldn't and that was the end on the spur of Hill B. And this we couldn't see. We couldn't cover it by machine guns. We could cover all the approaches to it, and this is where Sturm had his little headquarters, so he was stuck there. He couldn't put a head out or a foot out or anything, and there he was. And then we sent a platoon to occupy this place, and they captured him. So he was then brought to me and I think some of the books comment, that I was a German scholar and I could translate all the orders and the mortar and I translated the Operation Order, to try and see whether there were reinforcements to come and how many we got against us. I translated the mortar manual so that we could shoot their mortar, and then I interviewed all the prisoners as far as I could.

I had a very unpleasant interview with Sturm. He was far older than I was and he couldn't talk English and I could talk German, and I had his Operation Order which he didn't like and he'd lost his brush and comb set and he was a very frightened man! And he didn't like me at all! He wasn't very cooperative. He wanted to see whose Operation Order I had, and I wouldn't show him. Because, of course, you are not allowed to take an Operation Order into battle, for if you are killed or captured, this gives your plans away and tells how many troops are against. So one of his officers had disobeyed this rule but he got killed and we got his Operation Order.

Verbal testimony of Ray Sandover, Australia

The Battle of Rethymnon

The fighting intensified this morning, 21st of May. At one point, around Rethymnon, bright sparks from tracer bullets sped by me. "They've located me", I said to myself, as the bullets buzzed around my ears. I felt as if I was in a bee-hive. Thinking that the end was near, I said to the boy who was with me: "Giorgo, get out of here, I don't need you anymore". "Sergeant, I'm staying with you. Whatever happens to you, happens to me too", he answered. Finally however he had to leave and transfer the machine gun to protect the Gendarmes' company, which, however, had already extended down the line.

The new enemy squadrons became aware of the danger that lay on the road and attacked from various points. But the machine gun had been placed in such an advantageous position and its gunfire was so intense that it was impossible for them to advance. I can honestly say that if it wasn't for that machine gun the Germans would have entered the city in the first few hours, with no resistance, as the only combat unit in the city was the Gendarmerie School which had delayed getting into action.

Meanwhile several free range marksmen, mostly grey-haired old men with primitive weapons, had zealously gone into battle, ready to fight and to sacrifice themselves.

Thus, from defence we moved to attack and began to neutralizing the area by wipping out the opposition. By the afternoon the remaining Germans had entrenched themselves round the church of Aghios Georgios, situated on a hill south of "Perivolia". Wiping them out was very difficult, because the enclosure was protected by walls and we needed mortar and grenades which we didn't have. We were at a distance of between 200-250 metres and the ground between us was bare. Charging across at this point would have meant severe losses and the chances of success were minimal.

Night fell and time was running out. I suggested to the officers of the Gendarmerie that they launch an assault wich I would cover with heavy machine-gun fire, because during the night the enemy would slip over and wreak havoc the next day. It was the only worth-while piece of territory that the Germans had captured in this area.

While we were deliberating about what to do next, my brother Manolis appeared. He was carrying a gun, which he'd got his hands on I don't know how. I always thought he was unarmed. It must have been about 7.30 on the 21st of May, when a hydroplane flew very low over us, heading for the city and firing. I turned my machine gun towards it and emptied a cartridge band. It circled the city and headed back towards us. I emptied a second cartridge and the plane lost its balance and plunged into the shallow waters near the beach at Perivolia. It was the second one I had hit successfully with the machine gun.

My brother got very excited and shouted: "We got them, let's go", and jumped into the trench. Some of the others also got carried away and raced across the bare ground to capture the Germans' fortified position. Unfortunately so intense was the German shellfire that they were annihilated immediately.

Ten minutes later, I too was hit through the knee. I din't know of course that my brother had been killed. A gendarme named Sisakis lifted me onto his back and carried me to the hospital. On the way there we met Chief of Staff Christos Tziphakis. On recognizing me he slapped his leg in desperation. The sadness and disappointment that I distinguished in his features in those few moments, was for me the greatest reward for my efforts.

I spent the following day in hospital. In the evening when everything had calmed down, my brother Georgios came to see me. I asked him about Manolis. He withheld the truth but for me there was no doubt about it. Manolis was dead.

Andreas Manouras, Heraclion

The situation worsens by the hour

The next day, the 22nd of May, my squadron divided into small groups under official command. They began cleaning the area round Heraclion within a 5 mile radius.

A group of special reserves, 150 men, continued their heroic action and under my direct command besieged a farm house and the fifty Germans inside it. After much resistance the Germans were forced to surrender. They were well supplied with all kinds of defence weapons and fought like heroes. When they finally surrendered, twenty five of them had already been killed and the rest were wounded. I congratulated them on their bravery and sent them safely by car to the town hospital.

A little while later, that very same day, a soldier from Archanes fell heroically in battle, after having fought equally bravely. Before his death, he had wounded a German commander (who was using a machine gun) with his weapon and rushed to capture him before he died. The German, admiring his courage and self-sacrifice,

Apostolis Bafatakis from Arta, while serving in the Suda Gendarmerie, 1941.

congratulated him warmly and said in the little Greek that he knew: "Truly you Cretans are brave". He then gave him some sweets and food from his sack and drew his last breath with a photograph of his children upon his lips.

159

The situation on the evening of the 22nd of May is as follows:

The parachutists launched an assault on Heraclion and failed miserably. Most of the Germans were killed, 150 were taken hostage and the rest, about 500 or so, were isolated beyond the River Yiofiri, unable to move and surrounded by danger from all sides.

Four kilometres away, at Heraclion airport, the British with two Greek battalions besieged and immobilized the rest of the fallen parachutists. Their position worsened by the hour.

Report of Antonios G. Betinakis to the Greek Ministry of Defence

Three soldiers in different uniform

The great German invasion of Crete. Images of hell. Terror. The stukas bombarded Chania ceaselessly. By morning we had each gone our separate ways my father and I, to work. I had gone to the General Administrative Office in Crete, housed in the Ministry of Foreign Affairs to which I was dispatched. My father had gone to the warehouses stocking the building materials belonging to the army, to act as interpreter for the British.

From the shelters, day and night people witnessed in agony the growing disaster. Their only thought was how to find a way to leave the city.

On the 22nd my father and I decided to go to our small country house in the village of Galagadi, in Akrotiri, where the rest of our non-working family were staying after the first Italian bombing. There were many fortification works in Akrotiri, belonging to the British. There were heavy cannons, all along the coast of Korakes, large anti-aircraft units in the Sterna area and numerous machine-gun positions over most of Akrotiri which together with the anti-aircraft guns of Malaxa were the guards of the port of Suda.

At the beginning of the road leading to Akrotiri, at Profitis Ilias, the British had established their Headquarters inside the Maxakis family's country house. Their auxiliaries resided next door at the Kalligiannis' country house.

160

My father and I and two other men whom we had met at the office suppplying the exit permits, all set off for the same destination -the villages of Akrotiri. The first man was called Halaris, the second man's name I don't remember. We hurried along, keeping a lookout for the swarms of German aircraft that were flying over us like hell.

Suddenly as we were turning onto the road leading to Headquarters the stukas began to fire. We all hit the ground. My father and the two men fell on the right side of the road and I fell on the left, into a ravine. As I fell I spotted the small bridge situated at the fork of the road ahead of me. I could see three soldiers. They were dressed in separate types of uniform, different to the familiar Greek and English ones. They had padded pockets on the outside of their trousers, something that I'd never seen before, as well as the maps, wires and some small iron boxes scattered under the bridge. I couldn't see their faces, only their feet. I didn't like this at all.

After the planes had departed, I told my father what I had seen and asked him to inform Headquarters. My father couldn't imagine that any Germans would be hiding there. He knew I'd never seen any Germans before and it seemed impossible that there would be any, hiding just 200 metres away from the fortified Headquarters. But I was positive. The others seemed doubtful too, saying that fear must have made me imagine this. I was so insistent however that I managed to persuade my father to ask to see the officer in charge, to whom he narrated with some reservation what I had seen. After the officer heard our story he said that he had serious doubts and felt it was impossible and illogical for the Germans to land without being seen; However he was obliged to investigate because of my unwavering insistence. He took me to another office of higher ranking officers and I was asked to describe what I had seen, in the presence of one of their Greek speaking staff. After that I was led next door. In the yard there was a trench shelter where a German messenger was being held. He had come from Chania carrying a white flag and the demands of the Germans. He was being guarded by a British sentry. The moment I saw the colour of the hostage's uniform I began to shout, saying that it was the same colour as those I had seen by the bridge. Ther German who obviously understood Greek, spat at me.

I was then asked to escort the heavily armed British officers to the exact spot. One of them climbed up the hill to the left, the other to the right and the third together with a few soldiers staying on the road, firing in both the upper sections of the bridge. The Germans emerged stooping down and raised their hands in the air. The British advanced and led the Germans back to Headquarters with their pistols on their backs. The rest searched under the bridge. What they found both surprised and perplexed them. Although delighted with their success they could not hide their astonishment. They all shook my hand and hugged me, thanking me repeatedly. They gazed at me in awe, their eyes full of gratitude.

We were told that the Germans had placed explosives along the road leading to Headquarters. They had worked during the night without being observed and had already prepared to blow up the road and British Headquarters. They intended to take prisoner all those British belonging to the anti-aircraft units, men who could not otherwise leave, except by the road that joined Akrotiri to Chania and the rest of Crete.

As a token of their gratitude and as a souvenir, they gave me part of the booty. A revolver with six bullets, used only by a special unit of Hitler's men, a camera, a pair of binoculars, a belt with a swastika, a helmet and two grenades that looked like acorns. They taught me how to use those in case of an emergency. I also received a pair of thick leather gloves.

I was delighted and the day's tensions wore away immediately. I felt light as a feather.

Everytime I crossed that road and saw the marks from the machine gun fire, I felt something special, something similar to pride.

I have only recounted this story to loved ones and never asked for it to be written. I considered it a meagre contribution on my part in my country's fight.

The reason I do write this, is because time goes by and some truths must be spoken now, now that they have nothing to add to the unintentional protagonists.

The small bridge no longer exists.

The shooting range of Akrotiri demanded large, wide roads and the plans for this project wiped out any remnants of this true story, which I doubt if it was ever recorded in the archives of the British Army of the time.

I would really like to know if it ever was.

Anna Th. Kassimati, Chania

The archaeologist John Pendlebury

Just prior to the battle, I had met John Pendlebury, then in uniform as a Captain. Pendlebury, although still a young man, aged 36, had been for ten years Curator and resident archaeologist at Knossos. He knew Crete far better than any other Englishman, and during this period, when there were no roads to nine out of ten villages, nor any other modern amenities, he had walked all over the island's 200-mile length and knew hundreds if not thousands of people. It was not surprising therefore that he had been asked by the War Office (though I did not know this at the time) to organise and lead resistance to the Germans in the event of Crete being captured by them. In addition to his unrivalled knowledge of the terrain and of the Cretans, he spoke Greek, and was young and fit enough to face the physical hardships likely to be involved. He was indeed an impressive man to meet, tall, handsome, athletic-looking and with an air of considerable authority. The distinction was added to by his having a glass eye (the result of a boyhood accident) and sporting a sword-stick instead of a swagger-cane. Pendlebury had in fact made detailed plans for resistance, based initially on the villages round Mt. Ida (Psilorites) and this explains why, on 21st May, he decided to get out of Heraklion in order to activate his resistance organisation, while the battle was still in progress and its outcome undecided. What has never been explained, and I for one have never been able to understand, is why so intelligent a man chose to leave the town by the West, or Chania Gate, and by car. All of us had seen the parachutists landing in the area beyond the Gate the day before, and it could be safely assumed they now controlled the main road. Pendlebury and his driver ran straight into a pocket of parachutists, he was seriously wounded in the ensuing

163

skirmish, and taken to a nearby house where his wounds were dressed by a German Army doctor, and he was left overnight. The following morning more Germans returned, and Pendlebury was taken outside and shot. The assumption is that he had been identified by the Germans as potentially their most dangerous opponent in Crete and that they decided to eliminate him there and then. To shoot a wounded and defenceless enemy in cold blood was of course a war-crime, but one which could not subsequently be pinned on any individual German.

Ralph Stockbridge, England

General Freyberg to General Wavell

22 May 1941

The position at Heraklion is that the enemy appears to have penetrated the town but, as far as can be ascertained, the aerodrome holds. At Retimo we are still in a position to deny the enemy the use of the landing ground but the garrison is being attacked from the east. A successful counter-attack was carried out this morning. At Suda we are occupying a perimeter defence and are in full possession of all our base organisation.

The position at Maleme is less secure. The enemy has made tremendous efforts to knock us out and I am bringing in help from Georgiopolis. Owing to severe bombing and heavy casualties one battalion withdrew from the defences in the immediate vicinity of Maleme aerodrome during the night of 20-21 May. Early in the day we still commanded the landing area with machine-gun, trench mortar, and artillery fire. However, at 9.15 a.m. the enemy dropped approximately 500 parachutists just west of the aerodrome, also another lot in the vicinity of the enemy's main concentration at the prison and on the road five miles south-west of Canea. At 4.15 p.m. 500 parachutists dropped behind the aeredrome defences and our field guns were put out of action by air action. At 5 p.m. thirty planes landed on the aerodrome and others on the beaches. I am hoping to reinforce Maleme tonight but the situation is now obscure and, I feel, perhaps precarious. Everybody here is determined to fight hard. Do all you can to damage the surface of the aerodrome.

The non-energetic Energiser tablets...

The first three days after the landing we had quite a bit of fun gathering up the containers which were dropped by the Germans' supply carrying planes which came over daily. We were very short of food ourselves and were grateful for fresh bread straight from Berlin, Mettwurst sausage, chocolate and cigarettes each day. It was apparent that the Germans were not sure of the position of their own men at the time and accordingly the containers were dropped where they thought they might be. Unfortunately for us they found out after three days and the practice ceased.

The famous Energiser tablets of which so much had been heard, proved to be nothing but a myth, as one day Bill Mortimer who felt very hungry ate about 25 of them, having gone round from dead Hun to dead Hun salvaging a few from each. When I heard he had eaten them I expected to see him lifting up trees like Samson, but as they had no ill effects on him, I decided to try some myself. I am quite certain they take the place of a sulphur tablet as we know it and probably contained a certain amount of sugar or some such vitamin and are used purely for endurance.

A motor-cycle and sidecar had been dropped right in our lines and came in for quite a bit of notice, as we had no M.T. at all and hoped to get it going. It was a heavy bike, rather like the Twin Harley and carried one spare wheel and three tyres and tubes. One wheel had been buckled when it hit the ground, but otherwise it was quite O.K.

The next evening we were ordered forward with C Coy to take up a position on the right and I feel sure the succeeding two days were the worst I have ever spent. We moved up under cover of darkness and were placed in a line running from the sea to right of A Coy who crossed the road. For cover all we had was an irrigation drain and the only way to ensure full protection was to lie absolutely flat as it was so shallow.

165

The next morning the blitz started and from about 7.30 in the morning until 7.30 at night, there were never less than 40 to 50 planes in the air, first dropping their load of eggs and then coming down and machine-gunning. They machine-gunned on the basis similar to a draught-board, all taking sections of ground first one way and then crossways. It was very unwise to look up at them as an upturned face can be clearly seen from the air, but it was necessary for me to do so as I thought possibly their ground troops would advance under cover of this barrage. At times they flew as low as 50 ft and one could see the Pilot and the Rear Gunner peering down at the ground to see where the troops were.

Late evening Colonel Sandover came up and asked me how the lads were going, as he knew it had been a particularly bad day. I said that one or two of them were a bit jittery but otherwise not too bad. He asked did I think they could stand another day of it, so I said we would and he promised to have us relieved the following night. During the night we moved back about 200 yds and took up a position in a market garden, as it was considered that if they were going to blitz us again, we were in much too open a position. I made my Headquarters amongst a patch of beans, but spent most of the day scratching the gravel trying to get a bit lower. The blitz started again first thing in the morning and it did not take them long to discover we had moved back and they concentrated on this patch of about 300 yds square.

About 3 o'clock in the afternoon I decided to move over to what had been the R.A.P. to get a drink of water and had just taken refuge inside when 4 Stukas came over and decided to dive bomb the house I was in. I took a very poor view of this as the first bomb blew the door down and all the windows in. I was between the devil and the deep blue sea, not knowing whether to stay put or make for the open ground. Fortunately for me all their eggs dropped all around and once they had gone I did not wait for any more to come but made a bee line for my little hole in the bean patch.

Gerald Wild, Australia

The foreign citizens

I was 12 years old at the time of the Cretan landings. I was confined to the house at the time. As a foreigner I was not allowed the freedom of moving around. I was born and raised in Crete. No, I had no problems with the Cretan children, on the contrary most of my friends came from Crete. We were all very close, down there at Heraclion. We co-existed very happily. I lived with my grandparents and other relatives who had settled in Heraclion. My parents had died before the war.

It was midday when the aeroplanes arrived, I remember. We had a cellar, it was more of a coalpit, under our house which we went to when the bombing started. We stayed there for three days and nights. I remember it well, the bombs falling all round our house, luckily none of them falling directly onto it. Most of the houses nearby, though, were flattened. The aircraft continued to drop bombs from dawn till dusk. They parachuted into Heraclion, but most of them were killed, so they bombed afterwards. Heraclion suffered the most damage. A great part of it was destroyed by the bombings.

One night, two days later, we decided to leave on foot: my grandfather, my 80 year old grandmother and all our relatives. We could not remain in Heraclion since we had no food nor water. As a German I cursed them of course because they nearly killed me in our hide-out. I had never seen any other Germans before. My grandparents were British citizens. My grandfather (from my mother's side) had adopted British citizenship before the First World War, because he was the head of the British Telegraph Office. If he had not become a British citizen he would have had to leave - to resign. The locals considered him a British not a German. He spoke Greek well though. My cousins too are British citizens. My mother was the only one who became a German again, because of her marrying my father.

We left Heraclion at night. The bombings stopped at night. We wondered "Where can we go?" "What can we do?" My grandfather who was a British citizen told us that Evans', the archaeologist's, country house was being used as a hospital. It was called the Villa Ariadne. We decided to go there. We walked all night. My relatives grew tired because of their age and since the German parachutists had landed near there in Knossos -at around midnight the same time we had arrived - we spent the night there at an inn, a coffee house near the Villa Ariadne on the road leading to Knossos. The coffee house was empty. There was noone at all. Everyone had gone and we decided to get some rest here, as it was unlikely that anything would occur. At around 6 or 7 in the morning on the third or fourth day of the German invasion of Crete, we suddenly heard a noise inside the coffee house. About twenty German parachutists burst in. That was the first time I had ever seen a German. They said: "Who are you? Put your hands up". There were quite a few of us and they wondered what we were all doing in there. They asked us for identification and I produced my German passport as a German citizen. On seeing my passport they grew troubled. What is a German boy doing here? They called for their officer in command. I spoke little German, almost nothing. When my father died I was only four, so I didn't learn any German. We did not speak any German at home. My grandfather of course told him that he was a British citizen, but of German descent. His daughter had married a German, while he was working at the British Telegraph Office in Heraclion. They allowed us to leave and even gave us military escort right up to Villa Ariadne, two kilometres away. The British were bringing the Germans into the hospital. The hospital was full and we remained outside in the garden, under a palm tree as I recall. We stayed there for five days. The Battle of Crete had ended. Then we left. It was the very day after the battle had ended in fact. We saw dead Germans lying in the streets.

Verbal testimony of Rudolf Gätlich, Athens

A RAZOR'S EDGE ESCAPE

The Royal Flight to Freedom

King George II and the Greek Cabinet, who just before the fall of Athens had moved to Crete, were now compelled to leave once again in order to avoid being captured by the Germans. On the night of 23rd May they left the island, last free Greek soil, to continue the fight from outside, jointly with the Allies. After being almost caught by the Germans and saved by a split-second escape, the King, Prince Peter, Prime Minister Emmanuel Tsouderos, the British Ambassador Palairet and various members of the King's entourage, took for three days the arduous road to Sphakia in southern Crete. They travelled on foot, on mule and donkey over the tortuous 7.000 feet high White Mountains. Finally, the party boarded the destroyer DECOY which brought them to Alexandria and to safety.

General Freyberg to General Wavell

21 May 1941

This place has become no fit abode for important people. The King and the Prime Minister were yesterday morning nearly taken prisoner when fifty parachute troops landed within 500 yards of their house in the hills. I learnt of their escape only from a faint signal picked up last night. With their New Zealand escort, which I can ill afford to be without, the party will be on the south coast as per my telegram of 18 May. They are now out of touch with us, even by wireless. As the enemy have landed motor-cycles the risk of capture is now increased.

A picture (see p. 171) painted by the New Zealand War Artist Peter McIntyre shows my Father in his Headquarters outside Canea with King George II of Greece, and the Greek Prime Minister, Mr. Tsouderos.

Paul Freyberg, England

An epic in field orders

That morning I had received a message from the General saying "Report Force Headquarters, paint portrait of King of Greece", which I think is something of an epic in field orders. I have kept it as a souvenir.

At the Governate, General Freyberg presented me to the King of Greece. I had never met a King before and I was most impressed.

I made sketches of the King and the General and E. Tsouderos, the Premier who joined them in conference. I did not know it at the time but there was history in the making. It was the 19th of May and the Battle of Crete began on the 20th of May.

Later the General and the Prime Minister left and the King asked me to stay and make another sketch of him. He chatted pleasantly of England and of the Army, asking me all sorts of questions about my work. I met him again later on in Cairo and he jokingly reminded me of what a fateful day our last meeting had heralded.

As I left the King's suite the guards sprang to attention. I thought the King must be behind me, so I stepped aside and stood to attention beside the guards, only to find that the salute was for me. I slunk off down the broad marble stairs feeling very much like Charlie Chaplin in those early films.

A few days later I reached the Governate - a great white building facing onto a square. Only a few days before, I had been there sketching the King of Greece in conference with General Freyberg. Now the trees were down in the square and the cars in front of the Governate were wrecked and burned or riddled with machine gun bullets. The drone of planes was coming again and I made for the nearest doorway, but somehow hesitated and then dashed across the square and down into a sort of cellar. The Gods were with me apparently for almost as I reached the cellar I heard the scream of a bomb and the most shattering explosion I have ever heard made the very earth heave and the concussion threw me across the floor. Later when I emerged into the street again I found that a land mine had been dropped in the square almost where I had stood. The crater was as large as a house. The Governate was a wreck.

Peter McIntyre, New Zealand National Archives

The Royal family in Crete
Recollections of Princess Katherine

When we first arrived in Crete, we stayed in Suda, in the Bank of Greece. We slept on field beds. Five to six days later the British informed us that it was dangerous to remain there, because the Germans were bombing Suda. So we took a taxi and went to the

171

village of Neapolis, where we stayed for a few days living on honey and feta cheese. Then the British told us to go to Heraclion, where we spent another five to six days at Sir Arthur Evans's home. He was the archaeologist who excavated the ancient ruins at Knossos. The British warned us to leave, for fear of the German parachutists. It is flat country there, you see. All the Royal family returned to Suda. My brother King George II of Greece and Prince Peter went to a building that looked like a fortress where they stayed until the very last moment. As soon as the parachutists appeared, the British took them up to the mountains fearing the Germans would take them hostage. They planned on going to a secret hideout in the mountains, until the British rescue arrived. From there they went to Egypt where we were there already and together we continued on to South Africa.

Verbal testimony of Princess Katherine of Greece

Escape to Egypt, 1941 A.D.

Apart from preparing for the German attack and meeting it when it came, General Freyberg had another concern at his HQ inland. Winston Churchill had instructed him that the safety of the King of the Hellenes and his Prime Minister, E. Tsouderos must be secured. They must neither be killed nor captured. With Canea under persistent bombing, he decided that the least bad course was to place the King and his Prime Minister together with our Military Attaché, Colonel Blunt and a small New Zealand guard in a farmhouse on a hill overlooking the Maleme plain. From there, in case of need, they could escape southwards over the mountains to the south coast and thence hopefully by sea to Egypt.

Meanwhile, we were to remain nearby General Freyberg's Headquarters. Reluctantly, at the end of the second day's battle, General Freyberg decided that the King must be advised to move next morning over the Samaria Gorge towards Aghia Roumeli. At the same time, he sent a telegram to Admiral A.B. Cunningham, the Commander - in - Chief of the Mediterranean, to say that the King would be due in two days' time at Aghia Roumeli in the evening and requesting that one of H.M. ships if possible should take him and his party off during hours of darkness. If that proved possible and a light were seen out to sea, there would be an answering signal from the shore. No reply to this message could be expected, since strict radio silence was being observed.

As the battle had developed, Sir Michael Palairet and the few of us with him at General Freyberg's HQ could not make our way in time to join the King and so in General Freyberg's message to His Majesty, it was explained that we would make a detour east and south to Sphakia and thence attempt to meet up in Aghia Roumeli in two days' time. This by good luck we did. Luck on both sides, for German parachutists were landing within a stone's throw of the King's refuge while he made his escape up the mountain with his party. Fortune on ours after our trek in the evening when enemy aircraft were less in evidence to Sphakia to find a benzina which would be prepared to take us round the coast westward towards Aghia Roumeli. We put up in a cave for the night and started again as soon as there was sufficient light to navigate so as to avoid being spotted.

After we had arrived at Aghia Roumeli, our first task was to find out whether the King would, in fact, succeed in reaching us before darkness fell. A few of us set off up the Samaria Gorge in search. Before we had gone many miles, a runner, Manolis Manousakis, came towards us shouting, "The King is coming, the King is coming". He later died fighting in the resistance in Crete, but not, as I later heard many years after, before taking some 20 of the enemy with him.

Thus reunited and with a ration of hot boiled potatoes in their jackets, we waited together on the beach for night to come and in the hope of spotting a light out to sea. An hour or so after dark sure enough a light did shine far out in the bay. Our Naval Attaché advanced to the water's edge with a large torch and flashed S.O.S. in morse code. The light went out and we waited. After a while the same light shone at about the same distance from the shore. Again the Naval Attaché flashed his reply. Again darkness and later again a light at nearly the same distance away. After what appeared to be a game of blind man's buff lasting at intervals over an hour or two, our anxieties began to grow. Was the ship really from a ship of the Royal Navy?

Might it even be a German raider who was hanging about to see what sort of fish he might catch signalling S.O.S.? In the end as hours of daylight began to approach when no Naval vessel would wish to be caught in offshore waters, it was decided to send out the benzina to investigate with myself on board. The thought was that I could at least claim diplomatic immunity, for whatever it might be worth, if the worst happened. To give me some protection, even at the expense of diplomatic cover, a corporal with a tommy gun came with me.

We chugged out into the bay. After we had been going for half an hour or more without any sign of life, the skipper of the benzina said that he intended to turn back for fear of running out of petrol. I persuaded him to carry on for a bit in the hope that the light might show at least once more. Our luck held. After a very few minutes we found ourselves in the arc of a sealight and a stentorian and all too obvious naval voice shouted through a megaphone "Who the bloody hell do you think you are?"

We identified ourselves and were hauled on board, where the Captain said that at this distance out to sea there could be no chance whatever of a light from a hand torch carrying and that he had had no intention of risking his ship coming further in shore until certain that he was not on a fool's errand.

Now led by the benzina, he edged his way forward and before long the King and our party were all aboard two destroyers. As we left, we could see the flashes over the mountains of the battle still raging in the plain round Maleme.

When we woke the next morning, we found ourselves, thanks to the Royal Navy, part of the destroyer screen of what was left of the Mediterranean Fleet on our way to Alexandria.

The balance of power and ill chance dogged the British forces in Greece and Crete. But however true that may be, we were among the few first in reaching Crete and then in getting to Egypt who had more luck on the way than any mortal should expect in a lifetime.

Harold Caccia
From a speech delivered at the Royal Overseas League, London, on the 13th May 1982, for the Anglo-Hellenic League

Where is the King?

I looked out of the window and saw the first parachutists descending from among the aircraft. They landed in the village of Aghia and a whole squadron of them arrived at "Bella Cabina", the place we had left the night before. So the King's suspicions had been confirmed. We thanked God that we hadn't stayed there and had managed to move to this house. Later on we found out from Merlin that those Germans that had landed at "Bella Cabina" were special commandoes. The parachutists launched their assault shouting:

-Der König! Wo ist der König? (The King! Where is the King?)

Merlin was arrested and interrogated severely. The Germans wanted to know where the King was hiding, but he refused to divulge any information. He told us that each German soldier was equipped with a silk handkerchief which had a map of Chania drawn on it, with a circle round "Bella Cabina" and a note saying: "König hier" (the King is here). We had survived as if by a miracle and Freyberg was proven right in believing that the parachutists would land here in order to arrest the King. We discovered later on that all the information the German Administration had gathered, concerning the King's whereabouts, had been supplied by a Greek, the Honorary Consul in Germany. It was at his house that Levides had once thought of harbouring the King. He had a secret wireless which kept the enemy regularly informed of what was going on in Crete.

Recollections of Prince Peter of Greece
Acropolis, Athens, 16-3-1978

Civilians who didn't wish to fight!

The King of Greece was in Crete and he had made a proclamation which we found on the walls of the houses, to defend the country, and all the people followed this proclamation. The funny thing was that the King was about five hundred metres from my first company. We saw his house but we didn't know that the King was in it, it was a farmer's house, a normal farmer's house. On the next day, the 21st, we saw a long, long column of civilians leaving the house. It was the King and his government, but we didn't know it, and we didn't shoot at them because we thought that they're civilians who didn't wish to fight, -so we left them!

Baron von der Heydte, Germany

Transcripts of interviews conducted for the documentary film 'TOUCH AND GO - THE BATTLE FOR CRETE, MAY 1941' written and directed by Tom Steel and produced by Jeremy Isaacs Productions for the New Zealand Broadcasting Corporation.

The then Prime Minister
Emmanuel Tsouderos remembers

As soon as the German parachutists started dropping, the British Colonel Blunt, who was entrusted with the King's safety, as well as the New Zealand soldiers in his command, insisted that we leave for the mountains. Captain Volanis and the other Cretan war veterans suggested we stay and take shelter in a nearby cave. It would be better to wait till after the initial surge of landings and attacks. They maintained that noone ought to move and be seen by enemy during the first hours of battle. Blunt, however, without awaiting orders decided to head for the mountains straightaway, followed by the King, the New Zealanders and some of our men. We suggested they went towards Panaghia in the Keramia area and told them we'd follow.

Barely ten minutes later I also left accompanied by various Cretan Captains and civil officers, among them Kyriacos Varvaressos, the head of the Bank of Greece. We took the correct route and it didn't take us long to see that the King and his party were heading east, towards Suda. The worse thing of all was that Greek soldiers mistook them for a German column of soldiers and fired at them. We sent my cousin Giannis Manouselis (employee of the Bank of Greece) to catch up with the King and set him back, onto the correct route to the mountains. When Manouselis got there the King was sheltering in a cave used by families during the exodus from Chania. They welcomed him, offered him coffee and afforded him every kindness possible. The

176

King declared that he wouldn't move unless Captain Giorgis Volanis himself came to escort him.

This is just what happened.

At about 6 p.m we set off for Therissos which had been the seat of Eleftherios Venizelos' revolution in 1909 against Prince George (cousin to the King). It was a strange coincidence. Our retinue consisted of one hundred or more people and was an amazing combination: New Zealanders, Greek soldiers, local police, Cretans young and old in local dress and many escaped prisoners from Aghyia. The invaders had opened the prisons. The fugitives with their "Zebra" clothing added great character to our column.

We arrived at Therissos late at night. The men were away fighting and the women had remained in their homes. The women who did not recognise us began to insult us. They wondered why we were in their village instead of being at war. When they found out who we were, they opened their doors and welcomed us warmly. The King and Prince Peter occupied the head of the community's house. The rest resided at the local police station taking up the gendarmes' beds.

We set off at dawn. We ordered the police and the civilians to return and forbade the "Zebras" to follow us. The Aliakes point is a lovely place covered in elm trees. It is cool and has many other trees and a wonderful view. Blunt arrived there on time with news and instructions. According to these instructions we had to be at Aghia Roumeli by 8 p.m the next evening, otherwise we would miss the ship.

We began our ascent immediately towards the peak of the White Mountains and at nightfall we reached a "mitato", where the Cretan shepherds kept their sheep. Our next problem was where and how we would sleep.

Finally the King creeped in the Colonel's sleeping bag and fell asleep in the open air. Prince Peter on the other hand dug a hole in the ground, spread some leaves in it and fell asleep there. He had learnt to do this while he was in India and it kept him relatively warm. He also had an old tattered blanket. I settled into a "doghole" and wrapped myself in a cape, which had been given to me by a kind shepherd. I accepted it willingly even though I was in danger of being bitten by the insects which may have existed in that peasant piece of clothing. I used a piece of handluggage that contained various documents and some

177

money for our journey, as a headrest. The King's Chamberlain, D. Levides, slept in another hole with two British officers. As many as possible gathered in the dairy, while about fifteen or so spent the night in the freezing cold, seated on the ground, their teeth chattering. They tried to keep warm by squeezing one another -they told me.

It must have been about 5.30 a.m when we set off. The march was unbelievably tiring. We walked on rocky ground wearing city shoes. A young shepherd who was nearby, held my hand to steady me over the uneven bits. We reached a slope which opened out like a precipice. As we stood at the top of the precipice my young guide said to me:

"My father's mule stumbled here and disappeared out of sight".

At Aghia Roumeli we met up with the British Ambassador and Mrs. Palairet, Admiral Turrell, senior members of the British Embassy, as well as others who had sailed from Sphakia, where they took shelter after their evacuation from Chania. Their escape had been less wearisome.

The King with some of the Platoon of New Zealanders who escorted him from Crete.
Imperial War Museum, London.

We said goodbye to the Guerilla Captains and the villagers who had escorted us. They were seated round the parapets of the café. Most of them had white beards and looked so peaceful that they resembled mythological characters. We told them that anyone who wished to join us, could do so. They however declared that they would stay and fight on the island.

At exactly 2 in the morning the British warship that was to take us away arrived. It was the cruiser DECOY. We managed to board the ship and abandon our home-land with the help of a small Cretan motor-ship belonging to Sifis Doumis from Selia, Aghios Vassilios, which happened to be there. According to regulations the warships were not allowed to send lifeboats to pick us up.

Handwritten notes taken from the diary of Emmanuel Tsouderos
Ilias Venezis, EMMANUEL TSOUDEROS

NAZIS FAIL IN ATTEMPT TO CAPTURE KING OF GREECE

LONDON, May 26.—King George of Greece and his Ministers have reached Egypt after having escaped Nazi parachute troops who attempted to kill or capture them in Crete.

The Courier Mail, Brisbane, Australia, 27-5-1941

The last edict

After careful review of the prevailing situation, in conjunction with our responsible advisers, we are persuaded that our prolonged residence in Crete was becoming an obstacle for the command of

179

military operations. That is why we decided, with deep sorrow, to withdraw from the heroic island where the allied regiments, together with all Cretans -regardless of age or sex- continued their fight with commendable bravery, in defence of their honour and freedom.

We move temporarily away from the island in order to proceed onto British soil where we have been invited. This is the only way we can fulfil the duties imposed to us by the national interest. Our aim is to dedicate all our energy to the service of our beloved country.

Have faith in the ultimate victory, which is ours. The honour awaiting you is great, because you are the last yet most glorious and, with God's help, invincible battlement of Hellenism. The whole Nation is turning their eyes on you with trust and admiration.

White Mountains, Crete, 23rd May 1941
King George II   E.I. Tsouderos

TOUCH AND GO

The Battle of Galatas

During the night of 24th to 25th May, the Germans advance in two groups beyond conquered Maleme airfield; one group advances east towards Chania, the other east as well, but in the interior of the island. A small village, Galatas, which stands on a ridge across a sea of olive trees, resists in a heroic yet desperate fight.

Despite the fierce defence, the village succumbed. The few could not overcome the thrust of the many. That was the end of free Galatas; but at a price, the high price of the Cretan deep sense of freedom.

The first attack

As we had no transport on Crete we had to fight as Infantry. The Defence Sector allocated to Petrol Company was westward from Canea to the Maleme airfield. My Section faced south to a prison in the valley across five or six hundred yards of flat ground planted with olive trees.

On the 20th May the show really opened, shortly after sunrise on a bright, cloudless day. I first saw a bomber towing seven gliders, then the troop carrying planes came up the Valley and started dropping paratroops. About half an hour after dropping the first paratroopers the enemy had a mortar firing on our positions. Then the troop carriers came towing gliders that were uncoupled overhead. He then strafed all around our area for about ten minutes to half an hour. On landing the Germans occupied the civilian prison in front of us expanding from the prison. Later they attacked us moving through the olive trees and grape vines. Their first flurring was met by a disciplined and devastating fire which forced them to withdraw leaving many dead. Our casualties were extremely heavy. The first attack on Galatas had cost us approximately fifty percent casualties, about half of whom were killed. All our officers were either killed or wounded in this first attack including our Commanding Officer.

We later learned that he was promoted to the rank of Major on the morning of the attack.

We had to retire to the base of "Pink Hill". Then a captain Michael Forrester ratly rallied a party of Greeks in a weird counter attack; what was left of us joined in and a number of Greek children. The Jerries broke and then the enemy retired into the gaol and of course we again took to retire. Later as a prisoner of war I had the opportunity of speaking with one of the Germans in the attacking party who said: "When we thought we would have to kill children we decided to retire."

Gordon Rex Stephens, New Zealand

Cold-blooded Kiwis and hot-blooded Cretans

On Ruin Hill we fought our way through Thursday and through Friday, losing more men and becoming always more tired. But we were never seriously attacked by a German force determined to dislodge us from our Hill. The action we could see and hear was in Galatas village which stood on a ridge across a sea of olive green trees, all square white houses and a tall church at its centre. We could spot the movements of New Zealand soldiers on the perimeter of the town, above the cordon of light barbed wire and in the cemetery that lay on the outskirts. Fierce fighting was going on all that Friday, but we could not tell which side held the town. All we knew was that intense machine-gun firing went on remorselessly, and then the constant strafing from the air ceased in the afternoon.

182

About five o'clock all of us were startled to hear wild cries coming out of the middle of Galatas village; a loud ululation, high-pitched like a mix of Maori hakas and Red Indian war chants. Everything stopped as we listened, puzzled by the strangeness of these excited human voices ringing over to us across the olive groves. On and on they went .... until at last we understood.

The New Zealanders had been pushed out of Galatas leaving the great church full of their wounded, and now they had returned with a vengeance. Bayonets had been fixed, the Cretan villagers had fastened knives and bayonets to old-fashioned rifles and had joined the Kiwis in a mad charge through Galatas. Their aspect must have been terrible. The troops were angry and cold-blooded, the Cretans proud and hot-blooded, and the result as we heard later, was a stunning victory - at least for that day. No German soldiers remained in Galatas on Friday evening. The perimeter was fully manned again. In our position on Ruin Hill we were glad because if Galatas had fallen we would have been on a salient by ourselves, with the Germans in command of the only road direct from the plain around the Prison to the coast and its road to the capital Canea.

J.D. Fraser, New Zealand

The decisive fifth day

For us the first days had been more or less days of defence, except for one point and that was the village of Galatas. The whole battle of Crete had in this area two points of real strategic importance- that was Hill 107 and Maleme, and the village of Galatas. The village of Galatas was attacked by our second battalion and the second battalion was almost annihilated, because the population and the New Zealanders in Galatas defended the village with all their strength up to the last. On the last day of this battle for Galatas, a company had to be sent to reinforce the German forces, and I was with the company. And it was one of the most interesting but most difficult fightings I ever had during the war. We came up to the village, entered the village, for half an hour, and then we had to leave it again to take out our dead and

183

wounded. Finally, there was one British tank, a small tank in the middle of the village and the end of the battle of Galatas for me was when one of my anti-tank guns had the chance to destroy this tank.

Supplying food was one of the most difficult tasks, because the German air-force had already enough to do bringing ammunition, and so we had ammunition but we had no food and we became very hungry, I must say, and even thirsty, as we didn't find enough water and we didn't even know if the water was drinkable or not.

The whole question for us was the question of ammunition, and in the evening of the first day we had no ammunition at all. The British troops and the Greeks attacked us all day long, and at the end, when we had no ammunition left, I ordered my whole battalion to sing; instead of shooting, we sang. And the British had been so astonished, they thought perhaps this would be some, er (laughs), some sort of, er....

We came very near to losing, I think nobody who fought here, no paratrooper who fought here believed up to the fifth day that we would win. But the fifth day was the decisive one.

After five days I was almost certain that we couldn't win, because we had been hungry and thirsty and to the limit of our strength. And at this moment suddenly a lieutenant of the mountain troops came to my post of command, which was on this hill, and it was for us, I should say, an appearance of heaven, a gift from heaven.

Baron von der Heydte, Germany
Transcripts of interviews conducted for the documentary film 'TOUCH AND GO-THE BATTLE FOR CRETE, MAY 1941' written and directed by Tom Steel and produced by Jeremy Isaacs Productions for the New Zealand Broadcasting Corporation.

Counter-attack to recapture Galatas

After the attack on Maleme had failed the Germans were beginning to press in from the place of Agia - outflanking us from the Prison - and I believe it was considered that we should take this village of Galatas in a night attack with what troops were left. Some of them were mixed units and so on, under Brigadier Kippenberger. I was sent up to support it with my two remaining tanks, having lost one at Maleme - and I had two left.

I said to Kippenberger that I'd like first of all to go through the village on my own, so that I could go through at full speed and without infantry with me. And I drove through the village very fast firing on each side of the street and it was just chock-a-block full of Germans - and in coming out my second tank was hit and two of the crew members were wounded, but the tank was still serviceable. So I called for volunteers for the second go, when I had to go in with the infantry, and some New Zealanders who'd never fired machine guns or operated tanks before volunteered. So we went in then again with, I think, Sandy Thomas's battalion and I tried to drive slowly so that I didn't get too far ahead of them. But I got about a hundred yards ahead nevertheless and my tank was suddenly knocked out in the village square, my gunner was badly wounded, I was badly hit. My driver was hit in the shoulder. He pulled the tiller too hard and the tank swayed broadside.

I then pushed everybody out through the driver's seat from the front and crawled out myself, and I was hit in both legs and my arm and hid behind a stone wall praying for the New Zealanders who were behind me to come up, and they were having tough fighting as they came through. They came in with fixed bayonets into the square. I remember shouting to them 'Come on New Zealand, clean them out', and Sandy Thomas, who eventually became a General, was wounded just at the entrance to the square on the other side of the street from me and we shouted at each other and he brought the German I think who probably got my tank, down from the roof with an incredible shot with a pistol, because it was dark. And then having taken the village, suddenly the orders came to withdraw. I was left behind and so were a lot of the other wounded.

Roy Farran

Transcripts of interviews conducted for the documentary film 'TOUCH AND GO - THE BATTLE FOR CRETE, MAY 1941' written and directed by Tom Steel and produced by Jeremy Isaacs Productions for the New Zealand Broadcasting Corporation.

The Galatas girls: self-denial and self-sacrifice

The girls from the village of Galatas displayed great self-denial and self-sacrifice. A group of girls led by a mother of four, Mrs. Katsoulis, ran and brought in the wounded. They took care of them and prepared their food, ignoring the enormous risks they were running. The battle had spread to Galatas. Many of them sacrificed their dowries. They tore new sheets to use as bandages. When asked why they were destroying those useful things, they replied in true Greek fashion: "What's the point of having a dowry if we become slaves? This is no time to worry about our dowries when our brothers are in danger".

Takis Akritas, THE BATTLE OF GALATAS

Last night at Galatas

Who among us remember the well in the gulley between our line and the Jerries? Firstly our unarmed water party carrying 4 gallon petrol tins and an assortment of dixies, would go down and fill up while both sides watched and waited.

Then a little later the Germans turn. Two or three would stroll down in an equally casual manner, fill their cans and bottles, pause and light a fag, and then slowly return to their positions with all the trust in that unspoken gentleman's agreement. Yes, actions spoke louder than words.

Came the evening when some idiot with more ammunition than sense had to have a shot at the Jerries. All hell let loose as the Germans replied, we were forced to take a hand and no more trust between men who after all were only doing their duty whatever side they were on. Water was a trifle short after that and so was trust. One hopes that bloke enjoyed what he created.

But these incidents weren't confined to us alone. The Germans had their black sheep as far too well we know.

The shambles of that last night at Galatas when men charged without bayonets on their guns, chasing the enemy back and out, only to be outflanked, forced to withdraw, given a really hurry up out of the place.

The Battle of Galatas.

Wounded were carried out on doors, stretchers made of battle dress jackets on two rifles, on their comrades back and even some made it on their hands and knees. Into the olive trees, digging in if one had a spade, finding a wide tree to hide behind, then to battle again. Pull back 3 miles and the same old grind again. A stand at 42nd Street then a stand at Suda Bay. No further withdrawals. The Middle East Commando will land and hurl the enemy back, but within an hour or so we were on an orderly withdrawal to straighten the line, as fast as we could get out.

Jim Hughes, "Crete in Retrospect",
Pow-Wow, New Zealand, March 1987

Germans seize Galatas

The battalion commander has become particularly attached to No 2 Company. He does not show any favour to it nor finds fault with the others, but he is specially fond of it. Whenever he speaks of that Company he says: "Once again it has its right leader". And the Second Lieutenant knows how to handle his men. They went with him through thick and thin till two days later he was killed while leading them in sight of Suda Bay. It became clear from this morning's briefing that No 2 Company would be the main effort troop in storming the Kastelli height of Galatas.

The massive white rectangle of the prison walls is deep down in the valley. To the right and left of it the high ground rises slightly towards Galatas, but breaks off shortly before reaching that place as though nature had purposely dug a deep ditch round the height so that the walls dominate the whole terain like a tower.

It is bound to be hard going. The British are thoroughly aware that the Galatas heights are worth a capital city. Once again we have to fight our way through this wretched olive grove.

Dense cactus woods and agave thickets shove themselves forward forming wide barriers covering the whole terrain and closing off the view of everything lying ahead.

Our heavy weapons are moving to their positions during the entire morning. At 9.45 a.m. the first bombs from aircraft crash down on Galatas and our fighters roar at low altitude across the hilltops.

At 11.45 a.m. artillery and machine guns hammer at the enemy positions for the second time. Blows are exchanged in quick succession throughout the whole of the afternoon. German aircraft dive uninterruptedly on the village. No 3 Company has an excellent vantage position with a clear view of the enemy defence lines. It guides the fighter bombers by marks indicating the ranges. This system works splendidly to the delight of the mountain troops.

"Lord, what splendid fellows those airmen!"

They release their bombs right over our heads, and we push our helmets to our necks, but the heavy bits go buzzing over our heads opening up deep fissures in the village and mountain.

At 16.45 there comes another massive dive bomber attack. Whenever we raise our heads the New Zealanders open frantic and murderous fire, and late in the afternoon they even launch a desperate attack on the left flank of No 1 Company. They are determined to break out at any cost from the grip of the Luftwaffe but without giving up the dominating height. Finally the only choice left to them is "withdrawal" forward.

We, too, had heavy casualties.

At 18.00 hours exactly horrible detonations fill the valley, racking even our nerves. This onslought is in support of the mountain troops attacking since 17.00 hours.

At 18.30 hours the battalion commander whose companies are in position here alters their deployment forward. He wants to lead in person the attack ordered by the regiment. He arrives just at the very moment when No 1 Company under heavy enemy fire has had to take cover on the slope of the Kastelli heights.

The main British field fortification before Chania is being defended by grenade throwers, artillery, snipers on trees. It is a main effort to which the British have committed all they have in this sector in men and weapons.

The capital of the island is being defended here at Galatas. The decision for the possession of Suda Bay is being fought for here. It is a battle for the huge supply and equipping base set up by the British to support 20,000 men and their equipment for six months.

The Lieutenant-Colonel is fully aware that in those very minutes the decisive moment for the possession of the height has come. He has been left with barely one hour for the crucial part of the attack before darkness falls. Should the mountain troops fail to advance now there will be dreadful casualties.

The airborne troops have had to pay heavily in blood during their valiant struggle for the height through several days.

There is no way back now, and there must not be one!

The experienced front-line officer rises in the midst of the enemy fire and yells at the Company: "Boys, look! There I am and am O.K. Come on, hurrah!" (In Bavarian dialect).

And the lads jump to it, reverse their rifles with buts forward, break into the British position and with their commander in the lead capture the dominating height of Eastern Galatas.

The British withdraw and knock into No 2 Company which has started attacking the height on the left flank. They break into the New Zealand positions with exemplary dash. The New Zealanders stand fast not yielding an inch. An immensely tall fellow comes up out of a fox hole with two grenades ready for throwing. While one of these severs his left hand he throws the other at the feet of the Germans.

The New Zealanders are not surrendering. No 2 Company fights on in close combat, fiercely and mercilessly, led by their Second Lieutenant to wrestle the Kastelli height from the British. The Company losses in this struggle are one Lieutenant and fifteen other Ranks.

When darkness impedes nearly all visibility we hear dull detonations from hand grenades from the North-West, and shouts of hurrah.

The Second Battalion has penetrated Galatas village and is engaged in house to house fighting with the British who are putting up a fight in the ruins of the poor village.

Every cellar and ruined house has to be flushed out. Enemy orders are: "Galatas has to be held at any price". Let it be said that it was held to the last man.

In the fading light before darkness set in we see stretching below us in the fertile plain the houses and gardens of Chania. In the far distance, as the sun is setting, we glimpse Suda Bay, hide-out of the British Navy.

Dusk comes quickly, enveloping olive trees with strange full purple hues.

Pickets are posted and patrols sent for the night to keep an eye on the enemy. Stretcher-bearers take wounded comrades carefully down to the valley.

Kurt Neher, war correspondent
VON SERBIEN BIS KRETA

THE FATE OF CRETE IS SEALED

The last days

Despite the heavy losses and the gloomy prospects lying ahead of them, the Allies and the Greeks fight on. Heavy battles take place during the next few days in and around the main towns of Chania, Rethymnon and Heraclion.

The conquest of Galatas had opened the way to Chania. On Sunday, 25th May, the town was bombarded, burned. Brigadier Hargest found it "transformed from a pleasant little town to a smouldering dust heap with fires burning but otherwise dead." Chania, the capital, was finally captured on the 27th May, after a valiant resistance of the armed force and the whole population. It had not capitulated.

After the capture of Chania the German troops were shifted to relieve their forces still engaged at Rethymnon and Heraclion. Rethymnon was taken on the 28th May, Heraclion on the 29th.

The fate of Crete was sealed by Student's airblitz army during the night of 31st May to 1st June. OPERATION MERCURY had ended. On Sunday 1st June the sunlight could not pierce the sombre veil covering the Cretan hearts. The swastika, victorious, was floating over the battlements of the island, and it was there to stay for almost four years.

General Freyberg to General Wavell

23 May 1941

Reference your telegram of 22 May (No. 414). The situation at Maleme is really serious. Send all available air help.

A 19-year old Maori remembers

With daylight waves of German reinforcements arrived. One hundred and thirty troop-carriers landed under the escort of clouds of fighters. Two hundred dive-bombers attacked us. The Germans stabilised themselves in positions we cleared during the night.

With the return of darkness we again fixed bayonets, charged again and cut the enemy to pieces. This went on for four days and nights. Parachutists were dropped behind our lines, and we had to give ground bit by bit and take up fresh positions.

Eventually during an attack against enemy machine-gun posts just before dark one evening my company commander was shot dead in front of me. I carried on, but was shot by a Tommy-gun and crawled to our base, where I underwent an operation on the dining-room table of a shattered Greek house.

The Mercury, Hobart, Australia, 2-6-1941

Where is the starry sky

Where is February's starry sky
That I may take my gun, my beautiful mistress,
and go down to Maleme's airport,
to capture and kill the Germans.

Variation of the song "Pote tha kani xasteria" first sung during the Cretan Revolution 1864

Eratosthenes Kapsomenos, THE CRETAN SONG TODAY

The town was being bombarded every day

He who wrote these lines served as reserve soldier administering supplies to Empedon Battalion (basic training military camp) of Heraclion.

The town was being bombarded every day and the soldiers guarding the city walls and entrances faced many dangers from the Germans who tried to enter the city. Many of our soldiers holding vulnerable positions were killed by the bombs and gunfire of the stukas.

On the 23rd, a group of German parachutists entered through "Chanioporta" and advanced practically up to the centre of the town without facing any resistance. But there they were met by guards, soldiers and officers and they were wiped out.

After the great bombing of Heraclion during the night of the 24th, the administrator of supplies, the late reserve lieutenant I. Frangoudakis, accompanied by storemen, transported flour and food by military vehicles to a village called Peza. There the Battalion used a private bakery to knead and bake "Kouramanes" for the soldiers who fought in different areas outside the town, in Spilia, Profitis Ilias, Skalani, Babali and others. This transportation of goods endangered the transporters' lives as there were many German strongholds situated on hillsides, passages and road junctions from where they fired at the transporters and passers-by, citizens, women and children, who were walking along the main road.

Emmanuel Kardianakis, Ano Viannos

Capetan-Petrakogiorgis, one of the main guerilla leaders of the Heraclion area. Sketch by Patrick Leigh Fermor, England.

The army needs help

Our village is situated on the eastern peak of Psiloritis mountain, twenty-two kilometres from Heraclion. We could see Heraclion burning like a furnace, people were running here and there, panic stricken from the blast of the savage bombings. We did not know how to react. We wanted to help but didn't know how. Two days later on the 23rd of the month, as the same situation continued, Captain Christos Bantouvas, our fellow villager (who had been in Heraclion these last few days) arrived. Fully armed. He was exhausted from the two day battle. He told us that the Germans were dropping parachutists continuously and that the army needed help. He tried to get the villagers to follow him. When we asked where we could find the necessary weapons, he told us to take any weapons we could lay our hands on and that during the battle we could grab the dead Germans' weapons in order to fight them even more effectively.

That is exactly what happened. We crossed over to the villages of Kato Asites and Aghios Myronas and gathered another 15-20 men. We continued on foot till Yiofirakia Point, four kilometres from Heraclion. Many parachutists were landing in this area and all round Heraclion forming a circle, while the town was being bombed continuously. We, however, did not just stand there doing nothing. We slaughtered them mercilessly with their own weapons. We would draw near and, dazzled as they were we'd kill them as they landed and attempted to remove their chutes. We left Yiofirakia and moved to Agakou's Metohi. We managed to hold that position till the 29th of May 1941. Shortly afterwards we were forced to retreat, because Chania had been taken and the Germans had prevailed.

Apostolos G. Aghiomyrianakis, Heraclion

She carried me on her back

23rd of May. The Germans bombed the city. It has been decided to transfer the wounded from the hospitals to the villages.

Emilia, who was one of the few volunteer nurses carried me on her back to the truck that was to take me to Archanes.

Sifis Migadis, Heraclion

Photographs during the battle

You know that the Germans carried cameras in their aircraft and took photographs. The high ranking officers who landed with parachutes had cameras, too. I have no doubt that in this area at least, which I know well, they had photographed soldiers fighting. In fact, at Skalani towards Spilia, where the Germans landed and fought, there was a priest, an Archimandrite, who fought in his cassock along with 5-6 other men from Skalani.

A German officer had taken photographs. After they conquered Crete they went to Skalani and surrounded the area. They found the priest and two or three other men. "Follow me. Is that you in this photograph?" "That's right." They caught him and the others and shot them. No trial. Nothing. He only held the photograph.

Verbal testimony of Efstratios Saviolakis, Archanes

"I killed him and ran away ..."

A few days prior to the fall of Crete, the Germans tried to occupy my village, Kandanos. Kandanos is on the way to Palaiochora, which is a sea-port, so the Germans were most eager to get access. At the time none of the Cretan youth who had been fighting in Albania had yet returned home. Moreover, there were no weapons available, as Governor Metaxas - a few months earlier-, had issued a decree obliging everyone to hand over all arms to the authorities.

However, for some naive perhaps reason, -since the greatest part of Crete had already fallen, - we thought that we would be able to stop the Germans from going through our village. So, everyone, old men, women, youngsters, we all attacked the enemy with whatever weapons we had: Hunting rifles, old weapons used by our ancestors against the Turks, even farming implements. We managed to kill a lot of Germans which made them furious. It was here that the German boxer Max Schmeling was killed (sic) together with three others.

I was about 17-18 years old at the time. I remember an old man, around 80 years of age, who killed a German general. He had an ancient weapon and only two bullets made out of lead. He made a cut in them, so as to cause greater damage wherever they fell. He had been standing at the side of the street. "How did you know he was a high rank officer?" I asked him afterwards. "Well, he said, when I was fighting in Albania I often saw the generals who wore something red here. And now I saw this German sitting inside the motorcycle wearing this red sign, and I said to myself: He is high up. And I killed him, and I ran away."

Verbal testimony of Mrs. Marangaki, Kandanos

The battle of Kandanos

I was madly in love with Albert at the time. Being a Frenchman he had not been called up. He was staying in a village called Kandanos on the other side of the island. When the Germans launched their attack, communications automatically stopped.

One evening at the doctor's home I met a German called von Rosner. He was gorgeous! We spoke in French as I was just leaving the soeurs and he too spoke beautifully as did in principle all the Germans. As we were talking, I noticed a wound on his hand. I asked him how he'd got it and he said at the battle of Kandanos, that is where Albert was staying. We had not heard anything as yet. I naturally grew alarmed and he politely asked what was the matter. I explained that my fiancé was located in that village. "How old is he?" he asked me straightaway. "Twenty-eight" I said. "I have something very cruel to tell you", he said. "We were ordered by Hitler to kill all the young people in that village and set fire to their houses". Being by nature optimistic and knowing that Albert's family were French, I did not

196

ose hope. The German offered to go back to the village and find out what had happened to him. The very next morning he took his motorbike and rode back to the village asking news of the Prève family. Naturally all replied to his questions with "Kaput", fearing he might arrest them.

· That evening he informed me that no living soul had survived. Again, I was not convinced. Days later, the very same German drove me down to Chania in his jeep. The streets were covered in rubble and dead bodies. I finally found Albert and he was just fine!

Matilda Prève, Chania

CRETA SIEG DER KÜNSTEN

28th Maori Battalion

So we come to the night of the 26th when we got orders to move back once more to the line of the 42nd Street, in the vicinity of Suda Bay. There were all sorts of rumours, none good, but we trudged on until told we had reached our rest area. We slumped down among the olive trees and promptly fell asleep. We had been given to understand that a British brigade was holding the line on 42nd Street, so we felt quite safe and posted only a few sentries. We were to find out later that there were no such troops although we did pass through them the previous night. Where they got to, we certainly never found out.

Our rest was brief, and it was soon daylight, and with it the German planes, a sure sign that enemy ground forces were close. Soon sporadic small arms fire was heard, and close enough to mow the leaves off the trees overhead. We had received no specific orders, but under the cirumstances none were needed; here was more evidence of the discipline and great fighting instincts of our battalion. Within seconds every man was on his feet, rifle and bayonet at the ready, and without any words, heading in the direction of the enemy.

Major Dyer saw me on his left flank with my platoon and ordered me to hold back and take up a defensive position protecting the left flank of the battalion, in case of a German attack from that direction.

I watched major Dyer make off, walking stick in his left hand, and twirling his gabardine overcoat over his head with his right hand. A few yards further on, shouting "Come on D Company", he tripped and fell flat on his face and just as well too; about 20 yards in front of him a German in a kneeling position had his rifle aimed at Major Dyer. He must have fired just as the major tripped and fell. That was the German's last shot; the boys got him with the bayonet. On and on they went among the trees, their yells getting further and further away. Meanwhile, my platoon were reluctant to stop; they were steamed up and keen to keep going. Tainui and others had already found about a dozen Germans lying low in a ditch with a German shepherd dog; we had shot the lot and were looking for more; however, orders are orders, so I gathered up my men and settled down in a defensive position watching a village nearby at the foot of the mountain range on our left.

Eventually the boys came straggling back; their complaint was that the Germans wouldn't stand and fight, and those that weren't killed were too busy running hard to get away. The entire battalion had taken part in that bayonet charge; yells and hakas could be heard all along our front, a clear indication to the Germans of our eagerness to meet them hand to hand.

On the front I was watching, the only sign of the enemy were troops working their way along the mountain tracks above the village, moving to outflank us. The night before, we had picked up a Besa machine gun from a tank, a heavy lump of a thing which took two men to carry. I set this up on a rock and opened fire on these men. They must have been at least 1000 yards, and I had no way of knowing if my shots were close, but we had the satisfaction of firing belt after belt at the enemy.

The rest of the day was rest. We had no food, but there was plenty of water, so we had what we called a "Duck's breakfast, a drink of water and a look around".

That evening we were on the move again, to Beritiana and then up the mountains to Stilos, a distance of 15 miles. It was up and up, slowly, deliberately, nothing to say, "save your energy" until over the summit of the first range. Soon after, orders came to halt and rest for the night - or what there was left of it. In all, we had about three hours sleep when we were awakened by firing which turned out to be the 23rd battalion shooting the advance elements of a German force that had been moving to cut off our retreat. Apparently the Germans didn't want to pursue the argument and withdrew, so we had undisturbed rest for a little longer.

Rangi Logan, New Zealand

Maoris dance their "haka"

The Maori were big fellows usually, but not necessarily in height. They are brown, they are islanders, Polynesian and so on. They are lovely people, I like them, especially the rural Maoris.

I was with the Maoris once, it must have been Maleme, the airfield,

199

and they took it; then they got retreated, so the Germans took it over. Then they were given orders to take it again. So they went down the hill, I was walking by at the time, they went downhill, and they fixed their bayonets up and they did a "haka". A "haka" is a war dance, and you get so excited, I got carried away, I don't know why! And a big Maori pushed me behind to protect me, and they went with their bayonets and the Germans after about two minutes they ran away. They make those cries and their tongue comes right out there, brbrbr, it's to frighten the enemy.

Verbal testimony of Kenneth Stalder, England

Cretan donkeys carry the Parachutists' equipment.
Hauptman Piehl, GANZE MÄNNER.

Pz. II in action.
Photo by Randolf Kugler, Germany.

Under forty-five degrees in the shade

25th May: We have broken through the enemy line during the night. We have achieved a link-up with other units and lie in the mountains facing Heraklion airfield. We have been able to throw back an English attack with a counter-attack. We are without water. The waterpoints lie under heavy fire from enemy artillery. We are boiling among the pumice-stone. It must have measured forty-five degrees in the shade.

26th and 27th May: The situation is unaltered. Over the wireless we have got an offer from the enemy to hand over our wounded. We have accepted the offer. But whoever can still run stays where he is.

From the War Diary of Adolf Strauch, Germany

The spectacular evacuation

On this very day (27th May) the British ordered the evacuation of the island, and on this day too the British Navy suffered another loss by severe damage inflicted by bombs on the battleship BARHAM, 120 sea miles to the North-West of Alexandria.

The British evacuation of Crete, carried out between 27 May and 1 June, was spectacular. Its success and its scope had not been fully recognised by the Luftwaffe: 4 cruisers, 12 destroyers, 1 mine sweeper and a special purposes vessel evacuated 17000 men to Alexandria. But this too was costly to the enemy in material and personnel.

W. Gaul, "Operation Merkur"

28th May 1941. Battle of Apokoronas

When the Germans invaded my village, they locked all those they could find in the school. At dusk I came down to our house to collect some food and was shot at. It was a miracle that I survived.

That night the Nazis broke open the houses' chests and took the clothes (mostly girls' dowries). They slept on the roofs and in the yards, scattering guards everywhere who were firing at us continuously. The next day the 29th of May, the British retreated to Krapi. The Germans left my village to chase after them, taking trucks and our donkeys and mules.

During that battle 8-10 Germans were killed and were buried by their comrades at the Lakkos crossroads near the carriageway. They remained there until the end of the war.

Three British soldiers were killed and were buried by my fellow villagers the next day at Thyme. They mourned them as if they had been their own children. One villager in particular, G.A., who had children in Albania grieved for them like a true parent singing the famous Cretan laments.

I saw one of these soldiers still unburied, struck down among the cypress trees and thyme. He was a blond youth of about 22 years old.

His eyes were wide open, staring at the sun, and the Cretan breeze blew through his hair.

Poor lad. Your heroic death has surely brought victory to the Powers of Democracy in the Second World War. But when will World Peace be achieved as well?

Michael Galanakis, theologian in 1941 and now Metropolitan of Kissamos and Selinos Eirineos

Landing on Crete - The Italian version

Operations completed in Crete. The army began their landing on the Gulf late on the afternoon of the 28th May. It was completed a few hours later. The same night the army advanced towards the centre of the island. Their aim was two-fold: to advance towards the west and unite with the German forces and to then continue towards the south and get to the shores before the British had time to aproach from the other side.

One of the battalions advanced towards Heraclion having crushed the enemy's resistance, while the second one moved towards the southern shores and took outer Mouliani. The enemy was overcome after extremely fierce resistance. On their departure the Greeks left us about one hundred prisoners and a rich booty made up of arms and equipment.

Meanwhile the military landings continued under the protection of the airforce.

Cronache della Guerra, Rome, 14-6-1941

Not a single shot was fired

It's been written in various magazines that "when the Italians landed at Sitia, they fought hard in order to advance to the interior of

Heraklion Cave last day. 28th May 1941.

Sketch by Patrick Leigh Fermor, England.

ITALIANS LAND IN CRETE

South Wales Echo and Evening Express, 30.5.1941.

the island and oppose the Greeks and Allies, etc ..." It is all a pack of lies. The Gendarmerie School is at Rethymnon. Since the parachutists were landing at Chania, Rethymnon and Heraclion, the commander decided to transfer the School to Sitia, which was considered a much better place. When they saw the Italian naval forces approaching Sitia, all the officers came down from the School, not because they wanted to fight, they were outnumbered anyway, but rather to watch that peaceful laying down of arms. Not a single shot was fired. The gendarme cadets were arrested and taken prisoner and the commander, too, was arrested. Then they advanced steadily over the whole country. The Italians executed many men apart from the ones they had taken prisoner.

Verbal testimony of Stylianos Koundouros, Aghios Nikolaos

May 26: "No news". May 31: "We are slaves".

26-5-41
No news. Much sorrow because we realise the enemy has prevailed.

27-5-41
Hopeless situation.

28-5-41
Is it despair? Or agony?

29-5-41
Morale is low among people. Moral distress and fear of death.

30-5-41
We must accept that the enemy has prevailed.

31-5-41
We are slaves.

From the Diary of Dimitrios Lionakis, Kolimbari

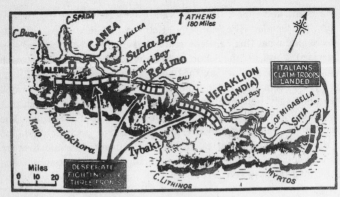

HEAVY LOSSES IN HAND-TO-HAND CRETE BATTLE

The Daily Telegraph and Morning Post, London, 30.5.1941.

Mountain-troops on their way to Chania marching through the olive groves.
Bundesarchiv - Militärarchiv, Freiburg, Germany.

View of Rethymnon. "Always watchful" is the subtitle to this photo,
first appearing in the book KRETA, SIEG DER KÜNSTEN.

"We must succeed." They did...

28th May: After a special heavy air attack on the town we are going to
take airfield and town by storm tomorrow. We must succeed or give
in.

29th May: The enemy have taken themselves off. Airfield and town are
in our hands. We don't stay in Heraklion, go further on to the West.

From the War Diary of Adolf Strauch, Germany

Last moments at Rethymno

Col. Campbell felt we could break through with a night attack -
movement by day was virtually impossible because of constant air
patrols. On the 29th we were ordered to close in on 2/1 position - the

Greek units had withdrawn - "C" COY and A/A Platoon were left as a covering force, but the guns in our area could not be moved - our new position could not be held in face of an attack from Retimo's direction. Some shelling had started late the previous afternoon and there were sounds of motor cycles. When German tanks appeared in front of us I spoke to Col. Campbell and he advised me that Heraklion had been evacuated (this was news to me) and that he proposed to surrender. I didn't feel I had the right to order a surrender and told him I proposed to give everyone a choice. Col. Campbell wished us good luck.

Ray Sandover, Australia
THE 2/11th AUSTRALIAN INFANTRY BATTALION 1939-45
Edited by Bill Brown

A PYRRHIC VICTORY

The aftermath

The Battle of Crete is over. After enumerating the total losses, George Orwell, in his war time diary on the 3rd of June, 1941 concludes: "And all this for absolutely nothing."

To an observer in those dark days, with no access to overall information and no Allied successes anywhere, the significance of the battle would very well appear to him as it did to Orwell. However, in restrospect, the majority of historians, strategists and politicians converge on the view that the Battle of Crete, for a variety of reasons, as we shall see, has not ultimately been fought in vain.

Moreover, the fear of an imminent invasion of the British Isles had now been effaced. The Nazis, after their razor's edge victory in Crete and the slaughter of the parachutists' élite corps, should now give up or indefinitely postpone their dream of invading England. Student was to say later: "The Führer was very upset by the heavy losses suffered by the parachute units. He often said to me: 'The day of parachute troops is over'. After Crete he refused to attempt another big airborne effort. I pressed the idea on him repeatedly but without avail."

In the last analysis, as admitted even by German strategists, the fight for Crete proved a Pyrrhic victory for Hitler's Germany.

Hitler's Greatest Gamble

the Military Correspondent

THE BATTLEFIELD

The Battlefield

Such are some considerations which the campaign of Crete evokes. But let me stress that all are minor considerations beside the single gigantic fact with which this new Hitler stroke confronts us. For if Hitler takes Crete, one thing alone is certain. THE NEXT ISLAND TO BE ASSAULTED IS OUR OWN. THIS EMPIRE DAY IS THE GRAVEST AND THE GREATEST HOUR FOR BRITAIN SINCE TRAFALGAR.

Evening Standard, London, 24-5-1941

Evening Standard, London 23.5.1941.

—by Illingworth

Invasion Rehearsal?

Another senior officer, who was acting as a liaison officer and saw the results of fighting in a number of separate areas told me that he considered that the lesson of Crete was that Germany could never capture Great Britain with parachutists and air-borne troops.

The attackers (he said) would have to contend in the United Kingdom with a powerful air force and highly organized ground forces, compared with the conditions in Crete, where there were scratch land forces and practically no air force. If the Crete show was really a rehearsal for an attack on the United Kingdom, it must have been a severe shock to the hopes of the German Command.

The Times, London, 3-6-1941

What the Battle for Crete meant

The victory in Crete cost the Germans some 22,000 troops, of whom 5,000 were drowned by the Royal Navy, and about 400 aircraft. I have seen it stated that the delaying effect of their attacks upon Greece and Crete not only interfered with Hitler's designs upon Syria and Iran; but eventually proved disastrous in their attack upon Russia. The German army reached the outskirts of Moscow in October, 1941, by which time the early frost had begun to interfere with its movements. Its arrival in front of Moscow five weeks earlier would probably have led to the capture of that city, the importance of which it is difficult to exaggerate.

Our defence of Crete, therefore, may have served its purpose in the overall pattern of the war.

A SAILOR'S ODYSSEY. The Autobiography of Admiral of the British Fleet Viscount Cunningham of Hyndhope.

The Battle of Greece and Operation "Barbarossa"

I was naval attaché to the British Embassy in Moscow from 1949 to 1951. The Swedish naval attaché to Berlin was General Jühlin-Danfeldt who had served in this post from 1933-1945. One day we were talking about his experiences as a trained observer who had followed the German army at Dunkirk as well as Moscow. I asked him why the German army had stopped advancing towards Moscow, especially when they had already reached the city gates and Moscow was there for the taking. He laughed and told me that the reason was really simple. They fell asleep that night with their tank axle - deep in mud, but when they woke their vehicles were axle-deep in rock. The temperature had dropped by 20 degrees and it was now impossible to move.

There is no doubt that the Battle of Greece was the reason behind the Germans' delayed attack on Russia - Operation "Barbarossa" as it was then known. If the Germans had reached the gates of Moscow a few days earlier, they would have surely taken the city. I am under the impression that this theory is common knowledge among historians.

R.I.A. Sarell, England

Tragically futile

The battle for Crete was one of those operations which appear in retrospect tragically futile. Crete was not prepared for defence and should not have been defended. Its loss was without strategic significance. So was its capture. It turned out that the possession of Crete made little difference to the conduct or course of the war one way or the other. Attempts have been made to argue that Hitler's need to clean up the Aegean postponed his attack on the Soviet Union and so saved Moscow at the end of the year; but their arguments are unconvincing. Events in the Middle East were uninfluenced by the German capture of Crete, just as they would have been uninfluenced by a German repulse. The struggle in the Mediterranean and North Africa was not perceptibly affected. People died: that is all. The very pointlessness of it makes Crete one of the purest of arguments against war.

Peter Calvocoressi, England

The crucial airport of Maleme

Unlike the Greek campaign, the Battle for Crete was not foredoomed. In the Duke of Wellington's words about Waterloo, it was to be "the nearest run thing you ever saw in your life".

Here let me go back to record a chance personal involvement. After the Italian attack from Albania, the Greek Government asked for British advice before making up their minds whether to move the Cretan division to the mainland to take part in the battle. The answer came that if it would help the Greek Government to make up their mind to redeploy the Cretan division, we could assure them that we would do our best to look after the defence of the island. In the

213

Minister's absence, I was the messenger who carried this welcome assurance. In the event, it looks with hindsight that in the throng of other things, Africa, the Middle East (Iraq) and the Western Desert, Crete became somewhat forgotten. In the six to seven months before the German attack on Crete, there were no less than six different British commanders on the island. During that period, there was no recruitment of Cretans who later showed at Galatos what they could have done. There was not even an appeal for a labour force and in consequence, as I passed by Maleme airfield two or three days before the battle, I saw Maori troops putting up the first defences. Perhaps most critical of all when the battle was engaged, there was no adequate supply of communications between forward troops and Headquarters.

Even so, at the end of the first day, May 20, General Student, the German commander, found his plans in disarray and casualties were high. But he saw with clarity that the hub of the battle was Maleme. For who commanded that airport might be able to reinforce and so win the battle.

Perhaps General Freyberg, the British commander was late to seize this, though he may well have guessed it by the end of the first day. Here the lack of adequate communications frustrated him. His orders to hold on at all costs around the airport never got through and the withdrawal of one New Zealand company from the hill overlooking the airport, enabled the Germans to pour in reinforcements despite much determined resistance.

Harold Caccia, England
From a speech delivered at the Royal Overseas League, London, on the 13th May 1982, for the Anglo-Hellenic League

The aerodrome is the key...

One knows what went wrong: There was one New Zealand Battalion sitting on the airfield, sitting round the airfield, dominating the Maleme airfield. And this battalion sent out two companies to chase up some paratroopers and they didn't come back those two companies for a while. Now there were Germans scattered all over the place. There were no wireless sets. If we had wireless sets we wouldn't have lost Crete. You'd sent a message, the C.O. of this battalion sent a message to brigade stating his position. Never got there. You see there were Germans, odd Germans, everywhere and you couldn't communicate, no telephones, you couldn't get in touch with brigade. It was every unit for itself at that stage there, because they couldn't pass information. So, anyway, the Colonel decided in the evening that he would have to withdraw, because his two companies were missing. So he withdrew and no sooner had he withdrawn and his two companies turned up flushed with success. They found he'd gone, so they went too, of course. And then the Maoris who were going to counterattack, they found that he'd gone and they retired as well. It wasn't, I think, fully realized, I mean, I can't speak because I was a long long way away and I only read the books, but it wasn't fully realized that there wouldn't be a sea-landing of any importance. And a lot of the reserves were kept in case there was a sea-landing. It wasn't fully realized how difficult the situation at Maleme had become, and how vitally important it was to hold the airfield. Otherwise, everything would have been thrown in to take it. What would have happened if it had been taken I don't know.

I went to New Zealand after the war and I had dinner with General Freyberg. He had an English Admiral and an English Air Vice Marshall and we stayed talking until about one in the morning. It all arose like this. They had a wise program about Crete, and they quoted the Australian Batallion numbers wrongly. I mean 2nd of the 7th instead of 2nd 7th. Freyberg felt very bitter about the failure to get Crete, well, that we were abandoned. Both the English Admiral and the Air bloke said: "Thank heavens you lost Crete. We could never have supplied it. It would have been an embarrassment. As it was, you tied up the German division for the rest of the war doing nothing, and if you recaptured it or if you'd won you might have inflicted a few more casualties on the Germans, but you would have tied down a British division there, and all the harbours were on the North. The Navy suffered enough trying to supply Crete, we can't bring in supplies from the South because the harbours just are not there, and it would have been some support for the operations in North Africa, of course, but thank heavens you lost it".

215

It wasn't up to Freyberg to agree or disagree. He'd lost the battle. But basically, of course, because of the lack of appreciation by him that there wasn't going to be a sea-landing of any importance, and that Maleme aerodrome and the aerodromes themselves were the key to the situation. A sea-landing, in point of fact, of course, there was. An attempt to do so, but it was very minor. And it was smashed by the Navy.

Verbal testimony of Ray Sandover, Australia

Recollections of a British Captain detached to the Information Service

I remember two instances when General Freyberg referred to the Greeks. I have no doubt that he expressed his admiration on other occasions, but I shall confine myself to my own recollections.

The first incident was when he spoke to me about how admirably the Greeks at Alikianos had driven back the dangerous German forces on the western side of the said "Prison Valley". The second incident refers to the famous attack at Galatas on the afternoon of the 22nd May, when about one hundred Greeks, including the villagers with their wives and children, charged across an open plain with such a frenzy, that they sent a large German unit into flight. The Germans had side attacked the New Zealanders' positions, but the Greeks' furious cries and ferocity sent them "fleeing without a second thought".

I interrogated several German prisoners in Crete. They were fit and well-trained but did not differ from the other German prisoners that I had met at the Western Desert. They had all been stunned by the resistance they had encountered on the island. Before the invasion they had been told that there were very few allied forces on Crete. This was not concocted to encourage them but rather what the German Military Administration really believed. The German Information Service was really terribly uninformed.

David Hunt, England

216

Civilians' Heroism Praised

Major-General Freyberg directed the last battle of Crete and the withdrawal from a cave, states the Cairo correspondent of the British United Press. The troops went to a secret rendezvous from which they embarked nightly.

The heroism of the people of Crete has been the subject of a special dispatch by Major-General Freyberg after the evacuation. It was delivered to the people of Crete, by the Greek Minister of Justice, who said that Major-General Freyberg had asked him to transmit to them the admiration of the British and Imperial forces for the great heroism, courage, and high morale shown by them during the German invasion of their island. Their fortitude had been really magnificent.

The Christchurch Star-Sun, New Zealand, 3-6-1941

Stepping-stones

General Student in a letter to lieutenant Carl Morris Tugwell in 1970 said: "According to my plan Crete was only a stepping-stone. Cyprus was the second. Our first main objective was the Suez Canal with Rommel advancing. I had won Goering over, he as much as I was an ardent opponent of the Russian adventure, but the army leaders supported Hitler. My plan was at any rate shattered by the heavy losses incurred in Crete."

Tugwell, in his book "Airborne to Battle" also quotes from Student that the Führer had said: "This affair will go wrong and will cost too many lives".

Ray Sandover, Australia

General Student, a brief sketch

German paratroopers are more or less the work and the invention of General Student. He was the man who had the plans and was commanding the first parachute division. I saw him before the battle in Athens at the briefing. He was, I would say, a man full of strength, full of confidence, when he gave us the orders. And then I saw him after the battle and he had changed completely. This battle had made him years older, he looked like an old man, like an ill man.

Transcripts of interviews conducted for the documentary film 'TOUCH AND GO - THE BATTLE FOR CRETE, MAY 1941' written and directed by Tom Steel and produced by Jeremy Isaacs Productions for the New Zealand Broadcasting Corporation.

'No Unattainable Isles'-Göring

Berlin, Monday. - Göring, in an order of the day to the Luftwaffe on the capture of Crete, says: "You have proved to all the world the words of the Führer: 'There are no unattainable islands' ".

"This first daring overseas operation must overwhelm the enemy like a thunderstorm. Parachutists, you have achieved superhuman feats." - Reuter.

Daily Mail, London, 3-6-1941.

Crete, a Pyrrhic victory

Goering gained only a Pyrrhic victory in Crete, for the forces he expanded there might easily have given him Cyprus, Iraq, Syria and perhaps Persia.

It was only our weakness in the air that rendered the German attack possible. The RAF strength early in May was 36 aircraft of which only half were serviceable. These were distributed between Retimo, Maleme and Heracleion, and were but a trifle compared with the overwhelming air forces about to be hurled upon the island. Our inferiority in the air was fully realized by all concerned and on May 19th, the day before the attack, all remaining aircraft were evacuated to Egypt.

Winston S. Churchill, and the editors of "Life", THE SECOND WORLD WAR

Hitler's mistake

Hitler declared on 19 August 1941 during an award ceremony of Knight's Crosses to those who had fought in Crete: "The days for paratroops are over. This is purely a weapon of surprise and this element of surprise has now been blunted". Since then, his paratroops were tied to the ground being used as élite infantry.

Der Żweite Weltkrieg, Heft 29

A new badge for paratroops

The "Crete Sleeve Badge" inaugurated on 16 October 1941, was the second special badge bestowed on Parachute Troops. Some hundreds of them were already wearing the Narvik crest for the Norwegian Campaign in the spring of 1940.

Günter Stein, "Arms of World War II, Special Issue"

The largest cemetery

Crete has the largest number of dead German parachutists on its soil. I shall not forget the time when the Cretan partisan said to the German General Bräuer: "You have fought well, accept my horse as a gift".

The emotional ties linking the Cretan guerillas and the German soldiers remain to this day very strong. You walk through the streets at Chania and suddenly a Cretan will stop you and ask: "Are you an ex-German parachutist?" "Yes". "I congratulate you, you are a good soldier".

A human touch links the brave Cretan guerillas to the German soldiers.

Verbal testimony of Rudolf Witzig, Germany
Contributed by Dimitrios Tsakonas, Athens

The airport will not last an hour

From the beginning of the war we had left the whole of Crete's defence strategy in the hands of our "friends" the British. On the afternoon of the 7th of May, together with Ambassador Palairet and Admiral Turle, we went to Castelli of Kissamos in order to find means of transportation for those British who had not yet managed to "bale out" of the Peloponnese.

As we passed the airport at Maleme, Palairet made a point of showing me an anti-aircraft machine gun. He wanted to emphasize how well protected the airport was from an aerial attack. At that time we were expecting a German air-landing operation at any moment. "The airport won't last an hour under a heavy enemy attack", I replied emphatically. Something which sadly became a reality ten days later.

Admiral Alex. E. Sakellariou, ON MY TRAVELS ...

6 WASTED MONTHS
Suda Bay Left Defenceless, Maleme Unfortified

Suda Bay Left Defenceless, Maleme Unfortified

From ALEXANDER CLIFFORD   **Cairo, Monday**

CRETE must not happen again. It was not only aeroplanes we lacked, it was foresight. The battle of Crete was lost not this May but last November. We occupied the island so that we could use Suda Bay as a naval base. But no serious attempt was made to fortify it.

After six months in Greece we had not got enough air fields even for our few planes. But within three weeks of occupying the country the Nazis had fresh landing grounds in use.

Daily Mail, London, 3-6-1941.

WAR HISTORY'S DISCLOSURES
Military Blunders Were Costly In Greece, Crete, Syria
By GUY HARRIOTT

Here are some of the conclusions reached by Mr. Gavin Long in his controversial second volume of the Army series of the Australian War History - "Greece, Crete and Syria" - published today by the Australian War Memorial, Canberra:

● The British Government failed to consult the Australian and New Zealand Governments before committing Anzac troops to the Greek expedition; General Wavell did not seek the opinions of General Blamey or General Freyberg.

●Thousands more troops could have been evacuated from Greece but for faulty and tardy planning by the British staffs.

●Crete could have been a victory instead of a defeat if Wavell had planned its defence properly and in time.

People's feelings changed overnight

By the time the battle had ended the Cretans had become very anti-British. Most people shared the same feelings of rage for the British. They considered them incompetent for not being able to make a stand. The Cretans felt contempt and exasperation. Twenty four hours later, however, the British had become heroes and semi-gods because the Germans started the executions and everyone was suddenly on the side of the British.

Verbal testimony of Manousos Manousakis, Chania

Forgotten?

I have very sadly reached the conclusion that the British Government does not wish to revive the Battle for Crete. Anniversaries of other World War II battles are brought to light, victory celebrations held, but not so poor old Greece and Crete. They seem to be forgotten, WHY? Our Government won't even grant us the privilege of accepting a medal from the Greek Government.

Frederick R. Turner, England

They glorified Dunkirk but not Crete

The Battle of Crete is one battle the British Government don't want to talk about; otherwise why don't they accept the Greek memorial medal which was awarded to the New Zealand and Australian Forces who served there? They glorify Dunkirk, but this was far worse. Ask any survivors. After all, it was the greatest airborne invasion ever by the Germans. The Cretan people were wonderful, looking after and helping our men in every way. I am most grateful to them.

S.A.J. Scott, England

"We both stood alone..."

It has been an affair not only of the heart but of the head too. My generation will never forget the experience we shared with Greece when for a whole year in the Second World War our two peoples stood alone in Europe's darkest hour against the might of the Axis powers.

Before Hitler's invasion of the Soviet Union and before the United States entered the fray we both stood alone against Fascist tyranny. Greek resistance was undoubtedly a factor in delaying the Nazi assault on the Soviet Union and that delay was fatal to Hitler's plans. For us Greece was then, as she is today, a friend worth having.

I shall never forget when on the 41st anniversary of the Battle of Crete I stood with a British Parliamentary delegation before a stone memorial dedicated to our men who fought and died there alongside their Greek comrades. Our guide whispered to me - "the man who gave the land for this memorial is here". I went over to him and said simply "Thank you for what you did". He seized both my hands and said, in Greek, "Do not thank me. I only gave the land - your countrymen gave their blood".

Bernard Braine, England
From a speech delivered at the House of Commons, London, on the 2nd October 1987, to commemorate the Battle of Navarino

These wretched young men

A few years ago I wanted to go to the place where the planes landed. There was a dry river bed where they came down and I wanted to see it. And a very kind man in Heraclion, I am not quite sure, took me there. And we stopped on the way at the German cemetery. And for the first time in my life I felt very sorry for the Germans. For the first time, I suddenly felt terribly sorry for them. Because there were these hundreds and hundreds of graves. And there were ones with no name. Two boys of about twenty one. No name. And again and again I came across these graves and I thought well, really, these wretched young men. It was a murderous war for the Germans, from the air.

223

The first soldiers were killed instantly. Just like that. I suddenly felt awfully sorry for them. And then I've heard that a Cretan who had worked with Paddy Leigh Fermor was in charge of the cemetery, who would have probably killed some of these boys during the war. And this young man was now one of the two custodians of the cemetery. And I thought that was terribly moving. One of them was George Psychoundakis. He is a very nice man, with a son who was educated in Germany. And it's so interesting that there's no feeling, you see. During the war there was bitter feeling, but now there is no anti-German feeling at all by these people who fought. I still have a little. Although I have German friends. And we didn't suffer here in England. My house was bombed but we haven't anything comparative with what happened in Greece. But I think quite a lot of English people feel like myself.

Psychoundakis was a runner. He must have walked, you know, forty miles a day. Extraordinary things. Crossing Mount Ida with messages!

It's a very very beautiful cemetery. I like it, I think it's more beautiful than the British cemetery. It's absolutely lovely, with a marvelous view, and terribly touching.

Verbal testimony of Dilys Powell, England

We respect each other, we can forgive...

Unfortunately I know how hard it is for us German soldiers to write about our past which many of us have still not been able to overcome.

Every soldier who has fought against us and everyone who has been hurt by us Germans by our war knows that their sacrifices have made sense and that victory over us was right and justified.

Young German soldiers of my generation have not only experienced defeat but they also had to cope with the shock from the realization that our leadership and their aims had ignominiously misled them, that we had been imposed upon and that our sacrifices and sufferings had merely served an evil cause. This is a grievous burden still carried by my generation to this very day. This is why many former soldiers are no longer prepared to talk about their past. I have turned towards "Christ" and now look upon my past from another point of view.

I consider it now essential to take you back with me to the past, to that period which I experienced as a German soldier. In May 1941 all German paratroops were volunteers and had joint the corps for idealistic reasons. They had been trained after very thorough selection. Any soldier who had committed offences against defenceless people or civilians was punished in accordance with the severe provisions of Military Law. Whoever looted, robbed, murdered or raped was punished with death.

I had been dropped by parachute at the Corinth Canal and was stationed in Nauplion from early to mid May. There we were at this time on almost friendly terms with the Greek population and I know of not a single case which marred this relationship.

When our task in Greece had been completed we were ordered to occupy the island of Crete and move thence to Africa. Of course we knew that we would have to fight the British and their Allies on the island. We were told that the island population would be neutral in their attitude. Not one of us had at that time thought that the Cretans would defend their island. It therefore came to us as a complete surprise when we landed to be attacked by armed civilians (the conception of "Partisans" was not then known to us). These combatants were not protected by our Military Law nor by the Geneva Convention.

After cruelties had been committed against German soldiers whom British war propaganda, referring to German parachute troops, called criminals and gaolbirds who would murder, loot and rape in Crete, the partisans were fought against with all severity. Also strict discipline was kept when we took Heraclion. I know that Cretans are now very proud of their fight for freedom waged against us. I respect their attitude and have an understanding for the sacrifices made by them. However, as I see it was a senseless shedding of blood as in May 1941 there had been no enmity from our point of view between all of us and the Cretan people.

After remembering those days I am happy that we understand one another now, that we respect each other and that we can forgive.

I was very happy when I could visit Crete with my wife in 1976 and when after a long search I found Maria Vassilaki in Gazi. In May 1941 during the days of intense fighting we had suffered greatly from lack of water and we were, therefore, especially grateful when girls from the village of Tsalikaki provided us with means to slake our thirst. Maria was one of those girls. Here is a picture of Maria and myself (1976). Unfortunately we no longer look as young as in 1941.

Adolf Strauch, Germany

Adolf Strauch, Germany, with Maria Vassilaki, Crete.

THE HEAVY PENALTY

War Casualties

"The fighting was of the most intense description", states the telegram sent from Cairo on June 2nd, 1941 by the Prime Minister of New Zealand to the Acting Prime Minister. "And though the proportion of dead to wounded is reported to be low, we must, I fear, expect heavy casualties. Most of the fit men and most of the walking wounded appear to have been evacuated, but a proportion impossible to estimate still remains in Crete, and it has been necessary to leave wounded cot cases."

Heavily wounded, invalids, dead, this was the sad account of the battle, the heavy penalty paid by Allies, Greeks and Germans alike. Faced with the tragedy of injury and death, however, there are no friends or foes. All fighters become the same. What prevails is the human element, compassion and grief, a helping hand reaching towards suffering and despair.

A nurse remembers

During the battle of Crete, I was working as a nurse in the Red Cross First Aid in Chanea. It was hard work, looking after the wounded soldiers who came from the mainland after the German occupation.

One week before the 21st May, 1941, the German Stukas dropped many bombs around the place and, as a result, there were hundreds of wounded civilians and soldiers. The city seemed to be on fire.

Part of an Australia and New Zealand hospital arrive in Crete. Some of these nursing sisters were wounded in a bombing raid whilst embarking, but they carried on uncomplainingly through the hardships of the evacuation.
Keystone Press Agency, London.

We had to transfer our clinic to the basement of the building, because it was more safe.

Early on the morning of the 21st May, we heard the news. The German paratroops were coming down everywhere. In Maleme, Galatas and the city.

The wounded poured into our clinic. Our white uniforms were almost red from the blood. All sorts of soldiers: English, Greek, German paratroopers and civilians. Women and children. A few died there before we were able to transfer them to the hospital. It was like hell, and the experience of seeing so many young people dying in front of us, was terrible. Some of them said a few last words for their families before they died. What a tragedy!

A young man came crying and said to me: "Come sister with me and help me; my wife is bleeding a lot at home and she is going to die." I went with him. The bombs fell down around us and we had to lie down on the ground for safety. We found his wife, a very young girl, having a miscarriage. She was covered in blood. I couldn't do much. We saw an army jeep pass by and we put her in and sent her to hospital. Later I heard that she survived.

Another time at the clinic I saw a young soldier with many wounds - I tried to dress them. He took my hand tightly: "Sister", he said "I don't want to die. I want to see my sister, my mother, again". But he died soon after.

I saw many tragedies. I helped a lot and suffered a lot seeing all this. I struggled to survive afterwards. I don't want to see any more wars. I remember all those happenings as a nightmare in my life.

Esther Petritakis - Torakis, Crete

Bundesarchiv -
Militärarchiv, Freiburg,
Germany.

A German remembers

It was in May 1941 that I jumped with German parachute troops near Maleme in the West of Crete. In the course of engagements in this area I was severely wounded during an attack near the village of Galatas. I received several hits from a British machine gun on I think the 25th of May. I was the only one of my squad to survive. I fainted from the loss of a lot of blood, nor do I know how long I lay there exposed to the fierce heat of the sun. I remember scarcely anything in the few moments that I came out of my unconscious condition caused by loss of blood and fever.

The first thing I became aware of was that I was being jolted and being carried or dragged on a stretcher by two British soldiers. Then I fainted again. The next thing I remember was that a blood transfusion was about to be made in a sizeable room and that there were British medical orderlies and presumably also a medical officer present.

Then I remember lying in a row with others on the floor on a mattress or something like it in a large room, possibly a school room, next to wounded British and German troops. Then all of a sudden there were again German soldiers about and we were loaded onto stretchers and then into a British ambulance. A wounded British soldier lay next to me on a stretcher. I came to occasionally from the jolting and the piercing pain during the drive. Then I remember being flown in a Medical service Junker 52 from Maleme to Athens. I recall finding myself lying in a bed with white sheets in the Military Hospital in Athens with a Greek medical sister standing by my bed. She addressed me in the little German she knew and it was then that I regained full consciousness. I remember that she was called Georgia and that she was very kind and friendly. I fell head over heels in love with her. However a few days later I was put on board an Italian hospital ship "Gradiska" where we were cared for by Italian doctors, Red Cross sisters and sailors. We were taken to Saloniki and transferred to a German field hospital. I think that after about two weeks in Saloniki I was taken in a hospital train to Vienna where I underwent treatment in various military hospitals till August 1942.

Natural humaneness prevailed over the then existing hostilities and expressed itself in the fact that hostility ceased where readiness to help an enemy in need prevailed.

Without this humane willingness to help I would most likely not have survived.

Unfortunately I no longer have pictures, letters and other things from those times as I was unable to return to my home after the war. My region became Polish in 1945.

Bruno Obloch, Germany

A stretcher-bearer remembers

On the second day of the battle the Luftwaffe was making low sweeping strafes. The noise was terrific, bullets thicker than hailstones - they even broke branches off the olive trees. And dead and wounded from both sides. Among all this carnage, along the cabble stoned roadway came a little old lady who stopped and showered all her pity on the 19-year old German paratrooper we were carrying to the Regimental Aid Post (R.A.P.) for medical attention. Over the years I have often wondered if the old lady survived the war and just where was she going that day in the midst of a battle.

I was losing track of days and my wound of several days was going bad, and with lack of food I was very tired and miserable. I crawled into some bracken that was growing against a wall, and went to sleep. I was awakened by terrifying yells. It was the Maoris going into their bayonet charge.

I was advised to seek proper medical attention so went to the doctor who had set up a R.A.P. in a house in the Suda Bay area. The doctor, who I think was English, had only his tools of trade, no bandages or antiseptic. A Maori who had a terrible wound in his hip was placed on the kitchen table. A Cretan woman was making bandages from household linen. I do not remember anybody speaking (it took energy to speak). The only people apart from the wounded were the army doctor and this Cretan woman.

The only thing to write on was a family photo on the mantlepiece, on the back of this the doctor wrote the instructions that I be evacuated from Crete.

R. Kennedy, New Zealand

A Maori's death

I'll tell you about a dying Maori. He was badly wounded, and I said I'd give him a blanket to bury him in. And I was frightened, of course. There were bombers and God knows what, and he was lying there. He knew he was going to die, so he took me by the hand. "Don't be frightened", he said, and he was dying. I gave him my blanket to bury him. Wonderful. He was comforting me and he was dying.

Verbal testimony of Kenneth Stalder, England

An English pilot remembers

The sun blazed down again. I had lost all sense of time. I must have been unconscious for most of that day and the following night. On the third day I had a spell of consciousness again.

There were men passing just by me. I tried to croak at them. They saw that I was alive and came round me. Six young German paratroops. My tongue was dry and swollen. They saw my need and produced their water-bottles. The first drops to pass my throat were more precious to me than life. I drank and drank. I seem to remember draining many waterbottles. Someone had cold tea with brandy in his. Another gave me some dried fruit from a cellophane packet. I was sick. And drank again. "Water" was the only word I could whisper through my cracked lips. Someone pulled a blanket over me and I was alone again. Only the craving for water remained.

I remember being carried in on a stretcher. We were passing the old headquarters. Every lurch of the stretcher was agony. I passed out again into merciful oblivion. Then I was lying among a crowd of other wounded and dying men in the village street. There was someone close by me on either side. One was silent; he was dead. The other was one of my own airmen. I was delirious.

Edward Howell, ESCAPE TO LIVE

Stretchers, stretchers, stretchers...

Eventually I dropped off to sleep.

In the morning I realised that the horrible stench that I had thought to be some corpse outside was coming from my leg. Someone had thrown a blanket over me during the night, and as I lifted it my gorge rose. I was terrified.

Presently a German orderly arrived with four stalwart stretcher-bearers and I was carried out and placed with other wounded on the back of an open truck.

When we reached the aerodrome the wounded were unloaded by some of our own men who had been prisoners at the airstrip for over two days.

I was carried down into the main airstrip. There seemed to be several hundreds of other stretchers lying in long rows on the edge of the runway.

We lay in the sun for nearly five hours. It was very hot and the stench of my leg and blood-soaked blanket was almost unbearable. The men near by complained that this stench made them feel sick and the orderlies moved them away from me. I felt lonely and miserable.

Later, one of the orderlies took pity on me and came over for a chat, although I was conscious that he kept his face well averted and sat to the windward. He described to me the scene on the aerodrome, how there were over one hundred planes crashed all round the edge of the airstrip, and how some of them near the beach still had their full crews and passengers seated stiffly in the positions they had been in when hit by our machine-guns. Planes were coming in and taking off continually quite unmolested.

A giant Junkers 52, a troop-carrying plane, drew out to the edge of the runway not far from where I was lying. I was carried over to it by four English medical orderlies.

W.B. Thomas, DARE TO BE FREE

Bullets were flying everywhere

June 1st, 1941

I am at Helwan Hospital in Egypt ....
I was wounded in the right shoulder last Sunday 23 May at about 4.30 in Crete ...

June 5th, 1941

Well, that happened while I was bringing a lot of ammunition from a trench across an open hill for our gun.

My word those men of the Red Cross are heroes. The bullets were flying everywhere, and they just went on, carrying men in and fixing them. No-one ever saw a more noble sight than I did while lying in the sunken road there and watching quietly as man after man was fixed, and they all came out of it safely. Wonderful, I do think.

I was put on a truck at dark, and all were brought to a hospital house, also to a big culvert over a road, or under a road, where even some operations were done! I left the next night and reached Suda Bay at 4.30 in the morning. The Red Cross men erected about 7 big tents and put out big Red Cross flags in the air and on the ground; and though the German airmen bombed all around for miles all day, they never once flew over our acre of new hospital camp, and that is fact, or else I would not be here. They only fire on them if anyone wears a tin hat or carries a rifle, or if the tents are under trees.

Well, we set out again at dusk for a very long night, and had a 7-mile ride at the end at daylight, so reached a hospital and safe again.

From the War Diary of Harold Loftus, New Zealand

A doctor's memories

During the operations in Crete I was medical officer to 33 squ. and was taken prisoner by German parachute troops, whilst attending to the wounded, at 1200 hrs. on 20 May 41.

I remained with the wounded (British and German) until dark, and then moved back with them to a village across the river, on the west side of the aerodrome.

That night I and about 50 wounded were put into a room about 16 ft. by 15 ft., and I was told to get on with the job. Many of the troops, including myself, were suffering from dysentery. I had no medical equipment, no water, and no food. I got a small amount of first aid equipment from the Germans.

I was in Crete until 1 June. During this time three other medical officers and I tended about 400 wounded with little help and next to no food from the Germans.

From the escape report of Thomas Henry Cullen
Contributed by Jean-Louis Roba, Belgium

Inferno

The medical dressing station is some distance but not far, from the regimental Command Post. As we advanced it was moved forward together with the signals. A small building, badly damaged by shell splinters, has become an operations theatre.

There is no room there for all the wounded, some of whom are stretched out in a lean - to by the house or in the garden. There seems to be no end to casualties being brought in on stretchers.

Senior Medical Officer Dr.B., wearing a surgical overall that was once white is operating in candle light and uses a torch as well. He is just operating a severely wounded casualty. Medical orderlies are helping, handing him surgical instruments and bandages.

"Tweezers", ... "Tetanus", ... "Bandages" ... These are handed to the surgeons in silence. The silence in the narrow room is only broken occasionally by groans from the wounded. Nearly all the badly wounded leave the operation room with a smile. The colourless liquid of the morphium syringe has relieved them for some hours from pain.

235

A parachute sergeant is being brought in. His breath comes in jerks. His chest has a gaping hole as big as a fist. The MO examines the unconscious man very carefully. The doctor's face displays anxiety close to hopelessness. A silent gesture of the hand-and we know that it is the end - medical skill is of no avail in this case.

They take him out - into the night and lay him down ... two hours later he died.

Those who after they jumped and dropped over Crete had not slept and had carried the attack forward under heaviest fire throughout the long day under a scorching sun, now dig a grave in the rocky soil. They bury their dead comrade in the light of bursting shells.

The forward dressing station serves as a place of refuge not only for the wounded but for others too in need of recovering strength. The regimental MO had provided for tea and food. This seems so very obvious, but a walking casualty tells me:

"Both doctors work without a break since early morning. Even though bits and pieces of the shed are sent flying and the flimsy structure sways and rocks - nothing makes the two flap. Occasionally artillery fire was so intense that the wounded had to be carried to comparative safety in the shelter of a rocky gully".

The British wounded follow the German casualties by being flown by the "Barbarians" in Junker aircraft to the Military Hospital in Athens. Many a Tommy shook our hands possibly with a changed attitude to the German soldier in contradiction to Churchill's propaganda.

Fritz Scheuering, SPRUNG ÜBER KRETA

Among the German wounded

A dressing was stretched across my body and stuck down with sticking plaster. I was then placed back on the stretcher, covered with a blanket and taken into an adjoining room where I was placed in a corner.

With what light there was I could see the room was crowded with bodies, one or two moaning and muttering, but it wasn't until morning that I discovered they were all German. Mainly, I found out later, paratroopers. It eventually turned out that I was the only English person in the house.

The first two days remain very vague. I was constantly being told by the German orderly (this was translated by the chap on the next stretcher, who spoke good English) that I must keep a tight hold on the operation or the clips would tear loose.

All the Germans in the room I was in had severe stomach wounds. Several of them could speak English. They surprised me by their friendly attitude towards me. We had several interesting conversations on the wastefulness of war. The chap on the next stretcher to me had been a student teacher of English from Munich. One day during a conversation he discovered I was in the construction industry. I shall never forget him exclaiming "Ha, construction, so much better than this destruction".

Being paratroopers, they all voiced the same complaint. They should have been allowed to reach the ground before being shot. Which sounded rather naive at the time. Though I could not really blame them when I thought of all the stuff we flung up at them. In fact anything from revolver to artillery.

Several days later we were informed that the post was to be evacuated and that we were all being flown to Athens. However, on the day of the departure a German soldier came marching in the room looking for the "Englander", and we were informed that I was staying put despite angry protests from the rest of the patients.

Several of them apologised as they went and left me books, shirts, trousers and socks, then I was alone, unable to stand and not knowing what was happening. This was so all day, then towards evening a truck pulled up outside, a German guard stamped in with two of our chaps, bellowing out for the "Englander", I was taken back to the prison camp where my mates were called for to come and take care of me.

Years later on a working party in Sudetenland I was fortunate enough to 'purchase' an illustrated volume of the Battle of Crete which I still possess. It was brought back to England by a pal I left it with when I escaped from the working party, and in it there is the German who operated on me.

Walking wounded
Bundesarchiv - Militärarchiv
Freiburg, Germany.

The mystery to me is, how did I come to be handed over to the Germans. How did the German surgeon (as he obviously must have) know my appendix had burst. Why was he able to operate, without anaesthetic, when our medics couldn't, and why was I the only Englishman there?

I only remember seeing the Doctor three times. The first time when he walked across the room to where I was tied spreadeagled on the table. He bent over me saying "ist gut"; he seemed an older person. I was just twenty two so he was probably in his mid thirties. He was tall with a lean face, with I believe two scars. Scars which seemed to belong to the face, not the type of scars made during the war. I am sorry I can't explain just what I mean, but he was the type of person who instilled confidence.

W.E. Parker, England

Feelings that can never be experienced again

I was in Crete during the battle and occupation of the island. I used the German I had learnt to serve as an interpreter for my compatriots. While I was there, I was approached by a German doctor who was eager to help me. But it was more of a spiritual feeling that bound us together. Every time he saw my mother he would ask:

"Wo ist die Maria?" (Where is Maria?) My mother realised that something was going on. One day she tenderly placed her hand on my shoulder, the first time she had ever done so, because Cretan mothers are not usually demonstrative, and said: "My child you must suppress these feelings otherwise you will get hurt. I will say Mass for you and help you with my prayers."

From that day on, I fought with myself. I suppressed my feelings. There are times in one's life that one can never re-live and feelings that one can never experience again. In the beginning I felt desperately lonely, but prayer and my philosophical view of life helped me get over it.

Years later I found out that he and his two brothers had been killed on the Russian front. I have kept the card that he sent before he left

239

Crete. He wrote his goodbyes discreetly and politely, careful to avoid mentioning his feelings of love. The card was written in German, it said:

> Honourable Miss Maria
> I wonder what the Future will bring
> Where is our destiny?
> Wherever it is, however, we shall endure it.
> My thoughts and warmest wishes accompany you
> for the rest of your life.
> Sunday, 24/9/1943.

I have no regrets. That was the way it had to be.

Verbal testimony of M. I., Crete

Greek, German and Italian wounded lay side by side

I was serving as a volunteer nurse at the hospital of Aghios Nikolaos in Crete.

The Battle of Crete was nearing its end.

During the last hours of the slaughter, many wounded were brought to the hospital of Aghios Nikolaos, mostly German parachutists and Italian soldiers who had landed on the shores of the County of Lasithi. Greek, German and Italian wounded lay side by side and were treated with equal care.

I was on the night shift at the time, and at some point I had to go and get medical supplies from the store room in the hospital basement. I fearfully began to walk down the pitch black corridors and stairs, carrying a candle in my hand. In order to get to the storeroom I had to go past the mortuary ward. There I knew there were Italian soldiers. They had been transferred there the night before. Each one was lying on a stretcher and was covered with a sheet. I made the sign of the cross and made a prayer. As I was about to move on, I suddenly saw that the sheet on one of the stretchers was moving and I heard a moan. I froze. Terrified I approached the stretcher and pulled back the sheet. By the light of the candle I could distinguish the angelic features of a twenty year old boy. He was an angel.... I was young, healthy and strong. I took him in my arms and holding on to the candle managed to drag him onto the first steps. Under these tragic circumstances I administered first aid. My position was a delicate one. There was no way out. I was saving the life of an Italian while the battle raged on and I was supposed to be getting medical supplies for a Greek. "Mama mia", cried the Italian. When he heard me speaking Italian, he calmed down a little. I left for a short while, to go and get the two Catholic nurses who belonged to the Nuns' school in Hania, which had been detached to our hospital. His name was Pasquale. It was the only thing I learnt about him and that he had been saved.

Virginia Galanoudaki
Acropolis, 2-8-1981, Athens

The wounded cadet

I had lost a lot of blood. The next morning I was transferred to the battalion's temporary first aid station, while the battle raged on all around. The doctor who was dressing my wounds was shot in the leg. In the afternoon I was moved to the Pananion Hospital at Iraklion. I had been shot right through the chest and the wound had become quite extensive. The hospital was full of wounded men: Greeks, British and Germans, some were even lying in the corridors.

I remained at Pananion for two days. On the third day the Germans bombed the city and the hospital was all but destroyed. All the wounded who survived the blast were transported to the town of Arhanes, where a small hotel had been transformed into a temporary hospital. I was one of the more seriously wounded. Two sisters belonging to the Greek Red Cross at Pananion helped me through my ordeal. I owe them my life.

After we had surrendered, the Germans moved all the heavily wounded Greeks and British alike, to Athens. We remained in a hospital in Athens for three months. We spent the first month at the Polytechnic, which was used as a hospital for prisoners of war. The circumstances under which we recuperated were very harsh: anyone who dared approach the window was shot by the guards. By the end of June the Red Cross had taken over and they transferred us to the

"Evangelismos", a branch of the 2nd military hospital. This hospital was also full of wounded men from Albania and the forts.

Upon leaving the Polytechnic in open topped cars belonging to the Red Cross, we were greeted by cheering crowds who had gathered outside. They shouted: "Take courage boys, we have not been beaten. The Italians who had already taken over as the Occupation Army forced the crowds to disperse.

It was a tragic sight. The victors enslaved by the defeated.

Agamemnon Gratsios, Athens

VIA DOLOROSA

Withdrawal to Sphakia

In view of the aggravation of the overall Allied position, the spectre of a new evacuation, the most hazardous of all, hanged over Freyberg's headquarters. Finally the "razor's edge" decision had to be taken. On the 26th of May, Freyberg cables to Wavell: "I regret to have to report that in my opinion the limit of endurance has been reached by the troops under my command. From a military point of view our position is hopeless. Provided a decision is reached at once a certain proportion of the force might be embarked."

General Scoulas, commanding the island's Greek forces, thought the same: "The position of the Greek forces is so difficult that they have begun to disintegrate as a result of the bad and constant struggle for so many days for lack of war material, food supplies and red cross material."

On the night of the 27th of May, Churchill's War Cabinet reluctantly admitted that "all hope of success was gone". The evacuation had started. To reach the village of Sphakia, however, which was the point of embarkation, the retreating army from Maleme and Chania had to face a formidable obstacle, the White Mountains. Earlier, as reported by Alan Clark, the 8th Greek Regiment, consisting of youthful cadets of the Military College of Athens (Evelpides), gendarmerie and civilians had successfully protected the road to Sphakia. "The heroism of this Greek unit", he writes, "was providential for they blocked a German move which, if successful, would cut the road to Sphakia."

So the Allies marched on, over some of the roughest country on earth. On all lips one word, one goal: Sphakia. As Freyberg wrote in his report:

"The road from Suda Bay over Crete to Sphakia was well described by someone that night as the 'Via Dolorosa.' Never shall I forget the disorganisation and almost complete lack of control of the masses on the move as we made our way slowly through that endless stream of trudging men."

Panorama of wreckage

Around Canea and Suda Bay there is a panorama of wreckage.

Olive groves are lying flat. Ten miles of the coastal plain are covered with dead and wounded and the wreckage of broken cars, guns, lorries, carts, village houses.

The Germans, who entered Canea on Tuesday after a continuous assault lasting 60 hours, found the town a blackened and smoking ruin.

The only people there were wounded whom a few British doctors and Greek assistants were caring for in underground shelters".

Daily Telegraph and Daily News, Sydney, 31-5-1941

The Cretans were turned out of their homes

Monday 26th of May 1941.

Far away, the fires and rumble of battle.

We left the road that led to Hania and followed the one that led to Nerokouros. It was a long way. Time went by quickly. We walked and walked, but the few belongings that we had, weighed us down. Nobody spoke, everyone was buried in their own thoughts. It was a very still night, none of the nocturnal birds could be heard, no insects were flying about, nothing except the monotonous sound of our tired footsteps. We felt that something disastrous lay nearby. Everything in sight bore witness of it. If only God could avert this disaster! Now and then we'd stop and rest our feet by the side of the road. If only we could finally get there. We were all so tired in body and in spirit. We arrived at Nerokouros well after midnight. The village was deserted. At the crossroads, we just lay flat out to rest. We couldn't bear it any longer. It was so good to be able to catch your breath. Tomorrow we would make an early start for the caves. We were so tired we couldn't sleep a wink. It was also freezing cold up here. Ahead of us in the distance we could just about discern the fires at Hania. Now and then lightening would strike at the sea and we could hear a distinct rumble. We wondered what was going on. Were they attacking from the sea?

Panos Papathanassopoulos
PARACHUTISTS IN CRETE, MAY 1941

The advance party to Sphakia

At about 4 p.m. that afternoon in Suda I was told to report to the CO's office. There I was introduced to an Australian officer and told I was, from then on, "seconded to" this Aussie's unit for all purposes and was to obey all orders whatever they might be. It sounded very ominous!

I got my "small" kit and drove the officer down towards Kalyves and from a road to the right we drove into the Aussie camp. I was "introduced" to a sergeant and told to get a meal from the cook house. On my return my lorry was loaded with tents, food, petrol, Bren guns, ammunition etc.

As darkness fell some Aussies climbed aboard my lorry and the sergeant sat next to me. All he said was "keep up with and follow the lorry in front - with no lights". After about half an hour the "convoy" of five or six lorries with me as tail end stopped and for the first time I was told our destination by the officer as follows: "We are the advance party to a village called 'Sphakia'. Defend it from German attack. It is the evacuation port/point for all troops. We are evacuating from Crete. If you are captured on no account give this name to anyone".

We carried on over the White Mountains "nose to tail". The journey was hair-raising, with a near vertical wall of the road on one side and a drop fall of hundreds and hundreds of feet on the other. All

"...Rather sad; it was in Prison Yard which eventually held German paratroopers. It shows two Cretan boys who worked there and "Blondy", a young navy signaller. "Blondy", and I am sure the other two, were killed with the first German bombs on the Prison".

with no lights. It seemed to go on and on. We flattened out on to a plain and finally started climbing again until all of a sudden there before us was the beautiful blue sea. As we started to dip down to the sea with a brilliant sun rise, the convoy stopped and the officer said: "This is Sphakia. After we have unloaded you can either drive your lorry over the cliff and be the first on the first boat back to Egypt, or you can (without my orders) return to your unit to be with them".

I next remember being awakened by the sergeant who said "now it is up to you". I had no hesitation in returning to my unit to fight on with my friends. I was only machine-gunned twice on the way back. I drove straight back at full pelt. Right into the "Prison" yard there was utter confusion. For no apparent reason our guns had been "spiked". A sergeant told me "orders are every man for himself, i.e. we're all equal, make for a place called Sphakia". I told him I knew! I'd been there!

Edward Frederic Telling, England

246

The Maoris are pushed back

After the New Zealand Maori Battalion had been pushed back from the airfield at Maleme after some bitter fighting I think everybody realized that we would not be able to hold the island and even though we weren't told that an evacuation was under way after what had been happening the preceding week we all realized that things were pretty serious. We were ordered to withdraw from our position up behind Suda Bay and make our way up to the top of the mountains and as everybody seemed to be making for Sfakia on the south of the island we joined in with the main force.

George W. Blanch, Australia

The Cretan base surrenders

What a sight is presented by our Mountain Infantry. Suntanned and parched, their uniforms in rags, caps flattened and caked with sweat and mud. Our mountaineering boots are patched up with insulating tape and leather straps, soles are worn through, nails torn out from jumping and falling. Arms and legs are grazed. Every group has its wounded and yet we carry on with unheard of élan. We no longer feel the heat and have overcome extreme exhaustion.

GEBIRGSJÄGER
AUF KRETA
Contributed by
Michael Xylas, Athens.

Ammunition and more of it is our daily prayer! More of it for the last blow. All day long supply columns wind their way up the mountains with ammunition loaded on donkeys and provisions also reach us. Water! Carriers bring this precious cloudy liquid in water bottles on donkey back from the wells down the valley to the forward positions where mountain troops are lying on bare rocks in wait for the enemy in that terrible heat.

Below us is the sea and the port of Sfakia with the white cubes of its serried buildings. The rugged mountain sides drop steeply to the ground below, Crete's southern coast towers over the blue waters of the Mediterranean like a cyclopean wall with mighty debris tumbled from it and then raised high by a giant's fist against titanic powers.

Kurt Neher, Germany
VON SERBIEN BIS KRETA

The gallant Cretans are deserted

As we marched through the night on our way to Sphakia, some villages were burning after being bombed by the planes and the people must have known we were leaving. I felt ashamed to desert such gallant people. Well on into the night, we came to a village with a well, without the means to draw up the water, so from our rifles we took the pull-throughs (used for cleaning the barrels) tied these together and lowered our sun hats down to the water and drank from the tin hats. I can still remember the taste of perspiration as I drank that water.

As daylight came, we scattered among shrubs and trees for shelter in case the planes came to bomb and machine gun us and, once again, we needed water. A mountain boy came, and we asked for water; he went away and came back with a large tin on his shoulder - it was a wonderful drink - and one of my friends had a sock full of sugar which we chewed.

I felt stronger after the water and sugar. We gave the Cretan boy some drachma to pay him, but he didn't want to take it - he was a handsome lad - perhaps 16 years old.

During the march over the White Mountains, we rested after every 50 minutes, for 10 minutes - we were so tired we had to be careful we did not leave any of our friends sleeping beside the road. Each time we halted, we could still hear the sound of the marching feet away down the mountainside.

I would love to visit both Greece and Crete again. I think the people must be among the most loyal people in the world. People who were poor, were risking their lives for freedom and helped so many British, Australian and New Zealanders who remained behind in Crete.

George Weelink, New Zealand

Bombers and fighters

Our officers in party told us to sit in square and no rifles or tin hats to be shown. A red cross flag was laid out. Sure as sin we heard planes and a Jerry formation came out of the sun. What a sight, bombers and fighters! All at once a fighter came down low and flew over us. We could see the airman, he waved, then flew to the rest of the flight. He found we were wounded, not combatants, so left us alone. But they dropped eggs into that gorge. The ground shook and dust flew up. This lasted about ten minutes, then all was quiet and they were gone.

Vic Kingdon, New Zealand

In three words

I would just like to sum the whole thing up in three words: A terrible nightmare.

S.A. Olliver, Australia

A wounded on his way to Sphakia

I was sent to hospital with shrapnel wounds in both legs. Was to have been operated that night, but before this an orderly came into the tent to say boats would be coming into Canea that night and if wanted could make the effort to get to the wharf. Made the effort and had my hand on the ship's side when an enemy plane flew over dropping two large flares, which made the night look like day. The ship pulled away leaving thrity-three of us behind, later taken to a hospital out on the way to Sphakia.

On the way to Sphakia, which I had to walk on my toes, the wounds stopped me walking normally. The first day kept going for nineteen hours, afraid may not make it to the coast. Kept to the road, put my small pack down at a well and lost it, plus all the films in it. Numerous strafing raids and near the end legs so sore couldn't be bothered to get off the road for shelter, just leant up against the bark.

The second to last afternoon was tough, in the .evening saw a monastery on the valley floor, made my way down to ask for a drink, was invited to have a cup of tea, the most pleasant taste had for days. That night slept in the graveyard on the windward side of a headstone. The following afternoon made my way down to the beach, spending the final hours in a cave.

Max B. Goodall, New Zealand

"The battle has not ended for us"

28th of May 1941.

We walked up the road towards the ravine at Nimbros. By the time we approached the village it was well after midnight. The village was shrouded in silence. The only sound we could hear was the rhythmical sound of our footsteps on the road echoing the beat of our hearts. Each one of us was lost in thought nurturing our fears with our bitter silence.

Near the village we were able to discern the outline of some shadowy figures waiting for us. As we approached they offered us a

View of Sphakia.

The last headquarters in a cave at Sphakia.
The embarkation of troops was conducted from here.
Contributed by John Tsatsas, Athens.

piece of hard bread, some olives and a glass of wine. These women were from Sfakia and had come here to fight. You would have thought them to be "Myrrhbearers" from the Annunciation. But these women were not carrying myrrh. They carried guns hanging across their strong shoulders. Their hands were rough and calloussed as they touched us. They wore headscarves usually worn by men.

One of them cried out to us:
"If there is anyone of you who can no longer carry his gun, he should either destroy it or hand it over to us, so that the Germans don't get their hands on it. Tomorrow we'll need it again. The battle has not ended for us".

Then we began to realize that all was lost and the end was near.

Some of our own men informed us that during the night the British boarded their warships and left. At Sfakia they had created their own safety zone and would not allow the Greeks to approach so that their men could leave first. Meanwhile the Germans sank many of their warships. Tomorrow was to be a crucial day for all those in that area.

From Manolis P. Siganos's Diary, Crete

*Sketch by Manolis P. Siganos,
Crete.*

252

THANK GOD FOR THE NAVY

Evacuation once again

There was a first evacuation from Heraclion. In the darkness of the 28th May two cruisers and six destroyers anchored off the port. Without the Germans being aware of their going, the garrison marched down through the desolate town which "was full of dead, debris, hungry dogs and wet roads from burst water pipes". The entire garrison boarded the ORION which was later hit and her commander killed. More than 500 crewmen were killed or wounded by the bomb blast.

At Rethymnon there was no evacuation and here the Greek troops, supported by the gallant Australians under Lieutenant-Colonel Ian Campbell and Major Ray Sandover fought till the last. Campbell's troops capitulated at dawn on the 30th, but Sandover thought it better to make for the hills and not surrender.

The massive evacuation of the Allied troops was effected from the village of Sphakia, point of embarkation selected by Freyberg. At the end of 'Via Dolorosa', the unassuming port of Sphakia mystified everyone as leading to salvation. Scrambling up to the warships was an elation, "an immense feeling of relief and pleasure, almost like the joy of coming back home."

The British Navy had done a feat in Crete. They managed to lift almost 12.000 men from Sphakia.

Only one officer and thirty-three returned...

28th May. We spent the day in our present positions and at dusk moved higher up the mountain sides where we could command a view of the country over which we expected the enemy to advance. We remained in these positions until first light and then began to withdraw down the road or rather metal track towards the village of Sphakia which we could see in the distance. Here the road held quite a few immobilised vehicles which had made an attempt to evacuate wounded and a few ambulances which had definitely been shot up by hostile aircraft. The smell of the dead in these vehicles was almost overpowering. We moved down the road a distance of some two miles until we arrived in a valley which contained quite a number of caves which proved to be a haven of refuge for the day. One very cheering sound coming from one of the caves which I learned later to be the headquarters of the late Brig. Hargest was the phut phut of the motor which was operating the radio and keeping in touch with the Navy which we found out was going to risk all for one more night in an endeavour to get us off the island. This news did a lot towards raising morale and troops thought that it was a very fine thing that their Bde Comd. who had opportunities to leave the island earlier had decided to remain to the last. We dispersed among the unoccupied caves and spent the day waiting and praying for the darkness and the Navy. Quite a number of the caves were already occupied by British wounded and medical orderlies. These unfortunates never left the island but remained until they were picked up by the Hun. There was a well quite handy to our area and many of the troops were able to bath for the first time in many days. There was no food to be had but personnel were not unduly concerned about this as minds were all the time on the arrival of the Navy. It was again decided to leave nothing to chance and as a safeguard against any enemy infiltration two strong patrols from 21 NZ Bn were sent up on to the high country above our positions to keep a sharp look out for any sign of the enemy and to remain there until recalled in the evening. No sign of the Hun was seen all day. There was the odd plane or two over our positions but no strafing or bombing took place. Towards evening we began to assemble for the march down to the point of embarkation. While units were getting into position to move off in the correct order of march about half a dozen Stukas came over and machine gunned the waiting troops. No one near me was injured although we spent some very tense moments. We moved off at dark with the Maori Bn in the lead.

We reached the actual beach somewhere about 23.00 hrs, and assault landing craft manned by naval personnel nosed their way quickly into the beach. They were loaded up as silently as possible and sailed quickly and quietly out to the waiting ships. We pulled along side HMS ABDIEL, a mine layer in the British Navy. After a few necessary formalities with regard to identification etc., we were quickly assisted aboard. The ship's company lined the routes that we were to take to our alloted parts of the ship and always when one started to stumble in the pitch darkness there was a sailor's hand ready to steady and guide. Many walking wounded were brought aboard and the ship was loaded with her complement of troops very quickly and quietly. Although we were still far from being out of danger a sense of security began to creep over us owing to the fact that we were once more in the capable hands of the Navy. Eventually the landing craft were sunk in the bay in Sphakia and the ship quietly weighed anchor and stole out to sea. Although there had not been sufficient time to commission the ship with regards to providing rations as a troop carrier, steaming hot cocoa and white bread and butter were handed around liberally. This was better than any feast. When daylight came I sneaked up on deck and had a glance around. I saw that in the convoy were also two destroyers. One was the AJAX and I never discovered the name of the other. I was told by one of the sailors that I was on board the fastest ship in the British Navy and she was certainly doing her stuff. It was difficult to stand on deck as she swung alternately to port and starboard to avoid torpedoes or bombs from enemy aircraft. At about 11.00 hrs a single ME 11c appeared overhead and started to dive in on us. All three ships opened up with everything they had and the pilot seemed to decide that discretion was the better part of valour as he pulled out of the dive to veer off and disappear. At 1500 hrs land was sighted and at 16.00 hrs we were berthed in Alexandria.

What a motley crew we were. Of my company, only 19 strong, I doubt if any two were dressed alike. We united with the members of the company who had come from the mainland of Greece via Cyprus and the company strength once more rose to the grand total of 34. Of four officers and 125 ORs who embarked for Greece, one officer and 33 returned.

Les Young, New Zealand

A Major of the 28th Maori Battalion remembers

The morning of the 30th dawned, the day was sunny and warm, and our only pastime, exercise or preoccupation or whatever you'd like to call it, was watching the columns of soldiers, or rather stragglers moving past us.

Later that day, Major Dyer returned from battalion with information, the battalion was to go off that night less a rearguard of 6 officers and 144 ORs which was to remain behind to protect force headquarters and be evacuated the following night. Major Dyer was in command with Capt. Rangi Royal as his 2i/c and four subalterns. Humphrey Dyer said to me with a smile, "of course you will stay with me." It was more a statement than a question; there was nothing to say; I certainly would not have left him and the D Company men required to stay behind. I quickly sought out the D Company men and told them I needed 28 volunteers to stay behind. Every single one volunteered, so Jack Tainui and I made the selection.

Later in the afternoon, our rearguard watched as the battalion filed past and made their way down the mountainside towards Sfakia.

Some time later, I heard there was an army food dump in Sfakia. I went to Major Dyer with the news and a request that I go down with a carrying party to get some. He sent me to Brigade to get a requisition signed by Brigade. When I told Brigadier Hargest what I wanted, he turned to his Staff-Captain and told him to write out a requisition for 200 men, 150 for us and 50 for Brigade HQ. I set off immediately with a carrying party of 26 men in all. We soon caught up with the tail of the evacuating troops and as I led my men past one column, a Tommy soldier in a panic caught hold of my arm and half-crying said, "you can't go past me Sir, I might get left behind. " Poor chap.

I turned on him, snarling, "we're going back up there (pointing up

256

the mountain) to fight while you bastards get off tonight; but now we're going to get some food." With that, I gave a back-hander. There was not another murmur as I and my men trudged past.

We eventually reached the fringe of Sfakia where we were told we could not enter Sfakia till after midnight when the evacuation was completed for the night, so we settled down to wait in the rear of the evacuating troops. In due course, midnight came and we moved down to the port area. I had no trouble finding the food store which was in the charge of a NZ Artillery Major (Lewis?). He was surprised to learn we were still fighting in the mountains and when he saw the requisition he and his men quickly gave us the supplies. He also asked if we had had anything to eat, and when I told him we hadn't had anything for days, he gave us extra rations on the basis of 2 men per tin of Bully beef and a packet of biscuits.

We carried our supplies up to the outskirts of the port to a flat rocky ledge with a deep well - it was more of a huge cistern. To get the water we tied a steel helmet to some signal cable we found nearby. While the boys were having their fill of water, Jim Warehi was issuing the Bully and biscuits. I should say at this stage that there was a decent moon which made what we were doing easy. According to custom in our battalion, the officers always ate last; if there was anything left, then the officer ate; so it came to my turn to drink. I remember kneeling by the well opening and gulping down the water. With spillage I drank four hatfulls; then Jim handed me a whole tin of Bully and a packet of biscuits.

When I protested that I should be getting only 1/2 tin and a 1/2 packet, his words to me were, "Shut up and eat". I am inclined to think that such conduct and such words can happen only in the Maori Battalion. There was a lovely relationship between officers and men.

Jim wasn't going to stand for any argument from me. So I ate, or rather, I emptied the tin into my cupped hands and just put my face into the meat. Bite and swallow, bite and swallow; then a drink of water, bite and swallow, a biscuit, more water, until all the meat was gone. That was my first food for four days, since the B Company area at Platanias, and that lot would not have fed more than a couple of sparrows.

We rested for a while after that magnificient repast, then we moved steadily along the mountain track up to a plateau. At this stage I must say that just before we left Brigade HQ the Brigadier told me that brigade and our battalion rear-guard would be moving down during the night to new positions nearer Sfakia and I could wait with my men till daylight to rejoin our unit. There was a large tree on the plateau and at the base of the cliff another 200 yards further on was a huge cave. I told the men to settle down and have a sleep around the tree, then Tainui Mathews and I moved towards the cave expecting to be challenged any moment. We had heard it was the command HQ of General Weston who was i/c troops following the departure of General Freyberg for Egypt. We got to the mouth of the cave without having been challenged; there were no sentries, no guards of any sort. We entered the cave; there were no lights, no movement, so we stood there surrounded by the snores of sleeping men.

After standing there for a moment or two, I tapped Jack and Guv on the shoulder, and we went out just as quietly as we had entered. Standing outside, I remarked that the entire command staff was at our mercy, and couldn't get over the lack of security. Then we settled down for a sleep, the time was 0300 hours.

Next morning we moved further up to the mountain, and it was not long before we found our rearguard dispersed among some caves by a ravine on the left flank and immediately above Sfakia. They were as pleased to see us as we were them, mainly I presume because of the rations we brought. After sending off a portion of the rations to Brigade, I rejoined D Company. I remember watching major Dyer sitting on a rock in a huge cave eating biscuits and jam, munching on and on with a contented smile on his face.

Later that day, we were moved to another area on the right of the defensive enclave around and above Sfakia. The rest of the day past uneventfully. Late aftenoon we started our withdrawal according to plan. Our problem now was not the Germans, but our own stragglers who would be trying to crash the evacuation columns. Major Dyer impressed upon me that he was putting me at the rear of the battalion force with strict orders NOT to allow any stragglers to join our line; his words were, "for every straggler you let pass, one of our men will have to stay behind. The Navy can take only the exact number and no more". So that was it, clear and precise.

At the tail of our column once again was the three of us, myself, Jack Tainui and Guv Mathews, I with my Luger and them with Thompson sub-machine guns. As the column moved slowly along the track, the stragglers pressed closely behind us, stopped only by the three of us and our guns. It was a sad sight; they were following in the hope of being accepted, and they knew too that to try and rush us would have been the end of dozens of them. There was even a group of our walking wounded who had struggled along after they had to abandon their 15cwt truck miles away. Luckily for them, the Brigadier himself came along and escorted them through and handed them over to Major Dyer. That was OK by me; it was his right to do that, and I was secretly pleased. We eventually reached Sfakia.

Nightfall and eventually the order to move.

In time I came to the water's edge and this was the last boat, loaded deeper into the water, the dark shape of the boat getting nearer; I reached out my hands, stifling a little feeling of panic - if the boat should move out now - and then my hands were on it.

I grasped the gunwale, nothing could make me let go now; I pulled myself out of the water and my boys pulled me into the boat - oh the relief, but then the boat was grounded because of the excessive load, so several of us got into the water again to push. It didn't take much effort and the boat was clear, and we hastened to clamber aboard again.

As the boat moved quietly away from the shore to the waiting ships, the evacuation from Crete was almost over; I was the last NZer to leave Crete in the official evacuation.

Rangi Logan, New Zealand

"We were pretty weak..."

The trying time was the march of 45 miles to the point of embarkation, over 7,000 feet mountains. We could only move at night and fortunately found dirty wells to drink from. When we finally got there we waited three days to get off, suffice to say the Navy were super as usual. One day my meal was a teaspoon of Bully beef and 2 biscuits. We were pretty weak on the last day and I was not in the selected

259

people to go to the ship. However Captain Caldwell just happened to meet the C.O. of the ambulance at 10 p.m. and he said there were orders all medical officers were to go - so here I am - rather close though!

From a letter by Tom Selby, Australia, to his family, 5.6.1941

The case of the stragglers

When we were going down to the beach, you kept your hand on the man in front of you, on his shoulder, so that stragglers could not break in between you. There was a register of the battalion, the number of the battalion and that register read off. If there was a hundred and twenty men, there was a hundred and twenty men, not a hundred and twenty one. The last chap got chopped off and he was left here, that's all. There were a lot of our own blokes left behind simply because they had not come down into the unit area at that time; and against that we had chaps that had fought with us right through from another unit whose name wasn't on the register, and they got left behind too. They weren't one of our men and although they'd been with us and done a good job, they were left behind simply because of the number that was your register, and that's all there was to it.

Clarrie Gordon, New Zealand

Transcripts of interviews conducted for the documentary film 'TOUCH AND GO – THE BATTLE FOR CRETE, MAY 1941' written and directed by Tom Steel and produced by Jeremy Isaacs Productions for the New Zealand Broadcasting Corporation.

Nicolas Racounas, a Greek, not a Cretan

Well, we weren't with the Greek Regiments very long but the short time we were which I imagine was three or four days only we got to know some of them very well and one particular boy, a fellow named Nicolas Racounas who was a corporal in the Greek Regiment and was a Greek not a Cretan - he spoke very good English and gave us a communications between the Regiment and us - he made things much easier. And he was a charming boy. I in fact got him out of Crete, he wore my uniform and I wore his to get on the boat.

Ray Minson, New Zealand

Transcripts of interviews conducted for the documentary film 'TOUCH AND GO - THE BATTLE FOR CRETE, MAY 1941' written and directed by Tom Steel and produced by Jeremy Isaacs Productions for the New Zealand Broadcasting Corporation.

Throwing their rifles

When we evacuated to board ship we refused to throw our guns away. We said "we have carried them all this time through Greece and Crete and now throw them away? We won't". They said "it's either 1.000 men with your guns or 1.200 men without them". So we threw them into the sea.

Verbal testimony of Edward Frederic Telling, England

Meanwhile, in Eastern Crete

On May 28th, Admiral Cunningham decided that the Heraklion garrison—five battalions and twenty-four guns— must be evacuated that night and Brigadier Chappel was so informed by Middle East Command. Orders were then issued and preparations began.

The cruisers ORION, AJAX and DIDO, and the destroyers HOTSPUR, DECOY, KIMBERLEY. HEREWARD, JACKAL and IMPERIAL had sailed from Alexandria at 6 a.m. on the 28th. In negotiating the 25-mile wide Caso Strait the ships had to run the gauntlet of air attacks as was expected; and about 9 a.m. AJAX was so narrowly missed by a bomb that a fire was started and she was ordered back to Alexandria without completing the passage to Heraklion. It was not until 11.30 p.m. that the remainder of the fleet arrived off the port. Only three and a half hours remained to carry out the embarkation before the approach of daylight would compel the ships to leave. The Navy lost no time. While the cruisers lay outside the harbour the destroyers went in to the main jetty and acted as lighters, ferrying the troops to the cruisers before taking in their own complements. In this fashion Brigadier Chappel's entire force, over 4,000 strong, was embarked, and the ships sailed at 3 a.m. on the morning of May 29th.

So far all had gone well. The enemy had made no sign. The first mishap was that to the destroyer IMPERIAL, whose steering gear broke down as the result of the bombing attacks during the outward passage. She was abandoned and sunk, the ship's company and the troops being transferred to the destroyer HOTSPUR. Then, soon after sunrise, when the ships had entered Caso Strait, the Luftwaffe struck and struck again. HEREWARD was hit and forced to steer for the Cretan coast where she ran aground, most of those on board eventually becoming prisoners of war. Damage to the DECOY caused speed to be reduced to 25 knots, and the cruiser DIDO was also hit. During repeated attacks the ORION, which carried 1,100 troops, was hit three times, losing her captain and 90 others killed and 275 wounded: one bomb passed through the bridge of this cruiser and exploded in the stoker's mess deck. Yet, so damaged as to be almost out of control, she staggered on towards Alexandria.

The ships were picked up by Fulmars of the Fleet Air Arm shortly before noon, and the German attacks, in which it was reckoned that over 100 aircraft were employed, gradually died away. We had suffered a grievous loss in troops and seamen—over one hundred killed and more than three hundred wounded—while the damage done to the ships caused difficulties in completing the evacuation which, with the departure from Heraklion, had only begun.

Christopher Buckley, GREECE AND CRETE 1941

Heraclion, 28th May

The news rather changed one's mentality. Previously we were all geared up to the idea of the last round and the last man but now our thoughts turned to the possibilities of an evacuation. The day turned out to be a most trying one. Sorties by German planes were more numerous and there were obviously heavy reinforcements being brought in, both of men and supplies. The thought that dominated us was whether the Germans were now going to launch a major attack which would scupper the evacuation. Another strain on our nerves at the first aid post was the presence of two of our guns in an olive grove close by. I think the gunners must have been aware of the evacuation and were using up their ammunition.

They were firing constantly and all the time German planes were trying to bomb them. The gunners only stopped firing for short intervals when the bombing got a bit too intensive, but as soon as the planes eased up they began firing again. All this meant near misses for us and there was no protection as at our fighting positions. But I never heard anyone at the post expressing a wish that our plane would stop firing so that the bombers would go away. I think that everybody was prepared to sweat it out so long as our guns were hitting the Germans.

Eventually, darkness fell and we prepared to move down to the harbour. I had said I thought I could walk but soon found I was only making a painful top speed of a mile an hour and was glad to accept a lift from a truck. We were dropped about half a mile from the harbour towards which I made my agonizing way helping another man who had a wound through his foot. Destroyers had tied up alongside the jetties and we filed aboard. When a destroyer was full up it moved away from the harbour and went alongside one of the cruisers waiting outside. I went aboard the ORION where I was given a bunk in a cabin. I then sought out the M.O. and asked him to look at my knee as it hadn't been seen since a dressing had been put on it at the airfield. (Looking back on this I think I must have had a bit of nerve to ask this as the M.O. had probably been working at full stretch for days).

Anyway, he stitched it up, put a splint behind the knee and gave me a mug of tea. I then went back through a gunhoist where I got another cup of tea and then to a gunroom where I found other Black Watch men, received yet another mug of tea and something to eat. After that I went to the cabin allotted to me. By this time I was exhausted. I said to myself, tomorrow is going to be hell but I do not care, I'm going to sleep now. I put my head down on the pillow and went straight out not waking until the gunturret above my head opened fire in the morning. Well, it wasn't hell, it was absolute, bloody hell! We were bombed for seven hours. The ORION received three direct hits. The steering was early put out of action and eventually the engines stopped working and we were taken in tow. But the worst part was the near misses. A raid would last about 10 minutes and the ORION was a principal target. The near misses were so frequent that it felt as if the ship was a train which had left the rails but was still proceeding at top speed and keeping upright over the sleepers. The vibration was such that one could not believe the ship just would not open up. Then after 10 minutes the raid would be over and into the silence would creep the noise of the steady beat of the engine. This calm lasted for 5 minutes when another raid began. All the time orders had to be passed by a line of sailors and soldiers from bridge to stern giving changes of course. One just marvelled at the steadiness of these men. There were a lot of soldiers up on deck firing with their rifles at the planes. I did not go up as I thought I would just get in people's way with my knee. And again, as at the first aid post on Crete there was absolute steadiness by everybody throughout a tremendous ordeal.

The Black Watch must have killed hundreds of Germans on Crete while only losing 15, but over 100 were killed on the DIDO returning to Egypt.

I still feel sorrow that we had to leave the Cretans to face the Germans on their own.

J.C. Donaldson, Scotland

Misfortunes at sea

At midnight on 28th May a Royal Navy force of two cruisers and six destroyers reached Heraklion. For three hours the destroyers ferried troops to the cruisers which lay outside harbour and themselves took on board the remainder. We were marched down to the harbour in batches, and I shall never forget the silence and desolation of the shattered town I knew so well. I took a vow at this moment to return to Crete as soon as possible and to help liberate its brave and wonderful people.

We sailed about 3.30 a.m. For six hours, from first light until noon, by which time we were out of range of the aircraft, we were dive-bombed continuously. The noise of the screaming planes and of the anti-aircraft guns was deafening. Both cruisers were hit, ORION losing her captain and nearly a hundred men killed among her crew and troops aboard. Of the six destroyers, IMPERIAL had her steering-gear hopelessly crippled; her crew and passengers were taken aboard other ships and she was sunk. HEREWARD was badly damaged and had to be run aground on the east coast of Crete; her crew and passengers became prisoners of war. On board JACKAL, where I was, we were packed like sardines, but suffered only near misses and minor damage. Towards nightfall we reached Alexandria, where good ladies with tea and sandwiches greeted us on the quayside.

Ralph Stockbridge, England

Lucky Mr. Whitbread

Wednesday, 28th May

Another blitz this morning and again this afternoon. Good news. At 4.00 we are getting off the island. Got aboard HMS DIDO at about 1.00, sailed at 3 am. Met Fred Rimmington on ship.

Thursday, 29th May

Raided from 6 am. and at 8 am. They hit our mess deck and killed the man next to me. I only got three small pieces and was lucky. About 35 killed. Arrived Alex about 5.30 after having been bombed nearly all day.

From the War Diary of J.E. Whitbread, England

NIGHT DRAMA OF THE CRETE EVACUATION

FIRST DESPATCH FROM AN EYE-WITNESS

SHALLOW BOATS TOOK 50 MEN AT A TIME

DIVE-BOMBING FOR WHOLE OF SEA-TO-SEA MARCH

From CHRISTOPHER BUCKLEY,
Daily Telegraph Special Correspondent
AT SEA WITH THE BRITISH FLEET IN THE
EASTERN MEDITERRANEAN, Monday.

This despatch, giving the first eye-witness description of the evacuation of Crete, in which some 15,000 British troops have been withdrawn, is being written aboard an Australian cruiser.

A few hours ago the warship took off 1,200 men from Sphakia, on the southern coast of Crete.

It was an eerie, yet intensely impressive, process. In the dead of night we had lain off the little Cretan village of Sphakia—it cannot be called a port—where a week earlier the King of the Hellenes had made his dramatic departure from Greek soil.

We formed part of a fairly big convoy of cruisers, destroyers and a troopship engaged on the same task.

For three hours we lay alongside while our boats—large, flat-bottomed, and shallow-draughted, so that they could be run right on to the beach—plied backwards and forwards, carrying fully 50 a-piece, across glass-smooth waters under a tranquil starry sky.

The stillness of the night was not broken by a sound, and one might have thought that the ship was sleeping instead of being intensely and throbbingly alive.

Worse than Dunkirk

The black mass of the island was totally unrelieved save for an occasional flash from the beach, answered by a recognition signal from the ship.

Boatload after boatload drew alongside, discharging silent cargoes of weary, stumbling, khaki-clad figures carrying what equipment they had been able to retain during their arduous trek across the bare Cretan Mountains from sea to sea. For these men British and New Zealanders, had arrived from the Maleme-Canea sector.

They had been bombed and machine-gunned ruthlessly from the air without intermission day after day under conditions which, in the opinion of those who had experienced both, made even Dunkirk seem a picnic by comparison.

As the men came aboard they were guided between decks and given hot cocoa and biscuits. For the most part they were content to sit almost silent while they stretched their legs and enjoyed the luxury of relaxing for the first time for days. Even of those who were not wounded the largest number were limping.

Daily Mail, London, 3-6-1941

The evacuation is completed

As I left Chania, I found by the roadside a New Zealander who was wounded in the leg. I helped him along to the crossroads. There we stopped a despatch-rider on a motor-cycle, and I persuaded him to take the New Zealander on his pillion. The walk-back was not improved by lowflying German aircraft and trigger-happy Australians hiding in a coppice by the road. That night I slept in a field. In the morning I rejoined Mike Cumberlege, captain of "The Dolphin", and we went together to deliver a report on a reconnaissance to the British H.Q., which was hidden by trees on the hillside. General Freyberg came out of his tent and called for an interpreter. As no one volunteered, I did so and had to translate a letter from a Greek commander who needed more ammunition. Freyberg groaned and remarked to a senior Staff officer that London's decision whether or not to evacuate was expected at any moment. We had all expected to defend Crete to the last man. Soon afterwards the order to evacuate came through. So back we went to the island in Souda Bay. There I laid the charges for the blowing up of a dump of special explosives and for the destruction of the engine and the gun of "The Dolphin". We commandeered a caique, "Miaoules", which had only one cylinder-head, cracked but functioning. The skipper and one hand agreed to come with us. We transferred our machine-guns and a cargo of explosives into her, fired the various charges and left soon after midnight. We headed for Dia, the island off Heraklion. Another withdrawal was under way.

Nicholas Hammond, England

General Freyberg to General Wavell

30 May 1941

I leave Crete tonight in accordance with your orders. I have handed over command to General Weston. I again urge you to do all that is possible to send ships tomorrow night to evacuate the gallant remnants of the British, Australian, and New Zealand troops who have borne the brunt of the fighting in the battle for Crete.

Destination Middle East

I arrived in Sfakia towards the end of the battle of Crete, a day after the retreat had been completed, as their British ships were coming and collecting the army. This ceased at some point because the Germans had arrived. I was caught prisoner along with the British army. I was returning from a mission with a British captain and we were captured together. I escaped straightaway. I left the area and made my way towards Kokkinos Pirgos at Timbaki, in the southern part of the county of Iraklion.

First I went to Aghia Galini. A group of us had gathered there with plans to escape to the Middle East. We bought a boat and prepared to leave. There was a British Hospital at Aghia Galini with many wounded, the doctors were unable to leave. One day a German officer arrived from Kokkinos Pirgos to meet the British Commander called Mc Nab. The British agreed to surrender. The very next day they slowly began to leave. When we heard they were going we decided to leave as well, but the British stopped us saying: "It's imperative to move those of the wounded who are unable to walk (no roads etc.) to Kokkinos Pirgos at Timbaki". I said: "Yes but the Germans will capture us with the boat". He said: "No, we have come to an agreement, they will let you leave". We took them with us regardless. I was supposed to be the Captain, although I didn't have a clue about boats. I had an airman who knew about engines, as a mechanic.

True enough, we took them to Kokkinos Pirgos, left them on shore and were allowed to leave. Unfortunately we did not know how to weigh anchor properly and were therefore unable to leave quickly. The sea began to get stormy and pushed us further inland towards the shore. At this point the Germans changed guard and a different commander arrived to tell us that we were being "detained". I said: "But we had an agreement". He said: "Not with me, you haven't". He ordered us to remain because he needed the boat to go round to the southern side of Crete to capture any Greeks, Britons or Allied Forces attempting to flee the island. "We cannot go through with this", I said to the airman. "The only way out is to try and escape". Some of the locals told us that the later the hour the stormier the sea would become, so we pretended to tie the boat up, but instead left the ropes loose and by morning the waves had sent our boat crashing onto the shore. The Germans accused us of sabotage. We said: "Why would we sabotage our own livelihood? We lived off that boat". I told them I was a merchant as well as a fisherman. He said: "All right you are to be detained anyway, until the boat is repaired. He ordered a guard with a machine-gun to keep an eye on us and said: "He's here to guard you, don't try to escape". We pretended to get to work. "Yes but we have no tools", we said. "We'll have to go to Aghia Galini to get them". They said: "We cannot allow you because you will try to escape". "But why should we try to escape and leave our entire fortune behind?" They kept a close watch over us and said: "You may go and get your tools". Meanwhile they also asked me for the ship's papers and since I did not have them I had to get someone to draw them up for me on my way to get the tools. On our return we brought the tools, pretending not to have noticed the Germans keeping a watch over us. The German looked at the ship's title-deed, put his finger on his tongue and pressed it onto the signature. "You signed this last night", he said. "Yes indeed we did, because I couldn't find the original and I had to have a new one drawn up". I got away with it. After supposedly attempting to repair our boat we said: "It's no use, unless we get a specialist to come and do the job. Otherwise we are just wasting our time. You won't be able to get on with your work and neither will we be able to manage". They had become enheartened and said: "Allright, go and get him from Aghia Galini". That was it. We never set foot there again. We escaped and took to the mountains.

Verbal testimony of Themis Marinos, Athens

She rowed more than 50 miles

A British naval officer has now reached hospital. He set out to cross open sea to safety, with a Greek girl in a rowing boat. The boat was partly stove in and flooded by machine gun attack from the air. Part of the officer's side was blown away. To stop the bleeding and gangrene the girl forced him to lie with his wounded side in the bilge-water at the bottom of the boat and herself rowed him more than 50 miles to an Allied island."

The Times, London, 31-5-1941

They left during the night

Two small ships had come here from Cairo. Between 15 - 17.000 English soldiers had gathered here from Hania and Iraklion, but they would only take the officers. The poor soldiers were left behind to be

270

While the Destroyer KIMBERLEY was en route to Tobruk, she sighted a small rowing boat drifting aimlessly. The Destroyer stopped and investigated the occupants, who turned out to be soldiers who had been hiding in Crete since we had evacuated it. Their only means of navigation was a sixpenny compass and a map torn from an Atlas. Photo shows the Destroyer approaching the rowing boat, and taking it in tow.
Imperial War Museum, London.

taken prisoner by the Germans. We helped them a lot. The Germans killed many of us because of this. We would hide them somewhere until some traitor or other betrayed us to the Germans and they would have us shot. I was about 12 or 13 years old at the time, but I would make my parents and relatives tell me these things. These small ships were called torpedo boats. They could take only five people each. They left at night, a bit further down, at Plakia, there is a gulf called Rodakino. A submarine would come and take them to Cairo and then return. They would signal each other with the use of torches and transmitters. They had everything.

Verbal testimony of Sifis Kouridakis, Sfakia

Heroic marines in Crete

General Wavell to General Weston, of the Royal Marines, May 31:

You know the heroic effort the Navy has made to rescue you. I hope you will be able to get away most of those who remain, but this is the last night the Navy can come. Please tell those that have to be left that the fight put up against such odds has won the admiration of us all, and every effort to bring them back is being made. General Freyberg has told me how magnificently your Marines have fought, and of your own grand work. I have heard also of the heroic fight of young Greek soldiers. I send you all my grateful thanks.

The War Illustrated, London, 4-7-1941

Sunday, June the first

The British Navy, and some of the British Army, left the island of Crete - but I didn't. Nor did several thousand other dejected lads. Sunday, June the first, was a black day indeed for many assorted British huddled in valleys back from the beach at Sphakia, a small village on the south coast. They were faced with the alternative of swimming two hundred and fifty miles to Egypt, or of just waiting. So they just waited-quietly, reflectively, unhappily.

No one even spoke. Everybody was too dispirited.

We all knew we should not have been in this plight. Although we didn't have nearly enough gear to match the German's airborne equipment, we did have the human qualities needed to outlast any enemy soldiers, crack Austrian alpine troops though they be. We hadn't come ten thousand miles just to be discarded as obsolete; German High Command-for the use of-or misuse of. They just couldn't do this to us. But they had.

I have never felt so terribly as I did at that moment. In fact, I don't think that I had ever really felt at all till then. Any troubles I had had in the past were mere ripples compared with this tidal wave. I was disgusted; I was deeply disappointed; I felt frustrated and shamed - above all, ashamed.

R.H. Thompson, CAPTIVE KIWI

272

BEHIND THE BARBED WIRES

Captured on Crete

At the Sphakia evacuation over 6.000 men had to be left behind on the beaches. Many of them were hunted down by the Germans and taken prisoner. They "were marched down to Chania like a mob of sheep."

Even before the end of May, however, to quote C.L. Sullivan from the 2/11th Australian Infantry Battalion, "large numbers of Australian, New Zealand and British personnel were prisoners of the invading Germans and were subsequently transported back to the Grecian mainland by either boat or aircraft.

From southern Greece and camps near Athens most P.O.W. were transferred by rail (with the march over Brallos Pass) or boat to the notorious Salonika Camp. Very little food was supplied by the captors and hunger was the constant companion of prisoners.

In due course large groups of P.O.W.s were sent from Salonika by rail (the enclosed trucks still labelled 40 Hommes 8 Chevaux - 40 men 8 horses) to the main Stalags (base camps) in Germany. The main camps were VIIA Moosberg in Bavaria, VIIIB Lambsdorf in Silesia, XIIIC Hamilburg and XVIIIA, Graz, Austria".

How they filled their tummies

After our capture, we were handed on to some ground of the 7th General Hospital. We were all suffering from severe dysentery and had to make our own shelter of iron, wood and rags etc. The Germans

273

Prisoner of War Camp - Beach on Crete.
Contributed by Don Bailey, New Zealand.

encircled the place with barbed wire with "Goon Bores" (sic) at each corner and searchlighted. One night a companion and myself sneaked under the wire and contacted a Cretan family who gave us some food and the only thing we could obtain from them as a cooking utensil was a bedroom chamber for which we were grateful. We returned to the camp because we were too weak to escape. Next day some companions who went on a work party ordered by the Germans brought back some grapes. We ate some of them raw and attempted to cook the rest in this chamber or "...pot" with a little of our food. It was a humorous sight. The mess tasted horrible but filled our tummies.

Gordon Rex Stephens, New Zealand

Through the barbed wire

They brought the British and Allied Forces they had captured to the Italian Prisoner of War Camp and shut them up. The whole village

274

brought them what we could: bread, potatoes, despite having been forbidden to do so. Many of them left the camp during the night through the barbed wire. They were mostly New Zealanders and Australians. They would leave at night and we'd find them during the day because they usually made their way towards our neighbourhood. We offered them whatever we could. They used to joke about how they got away. During the night the Germans would stand guard in opposite directions, then they would return and meet midway. Every time one of the guards went to the right and the other to the left, the soldiers would slip under the barbed wire. I was told that the Germans didn't take too kindly to us Cretans, because we would take anything and everything we could into the camp: bread, potatoes etc.

They didn't like us at all. All this was happening in June. By the end of July they removed the prisoners but I have no idea where they were taken.

Verbal testimony of the inhabitants of the villages of Alikianos and Skine. Contributed by Irene Vosper, England

Sketch by Frederick Turner, England.

Life in the prison camp

The dread, implacable enemy of the prisoner of war is the oppressive monotony which dominates his life.

Day succeeds day with the faithful uniformity of a copy. A heavy boundless boredom and a morbid home-sickness take possession of the soul of the prisoner and undermine his spiritual poise. If you add to this the humiliations and privations of all kinds, and the endless suffering from cold, and from lack of sleep and cleanliness, you will have a vague idea of our life in prison camp.

Testimony of a non-commissioned officer of the British Army who was captured in Crete, May 1941
Hellas, London, 17-12-1943

The first British prisoners - KRETA SIEG DER KÜNSTEN

dropped down and crawled beneath the road, and lay there a few minutes, I heard the guard walking above, I was lucky, it was a tight squeeze, but good enough, a little farther and I saw the grapes vines in front of me, and freedom! still on my stomach I went through the vines until I reached the wood, fully a hundred yards away from the camp, and safe, looking around I saw a few small cottages on a hill quite near I decided to try there for some clothes and perhaps something to eat.

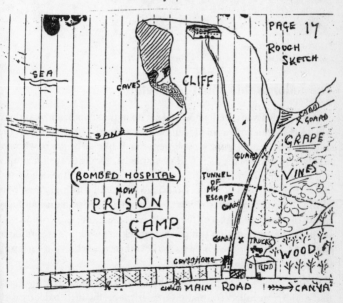

PAGE 17
ROUGH SKETCH

SEA
CAVES
CLIFF
SAND
CAMP X GUARD
GRAPE VINES
(BOMBED HOSPITAL)
NOW
PRISON CAMP
GUARD X
TUNNEL OF MY ESCAPE
GUARD X
GUARD X TRUCKS
WOOD
CAVE GATE
GUARD X MAIN ROAD →→ CANYA
GUARD X

From the War Diary of N. Nuttull, New Zealand
Contributed by George Logothetis, Athens

277

The first Greek prisoners on Crete
Bundesarchiv - Militärarchiv, Freiburg, Germany.

The indomitable spirit of Cretans

I was in Kalyves, in the hospital set up in the school, and was there when the surrender was made, and we became prisoners. As usual, the soldiers who actually took over were much like all soldiers who are involved in action- they showed no unpleasant animosity, but simply had a job to do. Owing to the stubborn resistance and the delays and losses, their organisation was a bit scrappy. But the ordinary members of the Cretan community shared with us their food and undoubtedly saved the lives of many, of the badly wounded and weak soldiers. I suppose the outstanding things that struck me were the indomitable spirit of Crete, and the kindness and brotherhood shown to us by all the people we came in contact with.

Later I was sent to the priest's house and it was while I was there that a German called Hermann Greiner sat on the little balcony with me and we talked of many things in the quiet and beautiful way in which men of the armed forces can do, in spite of a war. Only the

Gestapo roused aversion and hatred in men. At the end of our captivity we exchanged sentiments of good will with both the troops and the inhabitants of the village in which the camp was situated.

Rex Webb, England

Human relations among enemies

After the fighting in Crete, I was assigned to guard duty in a camp for soldiers from New Zealand and Australia. A New Zealander and an Australian were assigned to me to assist me in clearing up a variety of minor problems. In pursuit of the solution to these problems, it transpired that these soldiers and I spent endless hours together hiking through the trackless country. We ate, smoked, and drank together as if we were soldiers of the same unit and such friendly rapport developed among us that in the end we exchanged addresses, promising to resume contact after the war had ended. Alas, these addresses were taken from me when I was made prisoner in the Wesel area on the 24th of March 1945.

Adolf Strauch, Germany

... goodbye and good luck

An odd visit or two down to the prisoner of war compound made one grateful for the hospital accommodation. Men under old canvas some in tents to the number of 15 or 20, makeshift tin leantos, any old shelter at all, out in the open, the only bright point being that the weather was perfect. One chap sheltered under a door propped up by four sticks driven into the ground. One night one of the sticks was purloined and the language was outstanding as the door fell on the sleeping occupant.

The uncertainty of whether one was to be flown to hospital in Athens, left on Crete, or ship to Italy.

At last certainty. Walking wounded to parade, immobile to the trucks, a piece of bread, few figs, a small portion of goat cheese and goodbye and good luck.

Shuffling along to the shy and discreet waves of the civilians, frequent but short stops for rest, and then a grey grim steamer which was to be our home for three days.

Sick and wounded on deck, the fit P.O.W. down below, and in a short time that little island with its friendly people and the victorious enemy sank below the horizon.

Farewell Crete, one hopes to return one day to the isle of good and compassionate people of such wonderful courage. Kai Ora Kai Toa.

Jim Hughes, "Crete in retrospect", Pow-Wow, New Zealand, March 1987

Our thoughts...

And we who were there remember,
Those days of "hell" on Crete,
And hope that when our time comes,
Those pals again we'll meet;
And as we trudge along the road
Of life that is left to be,
Our thoughts will often turn to them,
Who sleep 'neath the olive-tree.

G.R. Eldridge, in "The Camp", 24-5-1942

The Kokinia "lazarett"

At the time of the retreat of the British Forces from Greece in April 1941, the Australian Fifth General Hospital had occupied a five-block Borstal prison in Kokinia, a suburb of Athens. There the most severely wounded soldiers from the Greek campaign had been installed, and several doctors had stayed behind to look after them - knowing they might become prisoners-of-war for the duration of the fighting. Each block of the old prison had four stories and was connected to its neighbour by passages, so that our hospital formed a single unit which could be patrolled by guards - if need be.

When the German troops took Athens, they also transformed the Kokinia Hospital into a prisoner-of-war "lazarett". Later, after the Crete campaign was over, more wounded came to fill the hospital and I was one of them. The Junker 52 which landed at Piraeus Airport was met by ambulances and I was soon thankful to be in a proper bed, my first since leaving the troopship in Port Tewfik, Egypt, in November 1940. That was June 2, 1941. We were well looked after, by New Zealand doctors and Australian male nurses. The supply of drugs and medical consumables must have been very limited, but an operating theatre was working and I never heard a complaint from a patient about the care of the staff, who did everything possible to look after their charges, twenty-four hours a day.

The weather was hot and appetites were poor, and just as well, because the food was sparse and of bad quality. We had Greek bread once a day, very old and very hard - so hard that it could not be chewed, but when sucked for a while it became soft enough to swallow. There was feta cheese too, white and crumbly, made from sheep's milk, strong tasting but doubtless nutritious, and gradually we came to enjoy its goodness. The other main food issue was boiled rice with a few raisins scattered through it; easy to eat but no substitute for the heavy meat diet of the New Zealand Division. Still, we were all more or less badly wounded and the temperature must have been over 80 degrees Fahrenheit, so food was not the major problem.

The New Zealand and Australian troops had been pushed out of Greece and out of the island of Crete: thus the morale of the patients was at a low ebb. A prisoner-of-war does not know when the war is going to end: he always hopes it will be soon, but in June and July 1941 all the aggression came from the German side, such as the invasion of the Soviet Union and the bombing of Britain and the advances of Rommel in North Africa. The inmates of this old Borstal building were lucky to have Bill Cole, an ex-London bus driver, who went to great lengths to amuse everyone. He was a Cockney, reputed to have been Joe Loss's drummer, large, fat and merry. He did not appear to have a wound, so he classified himself as a Masseur and stayed on the hospital staff. He was a natural entertainer and must have been the best known man in the whole complex. He was part of every sketch, every impromptu band group, and he was the principal character in every concert. Of course, when he went around the wards on his massage tour he simply oozed good-will and brightness. I class him as the major public asset of Kokinia.

For my part my luck held, because, although I must have had an incredibly close call when I was shot through the neck on Crete, here in Athens I had a New Zealand doctor who took a keen interest in keeping up my spirits. He was Dr John Borrie of Dunedin. He wrote my letters home for me, and always left me money when he visited me - unobtrusively beside my bed where I could not see it; but I was soon alerted by neighbouring bedmates that the cash was there, and available to buy the fruit that occasionally was brought in for sale in the hospital compound. Dr Borrie kept my spirits up; not only mine but those of a host of sick soldiers, for he was himself a fine entertainer.

I shall be ever grateful to him.

J.D. Fraser, New Zealand

From Suda Bay to Stalag VIII B

I can not remember just how long we were kept on Crete but from memory I think it was about one month. We were put on board a boat in Suda Bay, hearded on board like a mob of cattle about ten times as many as the boat was intended to carry, we all had dysentery and there was no toilet facilities on the boat all we had was a plank over the side with a piece of rope to hold on to, toilet paper was non existant so you can well imagine we were in a sorry state, from memory we were only on the boat for three of four days and during this time we had absolutely nothing to eat or drink so after a couple of days the plank over the side was not used very much. We were unloaded at a place in Northern Greece by the name of "Salonica" and put in old Turkish Barracks just out of the City. We thought the prison camp on Crete was the end of the world, little did we know what was in store for us at

Salonica, we were covered in fleas and lice on Crete but here we also had bugs. I had never seen a bug before but they were in this camp in millions, the old buildings had a roof, floor and walls but no windows or doors, there were thousands of Prisoners of War in this Camp. It seems the Germans were not prepared for the number of men captured in the fighting in Greece and Crete, we were given a cup of muddy lentil soup and a slice of black bread which was a full day's ration. When I enlisted in October 1939 I weighed 12 stone but after being in this camp at Salonica for a month or so I was down to about 7 stone. From memory I don't know for sure how long we were kept in Salonica, we were not allowed to use the toilets at night and those who did were shot, and next morning the German guards would say they were trying to escape. One thing I can still remember is the camp had water troughs which were used for watering the horses, us P.O.Ws used to strip off all our clothing and get into these troughs and wash ourselves and then sit in the nude and try and get the lice out of our clothing, I don't know what the Greek people thought of us but at the time we didn't care, all I can say about this Camp is if Hell is any worse I sure don't want to go there.

After we had been in this Camp for a few months the Germans loaded us into cattle wagons on the train. They gave us a tin of pork and half a loaf of bread, they told us they were taking us to Germany but didn't tell us how long we would be on the train, there were 50 P.O.Ws in each truck and only about half of us could lay down at a time. We were let out once I think it was at Belgrade and the Red Cross gave us a bowl of tomato soup as well as a slice of white bread, after what we had been through since we were captured this was like Christmas to us. Little did we know that we would be in those cattle wagons for eight days and nine nights, eventually we arrived at "Lambsdorf" (Stalag VIII B) just before Christmas 1941 and when they let us out of the cattle wagons the first thing I saw was what I thought was a heap of turnips and being a country chap I made a dash to this heap which I thought was turnips only to find out they were not turnips but sugar beet. I don't know if you have ever tried to eat sugar beet or not but take my advice and don't try. I can tell you we were a sorry sight to see as we had not had a wash for the eight days and nine nights and all with a week's growth of beard and our hair not combed since we left Greece. At that time of the war the Germans were on top of the world and they sure didn't show us mercy, it was night time and as most of us only had the clothes we were captured in we nearly froze as from memory it was some time in December and snow was everywhere, I just can't remember much about the first couple of days all I can remember we were pushed from pillar to post with the guards yelling at us all the time, eventually we were put into one of the buildings and we were in such a state we just fell down on the floor and went to sleep. Next morning before daylight the German guards came around and pushed and shoved us out into the snow to count us, after which we all had to go before the camp commander and given a Prisoner of War number. I don't know how many Prisoners of War were in Stalag VIII B while I was there but I believe it would hold about 17,000. At that particular time of the war Hitler was God in the eyes of the German people, he may not have had 100% behind him but he would have had 99.9%. I was sent out on three different working parties, the worst one was loading sugar beet at a railway siding, next I was sent to a Cement Works loading cement into barges where I received cement burns to my stomach and then I was sent to a Sugar Factory at Ottmahoe from where I managed to get into Czechoslovakia and lived and worked with a lovely Czech family for about four months.

George W. Blanch, Australia

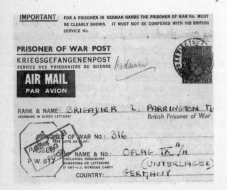

Imperial
War Museum,
London.

Don't forget me in your prayers...

30-8-1942

Dear Katy,

I have just received two letters from you, one with the photo and the other dated 24/3/42. Needless to say I was very happy to hear from you.

Seventeen months without any letter from you dear had me very worried and I finally gave up of ever hearing from you. Glad to know that everything and all is well at home. Yes, Katy Dear, I lost everything and I was very glad to receive that photo. The Red Cross are certainly doing a splendid job for which we are all very grateful.

Remember me to all friends and don't forget me in your prayers. Well Dear my love to all and I am glad to know that you receive my letters. Cheerio,

> Your loving brother,
> Bill

Letter written by Bill Thornton, from Stalag XIIIC

REGISTER FORMS FOR RECOVERED ALLIED PRISONERS OF WAR.

STOW	GEOFFREY WORSDELL	G.W.	BRITISH	(Print)
(Surname)	(First Name)	(Initials)	(Nationality)	
LIEUTENANT	NOT NOTIFIED	3609	1008 PIONEER Co CYPRUS REGT.	
(Rank)	(Army Serial Number)	(PW Number)	(Unit) (Regt)	
ARMY	STALAG VII A	6 DAYS	OFLAG VII B	
(Branch of Service)	(Present Camp)	(How Long)	(Previous Camp)	

ABLE
[General Physical Condition]

Evacuated by: Ambulance ___ Stretcher ___ Truck ___ Air ___

(Date Evacuated) U.K. (Destination)

1·6·41 CRETE
(Date Captured) (Place Captured)

29·4·45
(Date returned to military control) (Signature of Ex P. W.)

MIDDLE EAST William Mullett Capt
(Theatre in which captured) (Signature of Control Off.)

A.1.

From the collection of G.W. Stow, England.

No. Cas/5/KRRC
(If replying, please quote above No.)

Sir or Madam,

I regret to have to inform you that a report has been received from the War Office to the effect that (No.) 6897663 (Rank) Rfn.

(Name) Frederick Richard Turner

(Regiment) **THE RANGERS**
KRRC
was posted as "missing" on the 2nd June 1941

The report that he is missing does not necessarily mean that he has been killed, as he may be a prisoner of war or temporarily separated from his regiment.

Official reports that men are prisoners of war take some time to reach this country, and if he has been captured by the enemy it is probable that unofficial news will reach you first. In that case I am to ask you to forward any postcard or letter received at once to this Office, and it will be returned to you as soon as possible.

Should any further official information be received it will be at once communicated to you.

I am,
SIR or MADAM,
Your obedient Servant,

Mrs G. Turner.
39 Viaduct Bldgs.
Clerkenwell Rd.
Holborn E.C.1.

for Officer in charge of Records.

IMPORTANT.
Any change of your address should be immediately notified to this Office.

Wt. ...01-1/1249 400,000 (16) 9/39 KJL/8612 Gp 695/3 Forms B.104—63/9

From the collection of Frederick Turner, England.

286

THE SPIRIT OF CRETE

The wandering Allies

The fall of Crete marked the beginning of a long-lasting comradship between the Cretan population and those Allied soldiers who remained on the island, lucky enough to elude imprisonment. All these defying men mixed with the Cretans in the occupation years, hiding from the Germans and in many cases joining in the resistance. In the words of Winston Churchill:

"Upwards of 5.000 British and Imperial troops were left somewhere in Crete, and were authorized by General Wavell to capitulate. Many individuals, however, dispersed in the mountainous island, which is 160 miles long. They and the Greek soldiers were succoured by the villagers and country folk, who were mercilessly punished whenever detected. Barbarous reprisals were made upon innocent or valiant peasants, who were shot by twenties or thirties."

In hiding for twelve months - the Cretan way

On the night of 31st May 1941 we had seen the destroyers leave and we thought the next convoy would see us off. But on Sunday 1st June the Major said "this is the morning we show as much white as possible, as the British are surrendering the Island." When the planes came over, we all waved anything white and then they machine gunned us and killed quite a number including some of their own soldiers.

We were then marched back across the Island to Maleme to a makeshift prison camp. I escaped and made my way to Canea, where

287

the family of Mavrogianakis took me in and sheltered and fed me. After being there a while, the Germans commandeered part of the house. I used to go out in their vineyard early in the morning but come back in the evening to dine and sleep. After a while the family arranged for me to go to the village of Dracona, so they dressed me in the traditional black headdress and black dress as a woman.

We left Canea on a horse-drawn cart and when we got to Maleme the Germans stopped the cart and searched the men for pistols. I thought and feared for the people who were shielding me, but thank God the Germans thought I was a woman, so I was allowed to go on the journey.

When we arrived at Dracona I had difficulty in getting off the cart on account of the tight skirt, so the lady with me had to tell the driver that I was an English soldier. He then was delighted and wanted to give me what cigarettes he had and was thankful that we got past the Germans who were doing the searching.

After being in the village a while two more British came to visit me and invited me to the village where they were staying. While we were in a house in their village, a girl came and said the Germans were coming through the village. We made off across the fields and from then on we moved from village to village and then some villagers took us to a little shelter up in the hills where we slept at night and moved about in the day-time calling on villagers for food and drink. This went on for twelve months until we gave ourselves to the Germans to save the villagers being shot for harbouring us English.

James Baxter, England

Cretan hospitality and courage

For 2 1/2 months we lived in Khania, moving from house to house. Our main hiding place, to which we returned frequently, was the home of Mitsos Antonakakis and his wife Artemesia, near the harbour. They welcomed us as their sons, and here I began to learn the hospitality and the courage of the Cretan people. They showed us how to escape if the Germans should come to the house, knowing full well that they could not escape themselves, and that they and their family would certainly be shot. Behind them, with this same hospitality and courage, stood the whole Cretan people, ready to hide British soldiers after the German invasion, and to help us in the resistance regardless of the danger to themselves. We could move freely, knowing that the whole population was in support of us. I remember once travelling into Khania on the bus, and how we ran into a control post, where German soldiers lined us up and began a body search. I was carrying not only a revolver and spare ammunition, but also gold sovereigns and propaganda literature. My Greek friend, Marcos went ahead to be searched, planning to slip back and relieve me of these incriminating possessions - but the guard stopped him. I was now in line only six feet away from the search, and standing next to the open door of the bus. I slipped my revolver out of my pocket and dropped it amongst the driver's tools. He looked, in astonishment, first at the revolver, and then at me. He beckoned to a girl passenger, and sat her down on top of the tools. I got safely through the control, and when the bus was searched the girl was not asked to move. When we got to Khania, the driver sent somebody running after me with my revolver, and with the message "be more careful next time."

Stephen Verney, England

Ken alias "Pavlos"

On September 1st the round-up began, with thousands and thousands of Germans scouring the country on foot, and searching from the air.

Completely unperturbed, a friend of Dimitrios Kokkonakis (the Cretan who had been looking after me all this time) called Manoli Moundakis came and led me, riding this time a mule, up a narrow path, further on into the mountains above Tsiskiana. It was a hamlet of perhaps three or four houses, certainly not a village, and I was to stay here for two weeks. At this time, the German might was still evident; the low flying, slow reconnaissance planes circled, photographing; planes dropped supplies to the thousands who searched the mountains and valleys, hamlets and villages. But the Cretans hid me too well. Whenever a patrol made its way toward the houses, I would be lowered by rope into a cave, the entrance of which was just a hole in the ground. Once safely onto the cave floor about twelve feet below, a flat stone would cover the mouth of the cave. I hated it down there, but as a hidey-hole it was perfect.

Towards the end of September, I was issued with a Cretan identification card, or Taftotita. This had my thumbprint stamped on the bottom right corner, and was obtained from the mayor or president as he was known. My Cretan name was Pavlos Dimitriakis.

By this time I was able to get about quite well with the aid of a crutch. Now that I had my I.D. card, and being dressed as a Cretan, and even, apart from a ginger beard, being dark complexioned like a Cretan, I felt confident enough to venture a bit further afield.

In actual fact, Crete has never ended for me. I remember those people with deep affection and gratitude. We exchange cards, letters and photographs. As a people they gave so willingly and without thought of themselves.

Ken Little, New Zealand

Tipperary

The villagers would hide many British soldiers in their homes. In the evening however when the villagers brought them food and wine, they would drink some wine, you know, get drunk, go outside and start singing.

One evening my cousin and I came across an Englishman singing "Tipperary". There was a villager behind him shouting: "John you have given us away. John come back". They were afraid. The Englishman paid no attention. "It's a long way to Tipperary". That is how most of them were caught.

Verbal testimony of Marika Markantonaki, Chania

A tribute to the courageous Greek people

I was left behind and taken prisoner at Sfakia on the south coast then marched back to a P.O.W. camp near Suda where, with a friend Bill McCarrey, watched the movements of the German sentries for a few nights and took a chance to escape through the barbed wire.

Then began the long trip back through the mountains to the south coast. Being defeated we were doubtful about getting much help from local people and in fact the first night we stole some food rather than contact them, for they were also under threat of death if caught helping British Commonwealth troops. But our fears were unfounded. We were fed by the villagers and guided through mountains by the shepherds. Some people even gave us money, but it was never needed as no one would take money for the food, shelter and help provided.

Eventually we reached the Preveli Monastery where the head monk Agathangelos Lagouvardos and the resistance leader Michael Papadakis had organised shelter in the surrounding villages for hundreds of British Commonwealth troops and even though they faced the death penalty for helping us, it made no difference to these brave, courageous Cretan villagers. As the Germans sent out patrols, so they shifted us from one area to another.

Most of us were taken off by the British submarines THRASHER and TORBAY. We left the beautiful rugged island of Crete richer in feelings and memories of those indomitable Cretan people.

And now with the building of the white chapel on the hill overlooking the ocean and the village of Preveli in the south west corner of Australia, we can pay tribute to these courageous Greek people, making sure their sacrifice was not in vain and that their heroic deeds will live for ever more.

E.G. Edwards, Australia
From the Commemorative Publication on the Preveli Monastery

The Monastery of Preveli - a centre of resistance

The Commonwealth forces who had remained in Crete after the battle had ended, waited in the belief that the United Kingdom (steeped in naval tradition) would find a secret or even violent means of landing on the island and picking them up. They assumed this operation would take place in the southern shores of Crete. This was more convenient as it was nearer the Allied Bases in Egypt. It was also relatively deserted with many secret bays and suitable beaches.

The Commonwealth forces decided to gather at the Monastery of Preveli and the surrounding area. At the Monastery they received the unreserved hospitality of the monks and the locals. They were able to rest in secure hiding places and make sure of receiving help. Trained radio operators aided by the locals, would carefully come down to the sea and using whatever means they could would transmit danger signals towards the Libyan Sea.

Some men who had been abandoned at Sfakia and Aghia Galini by Admiral Cunningham (defenders of Crete) reached Egypt by boat. They reported of the gathering of their countrymen at the Monastery of Preveli and the surrounding area. They were caught however by allied craft and by the danger signals being transmitted off the shore. It was therefore decided by Headquarters in the Middle East to send the reserve lieutenant - commander Poole with the submarine THRASHER. Early in the morning of the 26th of July 1941, the submarine approached the Bay of Limni, belonging to the Monastery. Poole and his escort from Sfakia, Stratis, disembarked onto the beach and the submarine dissapeared. There were three Australians on the bay at the time, sending signals out to sea. They led Poole to the Lower Monastery of Preveli where the Abbot Agathangelos Lagouvardos was conducting High Mass at the church of John the Baptist. They waited for him to finish. Poole then appeared and introduced himself. The Abbot was very suspicious of him, taking him to be a German spy. The Australians hiding in the bay, as well as Stratis, had great difficulty in convincing him that he was a friend, not an enemy. Poole, in a private meeting with the Abbot, devulged that on the following evening of the 27th - 28th of July, the submarine would return to the bay of Limni, to take 80-100 soldiers back to Egypt. Poole would remain to verify certain matters which were of interest to

Headquarters. It should be noted that Poole spoke Greek very well. He had served for many years in Eastern Crete as a representative of Imperial Airways. One could not tell he was an Englishman from his appearance, he looked more like a Mediterranean.

The 80 officers of the Commonwealth were informed that they would be leaving. They were staying in the villages of Fratti, Vatos and Ardaktos and at the Monastery. At sunset on the 27th of July 1941, they all gathered in the Lower Monastery. They numbered about 150 people. The Abbot served all those who were present with a dinner consisting of meat and okra, at the Lord's Table in the Monastery. They wished each other well and spoke of unfulfilled desires. In the meantime it had grown dark and they made their way to the embarkation area at the bay of Limni. The convoy reached its destination silently at 21.30 p.m. A brave young Australian sub-lieutenant by the name of Jack, climbed onto the cliff overlooking the Limni and began transmitting signals towards the sea with the use of a torch and a petrol lamp. At exactly 22.50 p.m. the submarine came into sight about 100 metres from shore. The waters vary in depth around this area and the submarine began to submerge.

The Chapel of St. John the Theologian, Preveli Park, Margaret River, W. Australia. From the collection of E.G. Edwards, Australia.

Sub-lieutenant Jack made his way down from the cliff and crossed over to a rock west of the church of St. Savvas. He called to the Cretans and allied soldiers in the bay and showed them his hand, which was wrapped in a white handkerchief, so that it could be seen in the darkness.

"All English here, all Cretans here", he said slowly but clearly in broken Greek.

We could tell he was very moved because his trembling voice gave him away.

"All English, all Cretans, thank you, thank you, thank you".

He climbed down from the rock.

Presently there followed scenes which one does not often come across in world history. The gallant Australians did not know how to express their gratitude to their saviours - those men who had risked death and destruction to save them from the German reprisals. The Cretans bade farewell to friends they had made, under the harsh and deadly circumstances of battle. A battle they had all fought together against the horrific German war machine.

Michalis M. Papadakis, Crete

The first resistance centres

After the occupation of Crete, many of those fighters who had played a leading and undoubtedly distinguished part in this first stage of the Revolution, did not yield under German oppression nor did they surrender their arms. They made their way to the mountains continuing the tradition "Hainidon Revolutionaries", which originated during the Turkish domination.

This is how the first resistance centres were created during the summer of 1941. In the beginning they were limited to organising the gathering, protection and evacuation of those members of the allied forces (Britons, New Zealanders, Australians) who had been forced to remain on the island.

Dimitrios I. Melas, Heraclion

THE PRICE OF FREEDOM

The Cretan Resistance

It has been said that "the Cretan resistance sprang spontaneously into existence the moment the first enemy parachutist touched Cretan soil." For almost four years the invisible yet ubiquitous army of guerillas inflicted heavy blows on the Germans, thus obliging them to keep large numbers of soldiers on the island.

The fight never stopped; but the price was high, the reprisals atrocious. Death was at the doorstep of every household; death for them, for their families and in many cases mass executions and destruction of entire villages, burnt to the ground by the retaliating occupying forces. The villages of Mount Kedros, the province of Viannos, Koustogerako, Asteri, Anoyia and so many others remind us of the heavy penalty for freedom.

Heraclion in ruins

Up until the 15th of June we were living on the edge - not knowing what to expect. Those German soldiers who had survived, were given the right to a ten-day pillaging on the city. On the 1st of June they shot the first six men at Heraclion airport. They had been identified from photographs, as resistance fighters. Those fighters who escaped, fled to the mountains. That is how the first of the resistance forces began to materialize, in the summer of 1941. All the Germans' loot was piled on to aeroplanes and ships on its way to Germany.

All those houses at Heraclion that had not been completely

demolished, had been left wide open. Nothing had been left in its place, not a window not a door. We dared not go back to the city. The Germans would force anyone they found in their way to bury the dead and clear the rubble off the streets. In the middle of June I went to Heraclion in a cart with my father. Our journey lasted five days. We found our home half-ruined. It had been ramsacked. The neighbours told us the Germans had loaded three trucks. They were followed by locals who had also pillaged the area.

The village we took refuge in was overrun by the army. It grew very hot the first ten days and the half-naked soldiers would ramsack the houses, taking food, clothing, furniture and anything else they wanted. They would evict the inhabitants and occupy the homes they preferred. Our house was situated in an isolated part of the village and we were lucky enough to have escaped the initial flurry. We locked ourselves in and waited. Later on we were discovered and were forced down into the two rooms on the ground floor, while the Germans occupied the first floor. We did not like this at all, not knowing that there was worse to come. They did not take anything from our home.

In March 1942 my father was captured. The Germans blockaded the village. They had been betrayed by one of the locals and my father was identified as an accomplice to the resistance fighters. On the 3rd of June of that same year he was shot along with eleven others at Heraclion. On the 14th they shot another fifty men from the prison of Alikarnassos at Heraclion, in the act of reprisal against commandoes who had sabotaged the nearest airport and had set fire to fifteen German aircraft. Among the fifty men who died were my father's brother (a 70 year old priest), his son and his son-in-law.

Those members of my family who were left, returned to the derelict city of Heraclion in October 1944, after having spent four years as refugees.

Lena Sifaki-Stavrou, Heraclion

With the fall of the first parachutist

The resistance began with the fall of the first parachutist from the sky. The people's participation was unanimous. Each man was ruled by his heart and his conscience.

Verbal testimony of Zacharias K. Bantouvas, Heraclion

...may not come back, may not ...

After the Battle we were afraid, so we took to the mountain, Koustogerako. We were about 37 in all. We were afraid of the aeroplanes and at night we weren't allowed to light even a torch to see where we were going. Our leaders were afraid that in Palaiochora, which was visible, there might be some ships that could see us and fire at us. So we travelled from village to village, until we reached a cave which could take up to 500 people. We stayed there. We were given a cauldron and a slaughtered animal which we cooked. Luckily, my godfather was a notary and he had many connections around there. Here was where we stayed hidden, and cooked our meals, for about one week. One day we heard that such and such fellow-villager got killed, another day that someone else was blinded alive .... We heard so many things that we were scared to go back home. After a few days, however, we left the cave, and we went to a village called Rodovani, and afterwards we returned to Kandanos.

As soon as we reached the mountain ridge, we looked down and saw our village all black. We were out of our minds. Even from so high up, and you could smell it that Kandanos had been burnt. Already a month and a half had gone by since the Germans had burnt the place, and still the smell was terrible. Because all the oil which we used to keep in large, earthern jars, had been burnt. And wherever there was a field with a hole in the ground, it looked like a lake of oil. As the houses got burnt, the jars would break, and -don't forget-, these were huge, earthern jars, not iron barrells. As if the fire was not enough, the Germans also threw mortars inside the houses, for fear of any civilians left there hiding and ready to shoot them.

It was end of June when we came back. I had a lot of brothers and sisters, so my father made a small hut out of a plane-tree, at the foot of the mountain. He covered it up and then put on wooden legs, just like a village bed, with planks on top. Some of the children slept on the planks, the others slept underneath. So we stayed there until September, when the rain season began. In the meanwhile, the Germans had made a guardhouse in our village, and at night they would wonder around the neighbourhood, looking for anything they could get. We thought to ourselves:

"If they find the men, they will take them." But when the rain season started, we went back to our home; ours had not been burnt. Every time we would hear a German patrol, we would hide the men. In our garden there was a plane-tree with a large, round hole. This was my father's hiding place. We would pull a bush in front of him and no one could find him. This is the sort of life we've had .....

Later on, I had two brothers killed. The one in 1942, the other in 1943 ...

Anyway, I only hope that such days may not come back. May not come back, my Christ, may not come back ...

Verbal testimony of Mrs. Marangaki, Kandanos

German stark epitaph

"On the 3rd of June 1941 the village of Kandanos was raised to the ground, never to be built again. This was an act of reprisal for the brutal murders of German parachutists, mountain forces and engineer corps, by the men, women and priests who dared stand in the way of the Great Reich".

From the files of the archimandrite Stylianos Frantzeskakis, Paleohora

At "Ahlada"

Ahlada is situated in the White Mountains. During the 1930's the inhabitants of Koustogerako had built a dairy to carry the needs of the 15.000 livestock in the area. The battle I am referring to, took place in the White Mountains. All those Germans who survived, were taken prisoner and were then thrust into deep holes so as not to be in the way of the resistance fighters who had to move about freely in the mountains.

Stavros Georgiakakis, Chania

It fell upon me to perform the execution

After the battle at Ahlada we returned to the hide - out with our German prisoners of war. In the evening we tied them up and kept watch over them all night. The next morning we decided to execute them. We had no choice. We decided to draw lots and it fell upon me and Bassias to perform what the others had wanted to avoid doing. Bassias and I left first and went further up to Tafko's hole. It was there that we were to execute them. We sat and waited. We had tied all their hands together in order to transfer them to this spot. When they saw us standing there with our machine guns, they knew what to expect. Any hopes they might have had vanished from that moment onwards. In fact, that is how they must have felt the night before, when we had them in the hide - out and had given them food and cigarettes. We had even tended the wounded at the same time. This moment was indeed tragic and horrific for all of us. On the one hand this execution was contrary to our idiosyncracy since we were not in the habit of killing prisoners. On the other hand, however, we could not keep them alive because there was no chance of keeping them hidden in the face of the oncoming assault. I remembered how merciless they had been to those of our men who had fallen into their hands anyway.

By the time they had reached the edge of Tafkos, their morale had reached an all time low. Some began to cry, others covered their eyes with their hands and the execution began. The man who was shot first fell over backwards, as a result of which he dragged the rest along with him as he rolled down the cone- shaped hole. Most of them were still alive, as they fell into the hole.

We had to execute them very quickly so that the Germans would not find them the next day and vent their anger on the unarmed population. The hole was about 43 metres in depth. The late New Zealander "Vassilis", Dudley Perkins, even though wounded, wanted to climb down and finish them off, but I would not let him saying: "I'll go down, not you". We gathered the parachutists' tape strings and formed a rope about 50 metres long. They tied me and I began my descent from one end of the hole. At the very top, the hole was cone-shaped and the opening was about 10 metres wide. I had descended about 3-4 metres when suddenly I began to fall in a vertical line. The rope broke because of the sudden pressure and I shot down like a rocket and landed at the bottom next to the Germans. I suffered several fractures and a dislocated pelvis. All those who were standing at the top of the hole could not believe their eyes. My father burst into tears. Vassilis was wounded; I lay in an open grave; Manolis was away, probably at Iraklion, we didn't know if he was alive or dead; Costis was on a mission at Assi-Gonia. He had only two children left out of six. He couldn't bear it any more and cracked under the strain. Shortly afterwards they found some rope and formed a kind of "cable". They tied the rope round the unforgettable New Zealander and he began to descend into the hole in order to tie me and hoist me up. It was dark at the bottom and you needed a torch to see. One of the Germans who was very badly wounded, was moaning with pain and screaming. I couldn't stand listening to him. I was probably in more pain than he was and as time went by it grew worse. I took out my torch and switched it on. On seeing who was screaming, I pulled out my 32 and shot him on the head. He died instantly. I spotted another one with my torch, he was slightly wounded and thinking that I would not get out of there he said to me: "And now Greco we will die together".

I didn't answer him. I waited for the New Zealander at the bottom and pointed him out saying that he ought to kill him so that he would not remain the only one alive among so many dead. He tied the rope around me and called to the others to pull me out. My body had grown heavy and they had trouble pulling me up, but in the end they managed it. We sent Georgis Paterakis to Plemeniana to get Dr. Giorgos Hatzakis to administer first-aid, especially to the memorable Manolis Tzatzimakis who was the most badly wounded. The doctor however was delayed and since we were expecting the Germans to attack, we had to take him to Hania where he was betrayed and later shot by the Germans. The New Zealander Perkins had a bullet lodged in his left shoulder- blade which was removed using a Cretan knife. On the 22nd of the month 3.000 Germans arrived and surrounded Ahlada. They remained there for three days and were only saved by the thick fog and heavy rain. The Germans did not resort to reprisals against the unarmed population, (the first time they had not done so). This was probably because we had taken the identity cards from the dead men and had given the data to the Middle East. The next day Cairo radio announced the departure of the first German prisoners of war to the Middle East from Crete's White Mountains.

Antonios Paterakis. Contributed by Stavros Georgiakakis, Chania

They lined us up to be shot

On the 13th of August 1944 the Germans arrived at Grigoria, where those of us from the demolished villages had fled to. On the orders of the Gestapo squadron they arrested nine men; five from Margarikari and four from Kamares. I was among those arrested. They shut us up in the church of Aghios Grigorios in the village of Grigoria. Early on the morning of the 14th of August, fifteen Germans armed with machine guns escorted us to the village of Skourvoula, about ten kilometres away. It was the very same place at which two Germans had died in their attempts to kill groups of resistance fighters.

We found about 200 Germans there, all of them armed with automatic weapons and heavy artillery. We also found about 28 men and women whose names I don't know. They lined us up, all 37 of us (14 women and 23 men) to be executed. The commanding officer of the detachment said: "You have killed German soldiers here, in an act of dishonourable revenge. We have brought you here to kill you". The detachment soldiers bore skulls as a sign. They were armed with six machine guns for the execution, as well as the quick-firing weapons used by the rest of the Germans. I was fifth in line. When I saw the loaded machine guns I thought: "I am going to die either way", so I made a run for it before they started firing at us. Once I had got about 5 - 10 metres along the flat ground within excellent firing range, all six machine guns began to fire at me. I ran as if I had wings on my feet. I managed to get to a precipice about 20 metres high. The machine guns kept on firing. The olive trees and bean trees were riddled with bullets, but I was not hit.

I calculated that there must have been about 25 - 30 automatics, machine guns and artillery units, firing at me. I fell 20 metres down the precipice but did not get hurt. That is how I escaped death. I am alive today, almost eighty years old and work as a farmer.

The survivor Georgios Lenakakis, Margarikari
Contributed by Stavros Georgiakakis, Chania

A Cretan girl prisoner remembers

If I remember correctly, during the first few months of 1943, the radio transmitters belonging to Headquarters in the Middle East, fell by parachute in the area surrounding the Monastery of Toplou. The man in charge was called Emmanuel Tsagarakis. He was a Greek-Egyptian and a cousin from my mother's side. The radio operator was also Egyptian, he was called Giannis Matsakis.

From the moment they landed in Crete, they came into contact with the monks from the Monastery of Toplou. They assisted them in every way possible (both morally and practically) in order that their dangerous enterprise could be completed. Naturally they came into contact with many extremely loyal people from our city, people whose aim was to fight the oppressor. My own family was included among them.

In April 1944, the Germans discovered the radio transmitter and on the 29th of April at dawn, they arrested my brother Nicos and myself. (My elder brother Evangelos had escaped to Egypt six months earlier because the Germans had become very suspicious of him.)

We were taken to Gestapo Headquarters where I saw many people being detained. I found out that they were radio operators. After a routine interrogation in the afternoon, they let us go, probably in order to see whom we would come into contact with. Three days later

April 1942. Inhabitants of a Cretan village being interrogated by German troops. Contributed by John Tsatsas, Athens.

on the 2nd of May, they arrested us once more at dawn. They hauled us into a truck and transferred us to Aghios Nikolaos, to be interrogated. What I remember most vividly from the interrogation was my brother being tortured in the room next door to mine. I could hear the Germans beating him and my brother's cries had deteriorated into that of a groaning animal about to be slaughtered. I thought I was going to go mad. I also remember how they would give me no food for five days and then they would feed me but give me nothing to drink for two more days. I cannot begin to describe my hellish thirst. I began to hallucinate. In desperation I asked the woman whose room was adjacent to mine, to give me some water. Naturally the door was closed, so she was forced to spill some water on the concrete floor from under the door into my room. Although disgusted I spread my handkerchief in the dirty water and put it in my mouth, sucking it with relief. My unquenchable thirst subsided somewhat. We of course paid for this by being kicked and beaten by the Germans when they spotted

303

the wet floor and realised what had happened. Nevertheless I had managed to quench the thirst of two days.

After being interrogated at Aghios Nikolaos they put us in a truck and transferred us to the prison of Aghia at Hania. It had been used as a rural prison before the war. During the war it had become the Cretan people's Golgotha. We were all content deep down because the agonising interrogation had ended and the prison did not seem so terrible at first sight. It was made up of a group of buildings with a large courtyard full of flowers and plants. The prison was surrounded by beautiful fields that had been cultivated. We hoped that life there would at least be bearable. Our first disappointment: the courtyard was surrounded by about ten cells which were being guarded by heavily armed troops. Those cells housed all those who had been sentenced to death: Greeks, Germans and Italians, about thirty men in all. Further away there was another group of cells with its own courtyard which was isolated from the rest. It was enclosed with barbed wire as if the prisoners inside were cholera sufferers and had to be kept isolated. That group housed those of the Cretan Jews who were unfortunate enough to be arrested. A few days later these poor Jews left the prisons and Crete, crying woefully, to be transferred to German war camps.

Several days later it was our turn. The tribunal was to meet at Aghia. This was not good for us. We spent the whole day going back and forth from the court-martial's chambers. In the afternoon the tribunal announced its decision: six men were sentenced to death, four were found to be innocent; I was sentenced to exile in Germany's concentration camps.

From that time onwards until our departure we witnessed about 2 or 3 executions almost every day. We were at a distance naturally, but we lived every moment of the tragedy. We could see the preparations and we could hear the detachment's salvos.

The day came for us to leave for Germany. We said goodbye to our fellow prisoners with tears in our eyes and got in the cars that would take us to Souda, from where the ship was to depart. As we drove through the city's centre, we all began to sing simultaneously the Rizitico song: "Where is February's starry sky that I may take my gun?" This song had become Crete's National Anthem for all of us, myself included. The Germans were seething and screamed at us to stop. We carried on singing. The "Haniotes" (people from Hania) stared at us in amazement. People opened their windows and gazed at us thunderstruck. Some took handkerchiefs from their pockets and secretly wiped the tears from their eyes, others blew kisses at us, making sure not to be seen by the Germans, while others gave us the Victory sign. We, the youth of Crete, took to our feet and raised our voices defiantly "Where is the starry night?" The entire city of Hania was in a state of turmoil that day.

The 20th of July was an unforgettable day.

Katina Eleftheraki - Papadaki, Sitia

Top Secret

Information was continuously being passed on from the espionage detachment to Headquarters in the Middle East, concerning the convoys departing from Crete, which included the fully equipped aircraft destined for the "Africa Corps". They were destroyed before reaching their destination, by the allied airforces. Crete's importance as Rommel's supply centre justified the destruction of these aircraft. This proved to be invaluable to the Greek forces.

The most important piece of information passed on to Headquarters in the Middle East, was the contents of a top secret telegram by Rommel to Crete's military commander André, which the Greek secret service had managed to get their hands on.

The contents of the telegram were strictly as follows:

TOP SECRET

Impossible to continue advancing due to shortage of fuel, ammunition and light combat artillery.

Awaiting convoy as soon as possible.

Rommel

Immediately after this telegram had been sent, a large German convoy of about 40 fully equipped ships, left from the harbour of Souda and headed for the port of Tobruk. The well organised Greek secret service in Crete managed to inform Headquarters in the Middle East of the exact day and time of the convoy's departure, as well as the course they were to follow. The convoy was totally destroyed before reaching its destination by the allied aircraft. Only one ship managed to return safely to the port of Souda. The importance of the telegram was infinitely more valuable. The allied forces were now aware of the pitiful situation Rommel was in. He had been forced to halt at the entrance to Alexandria, in search of fresh supplies. The allied forces began to evacuate the city, only to stop doing so immediately upon being informed of Rommel's arrival. The 8th military division began to re-organize itself very quickly and prepare for an attack against Rommel. (The beginning of October 1942). This resulted in the well known victory of El Alamein.

Stavros Kaffatos in collaboration with Dimitris Bernidakis, Athens

"The City Andartes"

I owned a café in Neapolis, Crete. The café was situated on the main road. Every time the conquerors transferred their ammunition canons, food and supplies etc. they would have to go through Neapolis on their way down to Iraklion. I would spend my whole day in the café listening for the sound of the cars, so that I might go outside and see what they were carrying and where they were going. Entire "squadrons" were transferring supplies and I observed how large each "squadron" was and how many trucks were involved etc. I was too terrified to think what would have happened to me if I had been noticed. This was my post. There were two factions: the rebels in the city and the rebels in the village. I belonged to the ones in the city. I made a list of whatever passed through. Messengers would come by and collect them and have them broadcast through the various transmitters. My café had a basement which led on to another street, from which I could escape in case of an emergency.

Verbal Testimony of Dimitrios Kokkinis, Neapolis

"Death to the enemies of Crete"

Among the lighter moments I remember the time when I had a rendez-vous with Paddy Leigh Fermor at a monastery, to arrange for the reception of his party which was coming in to kidnap General Kreipe. It was a tiny monastery, a "metóchi" of Mount Sinai, with an Archimandrite, a nun named Porphyria and an acolyte named Stelios.

I arrived first and was very much looking forward to seeing Paddy again- we hadn't met for a long time, long enough for me to grow quite a respectable beard and the Archimandrite suggested that I should dress up as a monk. It was after dark when Paddy came into the dimly-lit room, having been warned by the Archimandrite that another monk had turned up from a distant monastery and that they didn't know whether he could be trusted or not. Paddy came over, kissed my hand and said something non-committal like "Death to the enemies of Crete" and retired to a dark corner of the crowded room where I could see him making sure that his pistol was free for action. All the Cretans of course by now were helpless with laughter so the deception did not last long and we had a memorable party. The next morning while the Archimandrite was doing his best to rouse Paddy by playing a record of Colonel Bogey at full blast on an old portable gramophone straight into Paddy's ear, I walked out on to the balcony and suddenly saw, to my horror, a German patrol marching down the road which led nowhere else but to the front door of the monastery. They were about 300 metres away but it was much too late to run so we hastily gathered up all our belongings and went down into the storeroom below which, of course, as in all Cretan country houses, was the ground-floor room. We hid behind the great wine barrels while the Germans halted outside and the officer and NCO went up the outside stone steps to our late bedroom. With age the floor boards had shrunk and it was possible to see the jack boots and hear every word that was said. It soon became apparent that this was just a routine patrol and that they had no idea of our presence in the neighbourhood, so we relaxed. The Archimandrite, the acolyte and Porphyria put on a perfect welcoming act and when the Germans asked for wine Porphyria came down to our hide-out to get it, so we all had a swig from the demijohn before it went up. After about half an hour the Germans departed with gifts of eggs, leaving behind an official commendation form praising the Archimandrite for his pro-Axis sympathies - we wrote a correcting statement in exactly the same terms, on the back of the form, with the same date. That notice exists to this day in the archives of the monastery.

John Stanley, England

Hermann's pleasant Sunday

15.9.41, Kalyves, Crete

Dear sister, Your last letter arrived here a long time ago. I know you write, we wait every day but no steamer brings us the letters.

Half his life the soldier is waiting, in vain.

On the 11th September I visited Canea. Official business in the morning, afternoon-coffee-cake for the week, they received cigarettes! Yesterday at 6 a.m. we drove to the mountains: Monastery Arcadi! Some donkeys afterwards; the Head of the Monastery welcomed us. Invitation to sight-seeing and Dinner (Pik!) He told us of the heroic history of the Monastery, the battle of the inhabitants against the Turks (20.000 1866!) All the peasants were in the Monastery for defence. The commander of the Turks allowed the wives and children to leave the place; they did not accept, they were blown up. The priests were murdered. After the church service we were invited for dinner. A pik and a special Cretan dish were served. Mavrodaphni and desert. It was for us, also, a pleasant Sunday.

Next Sunday our colonel will also visit the Monastery. He will be surprised. I am ready for my vacation to Germany, by plane (JU 52!).

Best greetings to you and my parents and little Ingrid,

Your brother Hermann

Letter by Hermann Otto Greiner, Germany

The kidnapping of the German General Kreipe

The kidnapping of the German General, according to the British, had been on the orders of the General Staff in Cairo. The two British who had come here were: Major Liférmos (Leigh Fermor) and Captain Moss who is now dead. They went to the dependency of the Monastery of Zografistos of Pandis (who had also taken part) and made their plans there. I was a policeman. On being notified I also

Visit to the Monastery of Arcadi,
Rethymnon, by German soldiers.
Among them is Hermann - Otto Greiner.

went there from Arhanes. I was assigned to observe the German. He used to eat here, at the school's club-house. The club-house was a tall building opposite the school. He was staying at Villa Ariadne and would come here to eat at the school and then leave. Naturally he would leave early and we never had enough time. I observed him for two weeks, from the beginning of April onwards. He was kidnapped on the 26th. That evening the Germans were to give a formal dinner in his honour, for some victory or other..... I went inside and asked the cook for a bottle. "I am busy now Stratis, leave me alone".

"Why are you so busy?" I asked her. "The General is coming to dinner and I am very busy". When I heard the word General I thought: Tonight is the perfect opportunity. "All right, I'll come and get the bottle tomorrow". "Yes, come tomorrow". I left and shortly afterwards went downstairs to the dependency to find the British and the others. I said: "Tonight is the perfect opportunity. They are giving a dinner in his honour, he will probably stay until quite late- at nightfall we will grab him". That is exactly how it happened.

We all took our positions along the branch road. As a policeman I knew the chauffeur, so I was to deal with him; one man was to deal with the General; someone else was to stand guard. Each man was assigned his own task and his own post. We had a man watching out for the car. He was to signal us with a flashlight. We saw the oncoming lights and kept a lookout. The British were wearing German uniforms.

They were supposed to be traffic police and they also spoke the language. As the car approached, it was stopped by the major. "The road is not safe further on" he said in German. We were hidden in the palm trees on either side. At the given moment we ran out, opened the car door, dragged out the General and his driver and Moss (who was an experienced driver) got in. We trussed the General up like a turkey.

The others took his driver and left. The General began to shout. He was told not to shout because he was a prisoner of the British commandoes. He was put back in the car and we all got in: The British, myself, Tyrakis and Paterakis. The rest of the men took the driver to Psiloritis, that is where we had arranged to meet the next day. As we left for Iraklion we came across 12 German guards. The Englishman was wearing the General's cap however, and we had the German flag in the front. On catching sight of the car, the guards stopped and saluted as we drove past. The General had travelled alone in the car with just the driver. On other occasions he normally had a major with him who travelled as a bodyguard. Fortunately that evening the major got drunk and was unable to accompany him. It must have been an act of God. The only thing we found was the empty machine-gun in the back seat of the car, which we confiscated. The next day we got into the car and drove to Rethimno, to Hania. We left him there. Major Liférmos had left the commander a note explaining how sorry he was that he could not keep such a beautiful car and that the General had been kidnapped exclusively by British and Greek commandoes from the Middle East. The Cretan people were not involved in any way. Inside the car they had left several bullets and a British cloak in the corner. The next day we met up at Anogia. As a policeman I knew the area well and had taken the General to a cave. By nightfall we were on the road once more. The road was steep and uphill. The General rode on horseback for part of the way and the rest on foot. In desperation he tried to commit suicide. At night he was under guard. He was commander of the 22nd military division as well as being in charge of fortification works in the Balkans. He was an important man. So I have been told. All that I saw however, was that he had numerous medals and swastikas as well as gold jewellery etc. At dawn we all met up and spent the day there. At nightfall we carried on climbing all around the mountains. We covered a large area: Anogia, Psiloritis, Sfakia and Rodakino. We stayed on the mountain from the 26th-27th of April, the day of the kidnapping, till 15th-16th of May. We covered all the mountains because the Germans had surrounded all of Crete. No arrests were made at Arhanes, although some were made on the mountain. They didn't know that the plan for the kidnapping had originated from Arhanes. They didn't know where it had started and how. No, no, they actually found out later on at Amari. The villagers suffered greatly. The so- called Gestapo burnt many of the villages at Amari. We left from the small port and made our way to the Middle East, to a place called Marsah-Matruh. The British General bestowed military honours on the German General; he presented arms. We did not see Kreipe again. We departed in separate cars.

Verbal testimony of Efstratios Saviolakis, Arhanes

The surrender of Crete-May 1945

As an officer with the Special Operations Executive I was working in the Nome of Canea as the British agent in charge of that area under the pseudonym of Dionysios. Fortunately, during the German occupation the representatives of the Allies, ably assisted by Cretans, had managed to keep the resistance movement fairly free from politics.

Athens, and even Heraklion, had been liberated and there only remained the German forces, consisting of about 11,000 heavily armed solders who had withdrawn to the Canea area. I was living in Kastelli and in touch with my Headquarters in Heraklion by radio. On the 8th of May I received a message to contact the G.O.C., General Benthag, and hand to him the Terms of Surrender. Fortunately, at this time Lieutenant Constantinos Mitsotakis, of the Greek Army, was

General Kreipe among his abductors, Dimitrios Tzatzadakis, Pavlos Zografistos, Stratis Saviolakis, Grigoris Chnarakis, Emmanuel Paterakis, Tyrakis, Nicos Komis and Zoidakis. Those who could recognize the General's vehicle were Michael Akoumianakis and Athanasakis. The British involved were Leigh Fermor, known in Crete as "Filedem" or "Michalis", and Stanley Moss, known as "Bill".
Demetrios Tzatzadakis, Crete.

with me as the organiser of the Greek Political Underground Movement for Canea, particularly as he spoke fluent German. Upon receipt of our instructions, Costa and I dressed in our Sunday Best, sent a runner to the nearest German outpost stating that we represented the Allied Forces Headquarters and wished to have a meeting with General Benthag. After some delay the answer came back that the General would see us and a staff car was sent to collect us.

Upon arrival in Canea we proceeded to the German Headquarters, which was the old family house of Mr. Venizelos. We were escorted to the General's office and found him with Colonel Barge, his Chief of Staff, and Lieutenant Wildhage, officer in charge of counter-

313

espionage, all in their best uniforms and looking very red in the face. The General informed me that he had just received orders from Admiral Doenitz at Flensburg to surrender to A.F.H.Q. and asked if we represented this H.Q. I introduced us and assured him that we did and that I had a list of points to which he had to agree.

The problem was that there were many armed Cretan Guerrillas surrounding Canea who were anxious to storm the area to liberate it and possibly take their revenge on the Germans. On the other hand, the Germans were very heavily armed and were more than a match for the Guerrillas. As, according to the Geneva Convention, a General can only surrender to an officer of equal rank, and I was only a major in the South Staffordshire Regiment, it was agreed that a Fairchild aeroplane should fly into Maleme Aerodrome with the aid of smoke signals let off by us for wind direction etc. The General would be picked up, taken to Heraklion to sign the official Surrender Document, make the necessary arrangements to receive the liberating force and be returned to his H.Q. without the local population being aware of this.

On the acceptance of the General to their Terms, I informed him, through the interpretation of Costa, I would relay this to my H.Q. and advise him of the arrival time of the plane. To this he pointed out that the matter was very urgent if there was not to be any skirmishes with the Guerrilas. I promised he would have my reply by the morning, which rather surprised him, and he asked how I was going to communicate with my H.Q. When I informed him that our radio was situated two or three doors away from his H.Q., so as to save us being picked up on their direction finders owing to the amount of traffic in the area, he seemed most upset.

That night we returned to Kastelli Kisamou to collect our belongings and my staff but, in any case, the 9th May was the birthday of Captain John Stanley M.C., who was in charge of the M16 network in the area and with whom we had worked very closely; needless to say, we celebrated his birthday and the liberation of Canea in true Kastelli fashion. John and I returned to Canea that day with my assistants, consisting of our wireless operator and two Cretan helpers, the senior of which was Pavlos Vernadakis, to take up residence in a flat next to the German H.Q.

314

I am pleased to say that the plan went off most successfully, although I fear the General returned from the Surrender Ceremony rather chastened as he realised that he and his forces were now prisoners of war.

On the 13th May the advance party of Press Force arrived consisting mainly of a Battalion of the Hampshire Regiment. This Force was joined by the Greek National Guard and on May 23rd they provided a first-class Guard of Honour and subsequently supervised the evacuation of the German Prisoners of War.

At this time, I was told I would be supplied with anything the Germans had available which we might require. One of my assistants was a young Cretan boy named Georgio Phindrilakis from the village of Asigonia who had been our runner and always looked after the heavy bag of gold sovereigns which we carried and who had never had any reward or recompense. When I asked him what he would like to receive most in all the world his eyes became misty and he replied in a whisper 'a German Army BMW motor-bike and side-car'. Next morning the young German officer detailed to look after our requirements looked a little surprised when I asked for such a motorbike to be sent round. Needless to say, 'Georgio' was thrilled beyond belief and was told to take it away and garage it. Unfortunately, this 'gift' rather repercussed on me as it appears that when the victorious Press Force arrived and was ceremoniously marching up the main street, the Brigadier was shocked to see a young Cretan Guerrilla trying to ride the bike and finishing up in the ditch in front of him. I was sent for next day and questioned about how this motor-cycle, requisitioned by me from the Germans, could have finished up in the hands of a young Cretan black marketeer.

However, I am pleased to say that when I explained the position to the Brigadier he seemed to appreciate the story and told me quietly to see it did not happen again. Unfortunately, a year or two later Georgio, was killed, so I was pleased that I had at least been able to grant him his wish.

D. Ciclitira, England

We knew we were making history

One of the Cretan villagers who saw how amazed I was at the bravery and self - sacrifice of the people of Crete, uttered these magnificent words:

"Why are you so surprised? We know that we are making history."

I do not know of any other country where the villagers can submit to such pain, sacrifice and personal destruction with such pride. This Cretan villager knew that there exists a value in this world far more important than life itself. A value that our whole nation fought and sacrificed itself for. Now, he also had to fight and sacrifice himself. This value is called history, in other words a posthumous reputation. Immortality.

A student called Mimis Lionakis was shot in the prison of Aghia, because he had fought against the Germans. Moments before he had asked for a pencil and paper to write to his parents this incredibly serene and brave letter:

My dear parents

I am writing to you shortly before I am to be shot. I die contented and in peace with myself, in the knowledge that I have done my duty to the full. I hope others will follow my example. Do not cry and do not be sad. I am not afraid. My courage has no limit. I have always feared death but now I embrace it with open arms ....

Such was the pain and heroism to be found in Crete.

Nikos Kazantzakis
Hellas, London, 28-12-1945

Who can ever forget them?

The Resistance was something which sprang spontaneously into existence the moment the first enemy parachutist touched Cretan soil. How well I remember our astonishment, only a little distance from where we stand today, at the sudden appearance - in the absence of the gallant 5th Cretan Division - of old men and boys beside us in the firing line! There is no need for me to sing the praise of the brilliant

Emmanuel Katsanevas with his son Lefteris,
from Perivolia - Chania, confronting the execution squads.
Museum of Contemporary History, Heraclion.

conduct of the Cretans in those fierce days, but I must recall one moment on the last evening of the Battle. An old and white-haired Kapitanios - one of the most famous - asked to see the Commanding Brigadier. "My son," he said, pacing his hand on the Brigadier's shoulder, "we all know you are going away tonight. Never mind! You will come back when the right time comes. But leave us as many guns as you can, to carry on the fight till then." Deeply moved, the Brigadier handed over all the arms we could collect.

In 1941 and 42, the fortunes of war were evil indeed. When all Europe had fallen, England and Greece had been left facing the enemy alone. The air trembled still, as it will tremble forever, with heroism and the glories of the Albanian War. We, your allies, had been retreated from Greece and then from Crete. England was being blown to bits by enemy bombs; the enemy were advancing on Stalingrad; Rommel's tanks were hammering El Alamein and it looked as if the whole Middle East might fall. They were desperate times. In Crete, great tragedies were almost daily events. And yet, members of the Allied Mission arriving here found no trace of discouragement or despair. We were astonished and inspired by the spirit and the resolution of the island, the conviction that one day we would win the last battle together. The mountains were filled with wandering Australian, New Zealand and British soldiers, hidden and fed by the Cretans at dire peril - just as though these strangers who had come from so far away to fight beside you and shed their blood in these mountains, were your own sons. We knew that we, your Allies, were risking no more than our lives, as in wartime all soldiers must, while the Greeks who helped our people so bravely and generously were risking not their lives only, but the lives of their families and the very existence of entire villages.

Who, of all of us here who had a share in those years, can ever forget them? The long night marches, the waiting for ships in lonely inlets, the plateau vigils waiting for arms and supplies to drop from the sky, the visits to the information networks in the towns, the expeditions with seaborne commandoes to destroy enemy aircraft and ammunition, the flights from enemy sweeps through the mountains - even once, the attempt at sea-sabotage in Herakleion harbour; the secret descent to the scores of villages that shielded us from harm, the

318

fellowship in times of crisis, the many dangerous operations undertaken together? The mountains - a hundred caves in the Lasithi and Herakleion mountain ranges - and, above all, on Mount Ida and Kedros and the White Mountains - were our ever-changing homes. It was in these snowbound lairs and in goatfolds like eagles' nests among the high crags, that we became accepted as part of the Cretan family. Our lives depended on the kindness and courage of the shepherds we lived among, and on the villagers and the priests and the schoolmasters of the hamlets below, and on all their families. Dressed in high boots, sheepskin cloaks and fringed headkerchiefs, we tried to become Cretans; and we almost succeeded.

Ideas change, men die, and, in time, all monuments fall. But perhaps something indestructable will survive; the spirit that guided the inhabitants of this island; something indefinable and noble and inspiring and inspired and as brilliant as the air and the light which shines on your mountains.

Patrick Leigh Fermor
From a speech delivered in Crete on the 25th May 1981 on the 40th anniversary of the Battle of Crete

Bibliography

This bibliography includes only publications from which quotations have been made with the permission of authors or publishers. References to all other sources are given in the text.

Ακρίτας, Τάκης. Η μάχη του Γαλατά. Αθήναι, Τυπ. Α. Κουβελογιάννη, 1949.
Βενέζης, Ηλίας. Εμμανουήλ Τσουδερός. Αθήνα, 1966.
Καψωμένος, Ερατοσθένης. Το σύγχρονο κρητικό ιστορικό τραγούδι. Αθήνα, Θεμέλιο, 1979.
Παπαθανασόπουλος, Πάνος. Οι αλεξιπτωτισταί στην Κρήτη. Μάιος 1941. Αθήνα, Πυρσός, 1946.
Πολιουδάκης, Μάρκος. Η μάχη της Κρήτης στο Ρέθυμνο. Αθήνα, 1983.
Σακελλαρίου, Αλέξανδρος Ε. Ταξειδεύοντας. Αθήναι, 1957.
Σιβετίδης, Μάξιμος. Η μάχη της Κρήτης συνεχίζεται. Αθήνα, Κέδρος, 1979.
Στρατηγάκης, Ιωάννης Εμμ. Σελίδες Κρητικής δόξης. (χωρίς εκδ. στοιχεία)
Φραντζεσκάκης, Στυλιανός. Οι αδούλωτοι. (Κρήτη, 1981).

Brown, Bill. ed. The 2/IIth Australian Infantry Battalion, 1939-45. Australia.
Buckley, Christopher. Greece and Crete 1941. 3rd ed. Athens, Efstathiades Group, 1984.
Churchill, Winston. (and the Editors of "Life"). The Second World War. New York, Golden Press, 1960.
Clark, Alan. The fall of Crete. 4th ed. Athens, Efstathiades Group, 1981.
Cunningham, Andrew. A sailor's Odyssey. The autobiography of Admiral of the British Fleet Viscount Cunningham of Hyndhope. London, Hutchinson, 1951.
Dahl, Roald. Going solo. London, Jonathan Cape, 1986.
Davin, D.M. Crete. Wellington, N.Z., War History Branch; Department of Internal Affairs, 1953.
Howell, Edward. Escape to live. 4th ed. London, Longmans, Green & Co., 1952.
Hauptman Piehl. Ganze Männer; vom Leben und Erleben der deutschen Fallschirmjäger. Leipzig, Verlagshaus Bong & Co., 1944.

Hunt, David. A Don at war. London, William Kimber, 1966.

Liddell Hart, B. H. History of the second world war. 2nd ed. London, Book Club Association, 1973.

Major Flecker, ed. Gebirgsjäger auf Kreta. 1942.

Ramcke, Bernhard. Vom Schiffszungen zum Fallschirmjäger-General. Berlin, Verlag die Wehrmacht, 1943.

Roba, Jean-Louis. Les Allemands en Egée. 1941-1945. Belgique, 1987. (Tome I, 1941).

Roon, Anton von. Parachute troops operations-Crete. Men of action. Münich, J. F. Lehmans. (In german).

Schenering, Fritz. Sprung über Kreta. Impressions and operations. Report by Guenther Mellerand. Oldenburg, Gerhard Stelling Verlag, 1944.

Stephanides, Theodore. Climax in Crete. London, Faber and Faber, 1946.

Thomas, W. B. Dare to be free. London, Alan Wingate, 1951.

Thomson, Richard Heywood. Captive Kiwi. Christchurch, N.Z., Whitcombe & Tombs, 1964.

Wason, Betty. Miracle in Hellas. The Greeks fight on. London, Museum Press, 1943.

Encyclopaedia Britannica. Chicago, 1978. (vol. III).

The Goebbels diaries; 1939-41. Translated and edited by Fred Taylor. London, Hamish Hamilton, 1982.

Kreta, sieg der Künsten. Graz, Steirische Verlagsanstatt, 1942.

Von Serbien bis Kreta. Herausgegeben von einer Propaganda Kompanie. Athen, Gedicht bei Aspioti-ELKA, 1942.

War at Sea. Introduction by Sir Herbert Richmond. London, Oxford University Press, 1942.

Index